STUDY GUIDE *PLUS*
FOR
HENSLIN

ESSENTIALS OF SOCIOLOGY
A DOWN-TO-EARTH APPROACH

STUDY GUIDE *PLUS*

FOR

HENSLIN

ESSENTIALS OF SOCIOLOGY
A DOWN-TO-EARTH APPROACH

GWENDOLYN E. NYDEN
OAKTON COMMUNITY COLLEGE

Allyn and Bacon
Boston · London · Toronto · Sydney · Tokyo · Singapore

Copyright © 1996 by Allyn & Bacon
A Simon & Schuster Company
Needham Heights, Massachusetts 02194

ISBN 0-205-18404-9

Printed in the United States of America

10 9 8 7 6 5 4 3 2   00 99 98 97 96

TABLE OF CONTENTS

CHAPTER 1: *THE SOCIOLOGICAL PERSPECTIVE* 1

CHAPTER 2: *CULTURE* 19

CHAPTER 3: *SOCIALIZATION* 35

CHAPTER 4: *SOCIAL STRUCTURE AND SOCIAL INTERACTION* 53

CHAPTER 5: *SOCIAL GROUPS IN A SOCIALLY DIVERSE SOCIETY* 69

CHAPTER 6: *DEVIANCE AND SOCIAL CONTROL* 185

CHAPTER 7: *SOCIAL STRATIFICATION IN GLOBAL PERSPECTIVE* 103

CHAPTER 8: *SOCIAL CLASS IN THE UNITED STATES* 121

CHAPTER 9: *INEQUALITIES OF RACE AND ETHNICITY* 139

CHAPTER 10: *INEQUALITIES OF GENDER AND AGE* 157

CHAPTER 11: *POLITICS AND THE ECONOMY* 175

CHAPTER 12: *MARRIAGE AND FAMILY* 193

CHAPTER 13: *EDUCATION AND RELIGION* 209

CHAPTER 14: *POPULATION AND URBANIZATION* 227

CHAPTER 15: *SOCIAL CHANGE* 243

TABLE OF CONTENTS

CHAPTER 1: THE SOCIOLOGICAL PERSPECTIVE 1
    Summary and Learning Objectives 1
    Chapter Outline 2
    Glossary of Difficult-to-Understand Words 6
    Key Terms to Define 7
    Key People 7
    Self-Test 7
    Down-to-Earth Sociology 13
    Answer Key 14

CHAPTER 2: CULTURE 19
    Summary and Learning Objectives 19
    Chapter Outline 20
    Glossary of Difficult-to-Understand Words 23
    Key Terms to Define 24
    Key People 25
    Self-Test 25
    Down-to-Earth Sociology 29
    Answer Key 30

CHAPTER 3: SOCIALIZATION 35
    Summary and Learning Objectives 35
    Chapter Outline 36
    Glossary of Difficult-to-Understand Words 40
    Key Terms to Define 41
    Key People 41
    Self-Test 42
    Down-to-Earth Sociology 47
    Answer Key 47

CHAPTER 4: SOCIAL STRUCTURE AND SOCIAL INTERACTION 53
    Summary and Learning Objectives 53
    Chapter Outline 54
    Glossary of Difficult-to-Understand Words 57
    Key Terms to Define 58
    Key People 58
    Self-Test 59
    Down-to-Earth Sociology 63
    Answer Key 64

CHAPTER 5: SOCIAL GROUPS IN A SOCIALLY DIVERSE SOCIETY 69
    Summary and Learning Objectives 69
    Chapter Outline 70
    Glossary of Difficult-to-Understand Words 73
    Key Terms to Define 74
    Key People 74
    Self-Test 75
    Down-to-Earth Sociology 80
    Answer Key 80

Table of Contents (*continued*)

CHAPTER 6: DEVIANCE AND SOCIAL CONTROL 85
    Summary and Learning Objectives 85
    Chapter Outline 86
    Glossary of Difficult-to-Understand Words 89
    Key Terms to Define 90
    Key People 90
    Self-Test 90
    Down-to-Earth Sociology 96
    Answer Key 96

CHAPTER 7: SOCIAL STRATIFICATION IN GLOBAL PERSPECTIVE 103
    Summary and Learning Objectives 103
    Chapter Outline 104
    Glossary of Difficult-to-Understand Words 108
    Key Terms to Define 109
    Key People 109
    Self-Test 110
    Down-to-Earth Sociology 115
    Answer Key 115

CHAPTER 8: SOCIAL CLASS IN THE UNITED STATES 121
    Summary and Learning Objectives 121
    Chapter Outline 122
    Glossary of Difficult-to-Understand Words 126
    Key Terms to Define 127
    Key People 127
    Self-Test 127
    Down-to-Earth Sociology 133
    Answer Key 133

CHAPTER 9: INEQUALITIES OF RACE AND ETHNICITY 139
    Summary and Learning Objectives 139
    Chapter Outline 140
    Glossary of Difficult-to-Understand Words 145
    Key Terms to Define 146
    Key People 146
    Self-Test 146
    Down-to-Earth Sociology 151
    Answer Key 152

CHAPTER 10: INEQUALITIES OF GENDER AND AGE 157
    Summary and Learning Objectives 157
    Chapter Outline 158
    Glossary of Difficult-to-Understand Words 162
    Key Terms to Define 163
    Key People 163
    Self-Test 164
    Down-to-Earth Sociology 169
    Answer Key 169

Table of Contents (*continued*)

CHAPTER 11: POLITICS AND THE ECONOMY 175
    Summary and Learning Objectives 175
    Chapter Outline 176
    Glossary of Difficult-to-Understand Words 181
    Key Terms to Define 182
    Key People 182
    Self-Test 183
    Down-to-Earth Sociology 188
    Answer Key 188
CHAPTER 12: MARRIAGE AND FAMILY 193
    Summary and Learning Objectives 193
    Chapter Outline 194
    Glossary of Difficult-to-Understand Words 199
    Key Terms to Define 200
    Key People 200
    Self-Test 200
    Down-to-Earth Sociology 205
    Answer Key 205
CHAPTER 13: EDUCATION AND RELIGION 209
    Summary and Learning Objectives 209
    Chapter Outline 210
    Glossary of Difficult-to-Understand Words 215
    Key Terms to Define 215
    Key People 216
    Self-Test 216
    Down-to-Earth Sociology 221
    Answer Key 221
CHAPTER 14: POPULATION AND URBANIZATION 227
    Summary and Learning Objectives 227
    Chapter Outline 228
    Glossary of Difficult-to-Understand Words 233
    Key Terms to Define 234
    Key People 234
    Self-Test 234
    Down-to-Earth Sociology 238
    Answer Key 239
CHAPTER 15: SOCIAL CHANGE 243
    Summary and Learning Objectives 243
    Chapter Outline 244
    Glossary of Difficult-to-Understand Words 249
    Key Terms to Define 249
    Key People 249
    Self-Test 250
    Down-to-Earth Sociology 254
    Answer Key 254

INTRODUCTION

Welcome to Sociology! You are about to embark on a fascinating journey in which you will discover all sorts of new and interesting information about yourself and the world around you. This study guide has been prepared to accompany the textbook <u>Essentials of Sociology: A Down-to-Earth Approach</u> by James M. Henslin.

Each chapter in this guide includes the following:

- a **Chapter Summary** that summarizes the main ideas found in the chapter.

- a set of **Learning Objectives** that provides statements concerning the main ideas of the chapter. If you want to check your responses, refer back to the page numbers listed with each question.

- a **Glossary of Difficult-to-Understand Words** that includes some of the words that may be unfamiliar, along with their meanings; the meanings are based on the context in which they are used. It is designed to be a resource for you to use as you read the textbook. If there are words that you don't know that are not included in this glossary, be sure to look them up in a dictionary. Your comprehension of the material is based on the assumption that you understand the words that are used.

- a listing of **Key Terms to Define** that contains all of the sociological concepts that are introduced within the chapter.

- a listing of **Key People** that includes some of the major sociologists whose work is discussed within the chapter. In some cases, these are early sociologists who contributed theoretical understanding and research insights to the discipline; in other cases, they are contemporary sociologists who are doing research and developing theory on the subject.

- a **Self-Test** that provides you with an opportunity to see how much of the information you have retained. Each self-test includes multiple choice, true-false, fill-in, and matching questions.

- a section entitled **Down-to-Earth Sociology** that asks questions about the material you have read so that you can relate it to your own life and the world with which you are familiar. Remember there is not necessary a right and wrong answer for these; rather, they are designed to get your opinion, based on your understanding of the facts you have read.

- an **Answer Key** that provides answers for all of the questions in the self-test. Check your answers against this; if you got the question wrong, refer back to the pages in the textbook and read those again.

In order to make the best use of the resources in this guide, here are a few suggesting for approaching the material in both the textbook and the study guide:

- Before reading each chapter, refer to the Chapter Summary and Learning Objectives that are found in the Study Guide. The Summary will provide you with a capsule statement of what the chapter is about, and the Learning Objectives will tell you how you should be focusing your attention. Then read the textbook.

- Rather than plunge headlong into the chapter, take a few minutes and orient yourself. Start with the chapter title. This tells you what broad area of sociology will be discussed. Keep the title in mind as you read through the chapter and try to create a mental picture of how the various parts of the chapter fit together within this broad area.

- Approach each chapter one section at time. Use the section headings to pose questions that you can ask yourself when you finish reading the section. As you finish a section, go back to the Learning Objectives in the Study Guide and try to answer the statement(s) that apply. If you can provide an answer, then proceed to the next section; if you can't, go back to the textbook and review the section you've just read.

- Pay attention to the concepts that are in bold-face type. The definition is provided for you; refer to that definition as you read. Try to think of some examples of your own; if you can relate the material to the world with which you are most familiar, you are more likely to remember it.

- Remember to read the boxed text; these pertain to the material in the body of the textbook and are included to give you insights into U.S. society as well as societies around the world. They are designed to bring sociology alive for you.

After you finish reading the textbook, you're ready to use the study guide.

- Review the Chapter Outline. This will provide you with a broad understanding of what ideas were covered in the chapter. If there is information in the outline that is still unfamiliar to you, go back to the textbook and reread that section. The outline can also be used when you are reviewing the material just before a test.

- Check the list of Key Terms to Define. Try and define each word and think of an example. Then check the definitions that are provided within each chapter of the Study Guide to see if you are correct. If you need help thinking of an example, refer back to the textbook chapter.

- Check the list of Key People. See how many you know and whether or not you can identify their contribution to sociology. If you can't, go back to the textbook and locate them within the chapter. (A quick way to do this is to refer to the Index at the back of the textbook, and then go directly to the page listed.)

- Take the self-test. Mark those questions that you got wrong, and try them again in a few days. Use the self-test to review the material just before a test.

If you attend class regularly, take good notes of material covered in class, read each chapter (ideally before the material is presented in class and then review the chapter as you are going over the material in class), and use the resources in the Study Guide you should finish the semester with an better understanding not only of sociology, but of yourself and your social world. I hope that you will enjoy your adventure and find that this subject opens new vistas of understanding to you. Good Luck!

Gwen Nyden, Ph.D.
Oakton Community College
Des Plaines, Illinois

CHAPTER 1
THE SOCIOLOGICAL PERSPECTIVE

☞CHAPTER SUMMARY

- Sociology offers a perspective--a view of the world--which stresses that people's social experiences underlie their behavior.
- Although it is difficult to state precisely when it began, sociology emerged during the upheavals of the Industrial Revolution. Early sociologists were Auguste Comte, Herbert Spencer, Karl Marx, Harriet Martineau, Emile Durkheim, and Max Weber.
- Sociology became established in North America by the end of the 19th century. Within U.S. sociology there has always been a tension between basic sociology and attempts to reform society.
- Because no one theory encompasses all of reality, sociologists use three primary theoretical frameworks: (1) symbolic interactionism--which concentrates on the meanings that underlie people's lives--usually focuses on the micro level; (2) functional analysis--which stresses that society is made up of various parts which, when working properly, contribute to the stability of society--focuses on the macro level; and (3) conflict theory--which stresses inequalities and sees the basis of social life as a competitive struggle to gain control over scarce resources--also focuses on the macro level.
- Sociological research is needed because common sense is highly limited and often incorrect.
- Eight basic steps are included in scientific research: (1) selecting a topic, (2) defining the problem, (3) reviewing the literature, (4) formulating a hypothesis, (5) choosing a research method, (6) collecting the data, (7) analyzing the results, and (8) sharing the results.
- Sociologists use six research methods (or research designs) for gathering data: surveys, participant observations, secondary analysis, documents, unobtrusive measures, and experiments.
- Ethics are of concern to sociologists, who are committed to openness, honesty, truth, and protecting subjects; sociologists are not supposed to misrepresent themselves or their research.
- Research and theory must work together because without theory research is of little value, and if theory is unconnected to research it is unlikely to represent the way life really is.
- Sociologists agree that social research should be value free, but recognize that, at any point in time, sociologists are members of a particular society and are infused with values of all sorts. One of the dilemmas for sociologists is deciding whether the goal of research should be only to advance understanding of human behavior or to reform harmful social arrangements.

☞LEARNING OBJECTIVES

As you read Chapter 1, use these learning objectives to organize your notes. After completing your reading, briefly state an answer to each of the objectives, and review the text pages in parentheses.

1. Explain the sociological perspective and discuss the contribution that it makes to our understanding of human behavior. (2-3)
2. Discuss how and why sociology emerged as a science in the middle of the nineteenth-century in Europe. (3-4)
3. Identify and explain the contributions that each of the following made to the development of sociology: Auguste Comte, Herbert Spencer, Karl Marx, Harriet Martineau, Emile Durkheim, and Max Weber. (4-8)

1

4.   Trace the development of sociology in the United States and explain the tension between social reform and sociological analysis and how applied sociology addresses this tension. (8-10)

5.   Explain the chief differences in the three major theoretical perspectives: symbolic interactionism, functional analysis, and conflict theory. (10-14)

6.   Compare micro-level and macro-level analysis and state which level of analysis is utilized by each of the major theoretical perspectives. (14)

7.   Explain why common sense is an inadequate source of knowledge about human behavior. (14-15)

8.   Identify the eight steps in a research model. (15-17)

9.   List and describe each of the six research methods. (17-22)

10.   Describe the major ethical issues involved in sociological research; demonstrate these issues by using the Brajuha, Scarce, and Humphreys research as examples. (22-24)

11.   Discuss how research and theory work together. (24-25)

12.   State the key issues in the debate about the proper role of values in sociology. (25)

☞ CHAPTER OUTLINE

I.   **The Sociological Perspective**
   A.   This perspective is important because it provides a different way of looking at life; and it contribute to our understanding of why people are the way they are.
   B.   Sociology stresses the broader social context of behavior.
       1.   Sociologists look at the social location--culture, social class, gender, religion, age, and education--of people.
       2.   Sociologists examine the relationship of one group to another.
       3.   Sociologists consider external influences--people's experiences--which are internalized and become part of a person's thinking and motivations, because all people have a tendency to take their particular world for granted.

II.   **The Development of Sociology**
   A.   Throughout history people have tried to figure out social life.
       1.   They asked questions about why there was war and why some people were richer or more powerful than others.
       2.   For much of history, the answers were based on superstition or myth.
   B.   Sociology developed in the middle of the 19th Century when social observers began to use scientific methods to test ideas about social life. Sociology emerged as a result of changes in European societies that were taking place at that time.
       1.   As result of the Industrial Revolution, both traditional society and culture were transformed.
       2.   As a result of the success of the American and French revolutions, new ideas about the rights of individuals within society were accepted, also upsetting tradition.
       3.   The natural sciences began to apply scientific methods to find answers for the questions about the natural order; the same methods were applied to questions being raised about the social world.

III.   **Early Sociologists**
   A.   Auguste Comte coined the term "sociology" and suggested the use of positivism--applying the scientific approach to the social world--but he did not utilize this approach himself.
   B.   Herbert Spencer, another social philosopher, viewed societies as evolutionary, coined the term "the survival of the fittest," and became known for social Darwinism.

C.   Karl Marx, founder of the conflict perspective, believed that class conflict--the struggle between the proletariat and the bourgeoisie--was the key to human history.

D.   Harriet Martineau studied social life in the United States and Great Britain, wrote *Society In America*, and helped to popularize Comte's ideas.

E.   Emile Durkheim studied the social factors which underline suicide and found that the level of social integration, the degree to which people are tied to their social group, was a key social factor in suicide. Central to his studies was the idea that human behavior cannot be understood simply in individual terms, but must be understood within the larger social context in which it occurs.

F.   Max Weber defined religion as a central force in social change, i.e. Protestantism encourages greater economic development and was the central factor in the rise of capitalism in some countries.

IV.   Sociology in North America

A.   Sociology was transplanted to the United States in the late 19th Century, first taking hold at the University of Chicago and Atlanta University.

B.   Since becoming established in the United States, there has been a continuing tension between social reform and sociological analysis.

     1.   Jane Addams was active in promoting social reform. In 1889 she founded Hull House, a settlement house that served the needs of Chicago's urban poor. Sociologists from nearby University of Chicago were frequent visitors.

     2.   W. E. B. Du Bois, an African American, created a sociology laboratory at Atlanta University in 1897, conducted extensive research on race relations in the U.S., and helped found the NAACP.

     3.   During the 1940s, the focus shifted from reform to theory; Talcott Parsons developed abstract models of society to show how the parts of society harmoniously work together.

     4.   In the 1950s, C. Wright Mills urged sociologists to get back to social reform; he saw imminent danger in the emergence of a power elite within the United States.

     5.   Sociology in the United States today is not dominated by any one theoretical orientation or single concern. At the same time, the debate about the proper role of sociology continues.

C.   Recently there has been attempts to blend sociological knowledge with practical results through the development of applied sociology.

     1.   The role of applied sociologists is to recommend changes.

     2.   Clinical sociologists become directly involved in bringing about social change through their work in various social settings.

     3.   Applied sociology is not the same as social reform because the goal is not to rebuild society but to bring about change in a limited setting.

V.   Theoretical Perspectives in Sociology

A.   Theory is defined as a "general statement about how some parts of the world fit together and how they work; an explanation of how two or more facts are related to one another."

B.   There are three major theoretical perspectives in sociology.

     1.   Symbolic interactionism views society as composed of symbols that people use to establish meaning, develop their views of the world, and communicate with one another. A symbolic interactionist studying divorce would focus on the changing meanings of marriage, divorce, and family to explain the increase.

2.   Functional analysis sees society as composed of various parts, each with a function, which contributes to society's equilibrium. Robert Merton used the term functions to refer to the beneficial consequences of people's actions, and dysfunction to refer to consequences that undermine a system's equilibrium. In trying to explain divorce, a functionalist would look how industrialization and urbanization both contributed to the changing function of marriage and the family.

3.   According to conflict theory, society is viewed as composed of groups competing for scarce resources. Divorce is seen as the outcome of the shifting balance of power within the family; as women have gained power and try to address inequalities in the relationship, men resist.

C.   The perspectives differ in their level of analysis:
1.   Macro-level analysis--"an examination of large-scale patterns of society"--is the focus of analysis for functionalists and conflict theorists.
2.   Micro-level analysis--"an examination of small-scale patterns of society"--is the focus for symbolic interactionists.

D.   Putting the theoretical perspectives together:
1.   Each perspective provides a different and often sharply contrasting picture of the world.
2.   Sociologists use all three perspectives because no one theory or level of analysis encompasses all of reality.

VI.   **Sociology and Common Sense**
A.   Common sense cannot be relied on as a source of knowledge because it is highly limited and its insights often are incorrect.
B.   To move beyond common sense and understand what is really going on, it is necessary to do sociological research.

VII.   **A Research Model**
A.   Selecting a topic is guided by sociological curiosity, interest in a particular topic, research funding from governmental or private source, and pressing social issues.
B.   Defining the problem involves specifying exactly what the researcher wants to learn about the topic.
C.   Reviewing the literature uncovers existing knowledge about the problem.
D.   Formulating a hypothesis involves stating the expected relationship between variables, based on a theory. Hypotheses need operational definitions--precise ways to measure the variables.
E.   Choosing a research method is influenced by the research topic.
F.   Collecting the data involves concerns over validity, the extent to which operational definitions measure what was intended, and reliability, the extent to which data produce consistent results.
G.   Analyzing the results involves the use of a range of techniques, from statistical tests to content analysis, to analyze data. Computers have become powerful tools in data analysis because they reduce large amounts of data to basic patterns in much less time than it used to take.
H.   Sharing the results by writing a report and publishing the results makes the findings available for replication.

VIII.   **Six Research Methods**
A.   Surveys involve collecting data by having people answer a series of questions.

1. The first step is to determine a population, the target group to be studied, and selecting a sample, individuals from among the target population who are intended to represent the population to be studied.
2. In a random sample everyone in the target population has the same chance of being included in the study. A stratified random sample is a sample of specific subgroups (e.g. freshmen, sophomores, juniors) of the target population (a college or university) in which everyone in the subgroup has an equal chance or being included in the study.
3. The respondents (people who respond to a survey) must be allowed to express their own ideas so that the findings will not be biased.
4. It is important to establish rapport--a feeling or trust between researchers and subjects.

B. In participant observation, the researcher participates in a research setting while observing what is happening in that setting.
C. Secondary analysis is the analysis of data already collected by other researchers.
D. Documents--written sources--may be obtained from many sources, including books, newspapers, police reports, and records kept by various organizations.
E. Unobtrusive measures involve observing social behavior of people who do not know they are being studied.
F. Experiments are especially useful to determine causal relationships.
1. Experiments involve independent (factors that cause a change in something) and dependent variables (factors that are changed).
2. Experiments require an experimental group--the group of subjects exposed to the independent variable--and a control group--the group of subjects not exposed to the independent variable.

IX. **Ethics In Sociological Research**
A. Ethics are of fundamental concern to sociologists when it comes to doing research.
B. Ethical considerations include being open, honest, and truthful, not falsifying results or stealing someone else's work, not harming the subject in the course of conducting the research, protecting the anonymity of the research subjects, and not misrepresenting themselves to. the research subjects.
C. Efforts by Mario Brajuha and Rik Scarce to honor their research ethics reflect the seriousness with which sociologists view ethical considerations. Research by Laud Humphreys raised questions about how researchers represent themselves to subjects.

X. **How Research and Theory Work Together**
A. Research without theory is of little value: it becomes a collection of meaningless "facts." Theory that is unconnected to research is abstract and empty, unlikely to represent the way life really is.
B. Sociologists combine research and theory in different ways. Theory is used to interpret data (i.e. functionalism, symbolic interaction and conflict theory provide frameworks for interpreting research findings) and it generates research. Research helps to generate theory.

XI. **The Dilemma of Values in Social Research**
A. Weber advocated that sociological research should be value free--personal values or biases should not influence social research--and objective--totally neutral.
1. Sociologists agree that objectivity is a proper goal but acknowledge that no one can escape values entirely.

2.   Replication--repeating a study to see if the same results are round--is one means to avoid the distortions that values can cause.

B.   The proper purposes and uses of sociology are argued among sociologists.

1.   Some lean towards basic sociological research that has no goal beyond understanding social life and testing social theory.

2.   Others feel that the knowledge should be used to reform society.

☞ GLOSSARY OF DIFFICULT-TO-UNDERSTAND WORDS

alleviate: make less painful (25)

armchair philosophy: to speculate about the nature things without ever doing scientific research (5)

bandied about: passed along without being careful (20)

bludgeoned: to hit with heavy impact (24)

Calvinism: one of the early Protestant religious groups whose followers believed that their fate after death was determined before they were even born (8)

collapsed: broken down, so they no longer are separate (15)

commonsense: things everyone should realize (15)

despicable: deserving of contempt (2)

disheveled: untidy, rumpled (2)

dissertation: a lengthy paper written in connection with obtaining a doctoral degree (24)

distortion: being twisted out of shape (20)

doctoral: of or relating to work towards a doctorate degree (23)

eerily: weirdly, disturbingly (2)

encompasses: contains within it (14)

falsification: changing something to make it appear different (22)

hallmark: a feature or trait that distinguishes something from everything else (25)

inalienable rights: rights that may not be taken or traded away (4)

inherent: naturally existing (13)

internalized: make part of your own thinking (3)

laudable: worthy of praise (24)

load the dice: unfairly influence the outcome (20)

misguided do-gooders: people who get in the way while thinking they are helping (5)

objectivity: expressing facts without consideration of personal feelings or prejudices (25)

overwhelmingly: many more people do than do not (20)

pathological: diseased (12)

preconceived: formed in advance (25)

rigorous: strict, precise (6)

Styrofoam cup: a rigid, lightweight cup (2)

subpoenaed: required to be produced in connection with legal proceedings (23)

swishing: moving through a liquid with a light noise (2)

treadmill: a revolving device on which you walk without getting anywhere (21)

unobtrusive: not getting in people's way (22)

urbanization: the movement from rural areas into cities (13)

vested interest: a situation in which a person (or organization) has a strong personal commitment to the existing arrangements (20)

☞ KEY TERMS TO DEFINE

After studying the chapter, define each of the following terms. Then check your work by referring to the answers beginning at page 14 of this Study Guide.

applied sociology	macro level analysis	society
authority	micro level analysis	sociological perspective
basic or pure sociology	nonverbal interaction	sociology
bourgeoisie	positivism	symbolic interactionism
clinical sociology	proletariat	theory
conflict theory	social integration	
functional analysis	social interaction	

☞ KEY PEOPLE

State the major theoretical contributions or findings of these people.

Auguste Comte	Laud Humphreys	C. Wright Mills
Mario Brajuha	Harriet Martineau	Rik Scarce
W. E. B. Du Bois	Karl Marx	Herbert Spencer
Emile Durkheim	Robert K. Merton	Max Weber

☞ SELF-TEST

After completing this self-test, check your answers against the Answer Key beginning on page 14 of this Study Guide and against the text on the pages) indicated in parentheses.

MULTIPLE CHOICE QUESTIONS

1. An approach to understanding human behavior by placing it in broader social context is: (2)
   a. social location.
   b. the sociological perspective.
   c. common sense.
   d. generalization.

2. A group of people who share a culture or territory are referred to as: (2)
   a. a tribe.
   b. a cultural grouping.
   c. a society.
   d. a nation.

3. According to the sociological perspective, people do what they do because of: (3)
   a. internal mechanisms like instincts.
   b. external influences which become internalized.
   c. a combination of internal and external forces.
   d. external forces which are shaped by internal mechanisms.

4.   The application of the scientific approach to the social world is known as: (4)
    a.   ethnomethodology.
    b.   sociobiology.
    c.   natural science.
    d.   positivism.

5.   The principle of "the survival of the fittest" was first stated by: (5)
    a.   Herbert Spencer.
    b.   Charles Darwin.
    c.   Auguste Comte.
    d.   Karl Marx.

6.   According to Karl Marx, capitalists, who own the means of production, exploit the: (5)
    a.   bourgeoisie.
    b.   proletariat.
    c.   masses.
    d.   peasants.

7.   Which of the following early sociologists studied social life in England and the United States? (5)
    a.   Emile Durkheim
    b.   Karl Marx
    c.   Harriet Martineau
    d.   W.E.B. DuBois

8.   According to Emile Durkheim, suicide rates can be explained by: (6)
    a.   social factors.
    b.   common sense.
    c.   the oppression of the proletariat by the bourgeoisie.
    d.   the survival of the fittest.

9.   According to Max Weber, the central force in social change is: (8)
    a.   technology.
    b.   economics.
    c.   religion.
    d.   immigration.

10.   One of the first U.S. sociologists to study race relations was: (8)
    a.   Jane Addams
    b.   W.E.B. DuBois
    c.   Albion Small
    d.   George Herbert Mead

11.   _____ study the symbols people use to establish meaning and communicate. (11)
    a.   Functionalists.
    b.   Symbolic interactionists.
    c.   Dramaturgical theorists.
    d.   Conflict theorists.

12. In explaining the high U.S. divorce rate, the _____ perspective would focus on explanations such as emotional satisfaction, the meaning of children, and the meaning of parenthood. (11)
   a.   conflict
   b.   functional
   c.   symbolic interaction
   d.   exchange

13. According to Robert Merton, an action intended to help a system's equilibrium is a: (12)
   a.   manifest function.
   b.   latent function.
   c.   dysfunction.
   d.   latent dysfunction.

14. Industrialization and urbanization have undermined the traditional purposes of the family, according to theorists using _____ analysis. (13)
   a.   conflict
   b.   exchange
   c.   symbolic interaction
   d.   functional

15. The idea that conflict is inherent in all relations that have authority was first asserted by: (13)
   a.   Karl Marx.
   b.   Auguste Comte.
   c.   Ralf Dahrendorf.
   d.   Emile Durkheim.

16. Conflict theorists might explain the high rate of divorce by looking at: (14)
   a.   the changing meanings associated with marriage and divorce.
   b.   society's basic inequalities between males and females.
   c.   changes which have weakened the family unit.
   d.   the loss of family functions which held a husband and wife together.

17. All of the following are true regarding the symbolic interactionist perspective, except: (14)
   a.   this perspective tends to focus on macro-level analysis.
   b.   this perspective tends to focus on micro-level analysis.
   c.   this perspective looks at social interaction.
   d.   this perspective focuses on communications--both talk and nonverbal interactions.

18. In studying the homeless, functionalists would focus on: (14)
   a.   what the homeless say and what they do.
   b.   how changes in parts of the society are related to homelessness.
   c.   the micro level inequalities in society.
   d.   the macro level inequalities in society.

19.   According to your text, which theoretical perspective is best for studying human behavior? (14)
    a.   the functionalist perspective.
    b.   the symbolic interactionist perspective.
    c.   the conflict perspective.
    d.   A combination of all of the above.

20.   Sociologists believe that research is necessary because: (14-15)
    a.   common sense ideas may or may not be true.
    b.   they want to move beyond guesswork.
    c.   researchers want to know what really is going on.
    d.   All of the above.

21.   _____ steps are involved in scientific research. (15-17)
    a.   Four
    b.   Six
    c.   Eight
    d.   Ten

22.   A relationship between or among variables is predicted: (16)
    a.   by a hypothesis.
    b.   by use of operational definitions.
    c.   when the researcher selects the topic to be studied.
    d.   when the researcher is analyzing the results.

23.   Reliability refers to: (16)
    a.   the extent to which operational definitions measure what they are intended to measure.
    b.   the extent to which data produce consistent results.
    c.   the integrity of the researcher.
    d.   the ways in which the variables in a hypothesis are measured.

24.   Based on the table in your text, all of the following are ways to measure "average" except: (19)
    a.   medial.
    b.   mean.
    c.   median.
    d.   mode.

25.   All of the following are research methods for gathering data, except: (17-22)
    a.   ethnomethodology.
    b.   surveys.
    c.   unobtrusive measures.
    d.   secondary analysis.

26.   A sample is defined as: (17)
    a.   a selection from the larger population.
    b.   a partial representation of the target group.
    c.   the individuals intended to represent the population to be studied.
    d.   subgroups of the population in which every member has an equal chance of selection.

27. The analysis of data already collected by other researchers is referred to as: (22)
    a. surveying the literature.
    b. use of documents.
    c. secondary analysis.
    d. replication.

28. In an experiment, the group not exposed to the independent variable in the study is: (22)
    a. the guinea pig group.
    b. the control group.
    c. the experimental group.
    d. the maintenance group.

29. Research ethics require: (22)
    a. openness.
    b. that a researcher not falsify results or plagiarize someone else's work.
    c. that research subjects should not be harmed by the research.
    d. All of the above.

30. Research which makes discoveries about life human groups rather than make changes in those groups is: (25)
    a. pure or basic sociology.
    b. applied sociology.
    c. clinical sociology.
    d. None of the above.

TRUE-FALSE QUESTIONS

T F 1. The sociological perspective helps us to understand that people's social experiences underlie what they feel and what they do. (2)

T F 2. Sociologists believe that internal mechanisms are very important in explaining an individual's thinking and motivations. (3)

T F 3. Sociology stresses external factors in trying to understand individual behavior. (3)

T F 4. Historically, the success of the natural sciences led to the search for answers to the social world as well. (4)

T F 5. Herbert Spencer believed that human societies evolve like those of animal species. (5)

T F 6. Karl Marx thought that a classless society eventually would exist. (5)

T F 7. Marxism is the same thing as communism. (5)

T F 8. According to Durkheim, social integration is the degree to which people feel that they are a part of a social group. (6)

T F 9. The ideas of Max Weber and Karl Marx are almost identical. (8)

T F 10. There are three major theoretical perspectives within the discipline of sociology. (10)

T F 11. Symbolic interactionists primarily analyze how our definitions of ourselves and others underlie our behaviors. (10-11)

T F 12. According to functionalists, the family has lost all of its traditional purposes. (23)

T F 13. All conflict theorists focus on conflict between the bourgeoisie and the proletariat. (13)

T F 14. Micro-level analysis focuses on social interaction. (14)

T F 15. Research generally confirms common sense. (15)

T F   16.   After selecting a topic, the next step in the research model is defining the problem. (15)
T F   17.   Sociologists have developed six basic research methods. (16)
T F   18.   Reliability is the extent to which data produce consistent results. (16)
T F   19.   Sharing the results is the final step in the research model. (17)
T F   20.   One of the first steps in conducting survey research is to determine a population. (17)
T F   21.   In survey research, it is undesirable for respondents to express their own ideas. (21)
T F   22.   The wording of questionnaires can affect research results. (20)
T F   23.   Secondary analysis and use of documents mean the same thing in terms of research methods. (22)
T F   24.   In an experiment, the experimental group is not exposed to the independent variable in the study. (22)
T F   25.   It is always unethical to observe social behavior in people when they do not know they are being studied. (22)

FILL-IN QUESTIONS

1.   The _____ stresses the social contexts in which people are immersed and which influence their lives. (2)
2.   The use of objective systematic observation to test theories is _____. (4)
3.   The idea of applying the scientific method to the social world is _____. (4)
4.   Durkheim used the term _____ to refer to the degree to which people are tied to their social group. (6)
5.   A _____ is a general statement about how some parts of the world fit together and how they work. (10)
6.   The theoretical perspective in which society is viewed as composed of symbols that people use to establish meaning, develop their views of the world, and communicate with one another is _____. (11)
7.   _____ analysis is a theoretical framework in which society is viewed as composed of various parts, each with a function that contributes to society's equilibrium. (11)
8.   Karl Marx believed that the key to all human history is class struggle between the _____, a small group of capitalists who own the means to produce wealth, and the _____, the mass of workers who are exploited by the capitalists. (13)
9.   Power that people consider legitimate is known as _____. (13)
10.   _____ analysis examines large-scale patterns of society, while _____ analysis examines small-scale patterns of society. (14)
11.   Hypotheses need _____, which are precise ways to measure variables. (16)
12.   _____ is the extent to which data produce consistent results. (16)
13.   The six research methods are: (1) _____, (2) _____, (3)_____, (4) _____, (5) _____, and (6)_____. (17-22)
14.   When the researcher asks the respondent a series of questions directly, either face-to-face or by telephone, this method is called a(n) _____. (17)
15.   A _____ is a concise way of presenting information. (18)
16.   _____ is a feeling of trust between researchers and subjects. (21)
17.   To conduct an experiment, the researcher has two groups: (1) _____ and (2)_____. (22)
18.   Research _____ require openness, honesty, and truth. (22)

19.   Research and _____ are interdependent, and sociologists combine them in their work. (24)

20.   _____ sociology makes discoveries about life in human groups, not to make changes in those groups. (25)

MATCHING QUESTIONS

___1. Auguste Comte
___2. Herbert Spencer
___3. Karl Marx
___4. C. Wright Mills
___5. Emile Durkheim
___6. Harriet Martineau
___7. positivism
___8. W.E.B. Du Bois
___9. Max Weber
___10. population
___11. sample
___12. secondary analysis
___13. documents
___14. dependent variable
___15. Robert K. Merton

a. *coined the phrase "survival of the fittest"*
b. *was an early African American sociologist*
c. *proposed the use of positivism*
d. *stressed social factors*
e. *believed religion was a central force in social change*
f. *believed the key to human history was class struggle*
g. *encouraged the use of the sociological perspective*
h. *published **Society in America** and translated Comte's work into English*
i. *the application of scientific methods to the social world*
j. *a factor that is changed by an independent variable*
k. *written sources*
l. *the target group to be studied*
m. *the analysis of data already collected by other researchers*
n. *used the terms **functions** and **dysfunctions***
o. *the individuals intended to represent the population to be studied*

"DOWN-TO-EARTH SOCIOLOGY"

1.   What insights do you think you might gain in your personal life by applying the sociological perspective?

2.   After reading "Sociologists at Work," can you think of some other ways in which sociological knowledge and the sociological perspective would be useful in the working world?

3.   Assume that you have decided to pursue a career in sociology. What research topics do you find most interesting? What methods would you most likely to use? What ethical constraints do you think you might face?

4.   Can you give examples similar to those in your text where researchers have loaded the dice to enhance the qualities of a product or a political candidate?

5.   The author provides examples of three different research projects that involved some ethical considerations. In each of these cases, did you agree or disagree with the position taken by the researcher? How would you have reacted in the same situation?

6.   What role do you think sociology plays in a world of turmoil? Do you understand why sociology makes some people uncomfortable? Does it make you uncomfortable in any way?

☞ ANSWERS FOR CHAPTER 1

DEFINITIONS OF KEY TERMS

applied sociology: the use of sociology to solve social problems--from the micro level of family relationships to the macro level of war and pollution

authority: power that people accept as rightly exercised over them; also called legitimate power

basic (or pure) sociology: sociological research whose only purpose is to make discoveries about life in human groups, not to make changes in those groups

bourgeoisie: Marx's term for capitalists. those who own the means to produce wealth

clinical sociology: the direct involvement of sociologists in bringing about social change

conflict theory: a theoretical framework in which society is viewed as composed of groups competing for scarce resources

functional analysis: a theoretical framework in which society is viewed as composed of various parts, each with a function that, when fulfilled, contributes to society's equilibrium; also known as functionalism and structural functionalism

macro-level analysis: an examination of large-scale patterns of society

micro-level analysis: an examination of small-scale patterns of society

nonverbal interaction: communication without words through gestures, space, silence, and so on

positivism: the application of the scientific approach to the social world

proletariat: Marx's term for the people who work for those who own the means of production

social integration: the degree to which people feel a part of social groups

social interaction: what people do when they are in one another's presence

society: a group of people who share a culture and a territory

sociological perspective: an approach to understanding human behavior by placing it within its broader social context

sociology: the scientific study of society and human behavior

symbolic interaction: a theoretical perspective in which society is viewed as composed of symbols that people use to establish meaning, develop their views of the world, and communicate with one another

theory: a general statement about how some parts of the world fit together and how they work; an explanation of how two or more facts are related to one another

ANSWERS FOR THE MULTIPLE-CHOICE QUESTIONS

1. b   The sociological perspective is an approach to understanding human behavior by placing it within its broader social context. (2)
2. c   A society is defined as a group of people who share a culture or territory. (2)
3. b   According to the sociological perspective, human behavior is shaped by external forces, that become internalized through the process of socialization. (3)
4. d   Positivism is the application of the scientific approach to the social world. (4)
5. a   Herbert Spencer first stated the principle of "the survival of the fittest;" however, it often is attributed to Charles Darwin. (5)
6. b   The proletariat is the large group of workers who are exploited by the small group of capitalists who own the means of production, according to Karl Marx. (5)
7. c   Harriet Martineau was an early sociologist who studied social life in both England and the United States; she published a book entitled *Society in America*. (5)

8. a Durkheim believed that social factors--patterns of behavior that characterize a social group-- explain many types of behavior, including suicide rates. (6)

9. c Max Weber disagreed with Karl Marx about the central force responsible for social change; he believed religion, rather than economic factors, was critical for social change. (8)

10. b W.E.B. DuBois was an early U.S. sociologist who studied race relations. (8)

11. b Symbolic interactionists study the symbols that people use to establish meaning and communicate with one another. (11)

12. c In explaining the high U.S. divorce rate, the symbolic interaction perspective would focus on explanations such as emotional satisfaction, the meaning of children, and the meaning of parenthood. (11)

13. a According to Robert Merton, an action intended to help a system's equilibrium is a manifest function. (12)

14. d Industrialization and urbanization have undermined the traditional purposed of the family, according to theorists using functional analysis. (13)

15. c The idea that conflict is inherent in all relations that have authority was first asserted by Ralf Dahrendorf. (13)

16. b Conflict theorists might explain the high rate of divorce by looking at society's basic inequalities between males and females. (14)

17. a The symbolic interactionist perspective does not focus on macro-level analysis but rather on the micro-level. It emphasizes social interaction and communication. (14)

18. b In studying the homeless, functionalists would focus on how changes in parts of the society are related to homelessness. Symbolic interactionists would emphasize what the homeless say and what they do. Conflict theorists tend to focus on macro-level inequalities in society--such as how the policies of the wealthy push certain groups into unemployment. (14)

19. d Since each theoretical perspective provides a different, often sharply contrasting picture of our world, no theory or level of analysis encompasses all of reality. By putting the contributions of each perspective and level of analysis together, we gain a more comprehensive picture of social life. (14)

20. d "All of the above" is correct. Sociologists believe that research is necessary because common sense ideas may or may not be true; they want to move beyond guesswork; and researchers want to know what really is going on. (14-15)

21. c Eight steps are involved in scientific research. (15-17)

22. a A relationship between or among variables is predicted by a hypothesis. (16)

23. b Reliability refers to the extent to which data produce consistent results. (16)

24. a Mean, median, and mode are ways to measure "average." (19)

25. a Ethnomethodology is the study of how people use background assumptions to make sense of life and, thus, is a part of symbolic interactionism. Surveys, unobtrusive measures, and secondary analysis are research methods for gathering data. (17-22)

26. c A sample is defined as the individuals intended to represent the population to be studied. (17)

27. c The analysis of data already collected by other researchers is secondary analysis. (22)

28. b In an experiment, the group not exposed to the independent variable in the study is the control group. (22)

29. d All of the above is correct. Research ethics require openness; that a researcher not falsify results or plagiarize someone else's work; and that research subjects should not be harmed by the research. (22)

30. a   The purpose of basic or pure sociological research is to make discoveries about life in human groups, not to make changes in those groups. On the other hand, applied and clinical sociology are more involved in suggesting or bringing about social change. (25)

ANSWERS FOR TRUE-FALSE QUESTIONS

1.   *True* (2)
2.   *False*. Sociologists focus on external influences (people's experiences) instead of internal mechanisms, such as instincts. (3)
3.   *True* (3)
4.   *True* (4)
5.   *True* (5)
6.   *True* (5)
7.   *False*. Although Marx stood firmly behind revolution as the only way for the proletariat to gain control of society, he did not develop the political system called communism, which was a later application of his ideas. (5)
8.   *True* (6)
9.   *False*. Weber agreed with much of what Marx wrote, but he strongly disagreed that economics is the central force in social change. Weber saw religion as playing that role. (8)
10.   *True* (10)
11.   *True* (10-11)
12.   *False*. Although functionalists do believe the family has lost many or its traditional purposes, they do not believe they have all been lost. Some of the existing functions are presently under assault or are being eroded. (13)
13.   *False*. Some conflict theorists use this theory in a much broader sense. For example, Ralf Dahrendorf sees conflict as inherent in all relationships that have authority. (13)
14.   *True* (14)
15.   *False*. Research often does not confirm common sense. The application of research methods takes us beyond common sense and allows us to penetrate surface realities so we can better understand social life. (15)
16.   *True*. (15)
17.   *True*. (16)
18.   *True*. (16)
19.   *True*. (17)
20.   *True*. (17)
21.   *False*. In survey research, it is always desirable for respondents to express their own ideas. (21)
22.   *True*. (20)
23.   *False*. Secondary analysis and use of documents are not the same thing. The data used in secondary analysis is gathered by other researchers while documents may be anything from diaries to police records. (22)
24.   *False*. In an experiment, the experimental group is exposed to the independent variable in the study. The control group is not exposed to the independent variable. (22)
25.   *False*. It is not always unethical to observe social behavior in people when they do not know they are being studied. However, there are certain circumstances in which the issue of ethics should be raised. (22)

ANSWERS FOR THE FILL-IN QUESTIONS.

1. The <u>SOCIOLOGICAL PERSPECTIVE</u> stresses the social contexts in which people are immersed and which influence their lives. (2)
2. The use of objective systematic observation to test theories is <u>SCIENTIFIC METHOD</u>. (4)
3. The idea of applying the scientific method to the social world is <u>POSITIVISM</u>. (4)
4. Durkheim used the term <u>SOCIAL INTEGRATION</u> to refer to the degree to which people are tied to their social group. (6)
5. A <u>THEORY</u> is a general statement about how some parts of the world fit together and how they work. (10)
6. The theoretical perspective in which society is viewed as composed of symbols that people use to establish meaning, develop their views of the world, and communicate with one another is <u>SYMBOLIC INTERACTIONISM</u>. (11)
7. <u>FUNCTIONAL</u> analysis is a theoretical framework in which society is viewed as composed of various parts, each with a function that contributes to society's equilibrium. (11)
8. Karl Marx believed that the key to all human history is class struggle between the <u>BOURGEOISIE</u>, a small group of capitalists who own the means to produce wealth, and the <u>PROLETARIAT</u>, the mass of workers who are exploited by the capitalists. (13)
9. Power that people consider legitimate is known as <u>AUTHORITY</u>. (13)
10. <u>MACRO-LEVEL</u> analysis examines large-scale patterns of society, while <u>MICRO-LEVEL</u> analysis examines small-scale patterns of society. (14)
11. Hypotheses need <u>OPERATIONAL DEFINITIONS</u>, which are precise ways to measure variables. (16)
12. <u>RELIABILITY</u> is the extent to which data produce consistent results. (16)
13. The six research methods are: (1) <u>SURVEYS</u>, (2) <u>SECONDARY ANALYSIS</u>, (3) <u>DOCUMENTS</u>, (4) <u>PARTICIPANT OBSERVATION</u>, (5) <u>EXPERIMENTS</u>, and (6)<u>UNOBTRUSIVE MEASURES</u>. (17-22)
14. When the researcher asks the respondent a series of questions directly, either face-to-face or by telephone, this method is called a(n) <u>INTERVIEW</u>. (17)
15. A <u>TABLE</u> is a concise way of presenting information. (18)
16. <u>RAPPORT</u> is a feeling of trust between researchers and subjects. (21)
17. To conduct an experiment, the researcher has two groups: (1) <u>EXPERIMENTAL GROUP</u> and (2)<u>CONTROL GROUP</u>. (22)
18. Research <u>ETHICS</u> require openness, honesty, and truth. (22)
19. Research and <u>THEORY</u> are interdependent, and sociologists combine them in their work. (24)
20. <u>BASIC (OR PURE)</u> sociology makes discoveries about life in human groups, not to make changes in those groups. (25)

ANSWERS TO THE MATCHING QUESTIONS

1. c   August Comte: *proposed the use of positivism*
2. a   Herbert Spencer: *coined the phrase "the survival of the fittest"*
3. f   Karl Marx: *believed the key to human history was class struggle*
4. g   C. Wright Mills: *encouraged the use of the sociological perspective*
5. d   Emile Durkheim: *stressed social factors*
6. h   Harriet Martineau: *published **Society in America** and translated Comte's work into English*
7. i   positivism: *the application of scientific methods to the social world*

8. b   W.E.B. Du Bois: *was an early African American sociologist*
9. e   Max Weber: *believed religion was a central force in social change*
10. l   population: *the target group to be studied*
11. o   sample: *the individuals intended to represent the population to be studied*
12. m   secondary analysis: *the analysis of data already collected by other researchers*
13. k   documents: *written sources*
14. j   dependent variable: *a factor that is changed by an independent variable*
15. n   Robert K. Merton: *used the terms **functions** and **dysfunctions***

CHAPTER 2
CULTURE

☞ CHAPTER SUMMARY

- Culture refers to the language, beliefs, values, norms, and material objects passed from one generation to the next. Culture is both material (buildings, clothing, tools) and nonmaterial (ways of thinking and patterns of behavior). Ideal culture refers to a group's values, norms, and goals; real culture refers to its actual behavior. People are naturally ethnocentric, using their own culture to judge others; cultural relativism is the attempt to understand other cultures in their own terms.

- Components of culture include symbols, language, gestures, values. norms, and sanctions, folkways and mores. Language is essential for culture because it allows us to move beyond the present, sharing with others our past experiences and our future plans. According to the Sapir-Whorf hypothesis, language not only expresses our thinking and perceptions but actually shapes them. All groups have values, standards by which they define what is desirable and undesirable, and norms, rules about appropriate behavior. Socially imposed sanctions maximize conformity to social norms.

- U.S. society is composed of a dominant culture and many subcultures. It also contains a number of countercultures which subscribe to values that set members in opposition to the dominant culture.

- Core values in U.S. society identified by Robin Williams emphasize personal achievement and success, hard work, and moral orientation. Values that are emerging as core values today within U.S. culture include leisure, physical fitness, self-fulfillment, and the environment. Ideal culture, the ideal values and norms of a society, exists in contrast to real culture, the norms and values that are actually followed.

- To the extent that some animals teach their young certain behavior, animals also have culture; however, no animals have language in the sociological sense of the term.

- As cultures come in contact with one another, groups learn from one another and adapt some part of their way of life; through this process of cultural diffusion changes take place in a culture. Today the technology in travel and communication makes cultural diffusion around the globe occur more rapidly than in the past, resulting in some degree of cultural leveling, a process by which cultures become similar to one another.

☞ LEARNING OBJECTIVES

As you read Chapter 2, use these learning objectives to organize your notes. After completing your reading, briefly state an answer to each of the objectives, and review the text pages in parentheses.

1. Define culture and explain its material and nonmaterial components. (31)
2. Differentiate between ethnocentrism and cultural relativism. (32-34)
3. Discuss the symbolic components of culture, including language and gestures. (34-38)
4. Define the following terms: values, norms, sanctions, folkways, mores, and taboos. (38-39)
5. Compare and contrast dominant culture, subcultures, and countercultures. (39-40)
6. List the core values in U.S. society as identified by Robin Williams. Identify the values that Henslin added to this list. (40-42)
7. Explain what is meant by value clusters and value contradictions. (42)

8.   Discuss the emergent values in U.S. society and analyze why core values do not change without meeting strong resistance. (43-44)
9.   Demonstrate how values act as blinders. (44-45)
10.   Explain the difference between "ideal" and "real" cultures. (45)
11.   Answer the question, "Do animals have culture?" (45-47)
12.   Define cultural diffusion and explain its relationship to cultural leveling. (47-49)

☞ CHAPTER OUTLINE

I.   **What is Culture?**
      A.   Culture is defined as the language, beliefs, values, norms, behaviors, and even material objects passed from one generation to the next.
            1.   Material culture is things such as jewelry, art, buildings, weapons, machines, clothing, hairstyles, etc.
            2.   Nonmaterial culture is a group's ways of thinking (beliefs, values, and assumptions) and common patterns of behavior (language, gestures, and other forms of interaction).
      B.   Culture provides a taken-for-granted orientation to life.
            1.   We assume that our own culture is normal or natural; in fact, it is not natural, but rather is learned. It penetrates our lives so deeply that it is taken for granted and provides the lens through which we evaluate things.
            2.   It provides implicit instructions that tell us what we ought to do and a moral imperative that defines what we think is right and wrong.
            3.   Coming into contact with a radically different culture produces "culture shock," challenging our basic assumptions.
            4.   A consequence of internalizing culture is ethnocentrism, using our own culture (and assuming it to be good, right, and superior) to judge other cultures. It is functional when it creates in-group solidarity, but can be dysfunctional if it leads to harmful discrimination.
      C.   Cultural relativism consists of trying to appreciate other groups' ways of life in the context in which they exist, without judging them as superior or inferior to our own.
            1.   This view helps to avoid "cultural smugness."
            2.   Robert Edgerton argues that those cultural practices that result in exploitation *should* be judged morally inferior to those that enhance people's lives.
II.   **Components of Culture**
      A.   Sociologists sometimes refer to nonmaterial culture as symbolic culture because a central component are the symbols.
            1.   Symbols are something to which people attach meaning--that people use to communicate.
            2.   Symbols include language, gestures, values, norms, sanctions, folkways, and mores.
      B.   Gestures, using one's body to communicate with others, are shorthand means of communication.
            1.   Gestures are used by people in every culture, although the gestures and the meanings differ; confusion or offense can result because of misunderstandings over the meaning of a gesture or misuse of a gesture.
            2.   There is disagreement over whether there are any universal gestures.

C. Language consists of a system of symbols that can be put together in an infinite number of ways in order to communicate abstract thought. Each word is a symbol to which a culture attaches a particular meaning.
   1. Language is important because it is the primary means of communication between people.
   2. It allows human experiences to be cumulative; each generation builds on the body of significant experiences that is passed on to it by the previous generation, thus freeing people to move beyond immediate experiences. It extends time back into the past, enabling us to share our past experiences, and forward into the future, allowing us to share our future plans. It expands connections beyond our immediate, face-to-face groups.
   3. It allows shared perspectives or understandings and complex, goal-directed behavior.
D. The Sapir-Whorf hypothesis states that our thinking and perception not only are expressed by language but actually are shaped by language because we are taught not only words but also a particular way of thinking and perceiving. Rather than objects and events forcing themselves onto our consciousness, our very language determines our consciousness.
E. Values, norms, and sanctions:
   1. Values are the standards by which people define good and bad, beautiful and ugly. Every group develops both values and expectations regarding the right way to reflect them.
   2. Norms are expectations, or rules of behavior, that reflect a group's values.
   3. Sanctions are the positive or negative reactions to the way in which people follow norms. Positive sanctions (a money reward, a prize, a smile, or even a handshake) are expressions of approval; negative sanctions (a fine, a frown, or harsh words) denote disapproval for breaking a norm.
F. Folkways and mores:
   1. Folkways are norms that are not strictly enforced, such as passing on the left side of the sidewalk. They may result in a person getting a dirty look.
   2. Mores are norms that are believed to be essential to core values and we insist on conformity. A person who steals, rapes, and kills has violated some of society's most important mores and will be formally sanctioned.
   3. One group's folkways may constitute another group's mores. A male walking down the street with the upper half of his body uncovered may be violating a folkway; a female doing the same thing may be violating accepted mores.
   4. Taboos are norms so strongly ingrained that even the thought of them is greeted with revulsion. Eating human flesh and having sex with one's parents are examples of such behavior.

III. **Many Cultural Worlds: Subcultures and Countercultures**
A. Subcultures are groups whose values and related behaviors are so distinct that they set their members off from the general culture. Each subculture is a world within the larger world of the dominant culture, and has a distinctive way of looking at life, but remains compatible with the dominant culture.
   1. U.S. society contains thousands of subcultures, some as broad as the way of life we associate with teenagers, others as narrow as skateboards and boating enthusiasts.

2. Ethnic groups often form subcultures with their own language, distinctive food, religious practices and other customs.

B. Countercultures are groups whose values set their members in opposition to the dominant culture.

1. Countercultures challenge the culture's core values.

2. While usually associated with negative behavior--heavy metal adherents who glorify Satanism, hatred, cruelty, rebellion, sexism, violence, and death, are an example of a such a negative counterculture--some countercultures are not--the Mormons would be an example of a counterculture because they challenged the core value of monogamy, and yet they were not seen as negative.

3. Often threatened by a counterculture, members of the broader culture sometimes move against it in order to affirm their own values.

IV. **Values in American Society**

A. Identifying core values in U.S. society is difficult, due to the many different religious, racial, ethnic, and special interest groups that are found in this society.

1. Sociologist Robin Williams identified achievement and success (especially, doing better than others); individualism (success due to individual effort); activity and work; efficiency and practicality; science and rationality (using science to control nature); progress; material comfort; humanitarianism (helpfulness, personal kindness, philanthropy); freedom; democracy; equality (especially of opportunity); and racism and group superiority.

2. Author Henslin updated Williams's list by adding education; religiosity (belief in a Supreme Being and following some set of matching precepts); and romantic love (as the basis for marriage) and monogamy (no more than one spouse at a time).

B. Values are not independent units; value clusters are made up of related core values that come together to form a larger whole. In the value cluster surrounding success, for example, we find hard work, education, efficiency, material comfort, and individualism all bound together.

C. Some values conflict with each other. There cannot be full expressions of democracy, equality, racism, and sexism at the same time. These are value contradictions and as society changes some values are challenged and undergo modification.

D. As society changes over time, new core values emerge that reflect changed social conditions. Examples of emergent values in the United States today are: leisure (including the expectancy of retirement benefits); physical fitness; self-fulfillment; and concern for the environment.

E. Core values do not change without meeting strong resistance. A major criticism of the emergent value cluster of leisure, physical fitness and self-fulfillment is that they encourage individualism at the cost of social responsibility. Hunters, builders, and business people feel that their rights are being trampled on as a result of concern for the environment.

F. Values and their supporting beliefs may blind people to other social circumstances. Success stories blind many people in the United States to the dire consequences of family poverty, lack of education, and dead-end jobs.

G. Ideal culture refers to the ideal values and norms of a people. What people actually do usually falls short of this ideal, and sociologists refer to the norms and values that people actually follow as real culture.

V.   **Animals and Culture**
       A.   Much of animal behavior is controlled by instincts, inherited patterns of behavior common to all normal members of a species. By definition, that does not constitute culture.
              1.   Anthropologist Jane Goodall discovered that chimpanzees made and used a form of simple tool (a blade of grass, stripped of its leaves and licked on one end) that they would stick into a nest of termites and then pull out, enabling them to eat the termites. This behavior on the part of the chimpanzees was a form of animal culture: learned, shared behavior among animals.
              2.   Other scientists have learned that the mating behavior of some animals is learned, rather than pure instinct. Young gorillas raised in captivity seem to want to mate, but don't know how; watching a movie of two adult gorillas mating changes that.
       B.   To the extent that some animals teach their young certain behaviors, they have culture. No animals, however, have language in the sociological sense of that term, although some animals apparently do have the capacity to learn language.

VI.   **The Global Village: Cultural Diffusion and Cultural Leveling**
       A.   For most of human history cultures had little contact with one another; however, there was always some contact with other groups, resulting in groups learning from one another.
              1.   Social scientists refer to this transmission of cultural characteristics as cultural diffusion.
              2.   Material culture is more likely than the nonmaterial culture to change as a result of cultural diffusion.
              3.   Cultural diffusion occurs more rapidly today, given the technology.
       B.   The world is being united by travel and communication to such an extent that there is almost no "other side of the world." Japan, for example, no longer is a purely Eastern culture, having adopted not only Western economic production, but also Western forms of dress, music, and so on. This is cultural leveling, the process in which cultures become similar to one another.

☞ GLOSSARY OF DIFFICULT-TO-UNDERSTAND WORDS

adherents: people who argue in favor of something (39)

arbitrary: making distinctions that may be incorrect (32)

bag of scum: an insulting expression, meaning someone is disgusting (36)

bilingual: speaking at least two languages (37)

burros: donkeys (30)

clamored: gathered around demanding something (30)

codified: systematically classified (37)

divergent: varying from one to another (40)

dweebs, dorks, nerds: people regarded as dull (38)

embodiment: solid example of (37)

ethnic stews: a mix of ethnic groups (37)

Fahrenheit: a scale for measuring temperature (30)

flailing: moving his arms around wildly (30)

flare-ups: sudden outbursts of anger (37)

hygiene: practices related to cleanliness (31)

hypothesis: a statement about the relationship between two phenomenon (38)

ingrained: forming an essential part of one's being (39)

inherently: involving the essential character of something (31)

interrelated: connected in various ways (43)

makeshift: crude and temporary; a substitute (30)

mecca: a place sought as a goal by many people (37)

microbes: very small organisms, such as germs (31)

microcosms: small samples (39)

monolingual: speaking only one language (37)

paleontologist: one who studies prehistoric life forms (45)

pervasive: spread throughout (31)

philanthropy: helping mankind, by giving gifts and doing good deeds (41)

precepts: rules of action or conduct (42)

profound: having deep feelings (31)

rudimentary: most simple (36)

satanism: the worship of Satan (40)

sequence: the order in which things appear (38)

shoo off the flies: driving flies away by sounds or gestures (30)

shorthand: using symbols for words or thoughts (34)

sidestepped: gotten around (42)

skateboarders: people who ride small boards on small wheels (39)

smugness: feeling extremely correct about something; very satisfied with yourself (33)

strange tongue: unaccustomed language (30)

succinct: stated clearly in a very few words (34)

superimposed: placed over something else (48)

surreptitiously: secretly, furtively (31)

temporal: worldly; relating to time rather than space (36)

unflinching: not moving or shrinking away (43)

weeded out: removed from something more desirable (33)

yardstick: a standard using in measuring (32)

☞ KEY TERMS TO DEFINE

After studying the chapter, define each of the following terms. Then check your work by referring to the answers beginning at page 30 of this Study Guide.

counterculture	ideal culture	real culture
cultural diffusion	instincts	sanction
cultural leveling	language	Sapir-Whorf hypothesis
cultural relativism	material culture	subculture
culture	mores	symbol
culture contact	negative sanction	symbolic culture
culture shock	nonmaterial culture	taboo
ethnocentrism	norms	value cluster
folkways	pluralistic society	value contradiction
gestures	positive sanction	values

☞ KEY PEOPLE
State the major theoretical contributions or findings of these people.

Charles Darwin	Edward Sapir	Robin Williams
Allen & Beatrice Gardner	William Sumner	Edward O. Wilson
Jane Goodall	Benjamin Whorf	

☞ SELF-TEST
After completing this self-test, check your answers against the Answer Key beginning on page 30 of this Study Guide and against the text on page(s) indicated in parentheses.

MULTIPLE CHOICE QUESTIONS

1. A group's ways of thinking and doing, including language and other forms of interaction is: (31)
    a.   material culture.
    b.   nonmaterial culture.
    c.   ideological culture.
    d.   values.

2. Material culture includes: (31)
    a.   weapons and machines.
    b.   eating utensils.
    c.   jewelry, hairstyles, and clothing.
    d.   All of the above.

3. All of these statements are true regarding culture, except: (31)
    a.   people generally are aware of the effects of their own culture.
    b.   culture touches almost every aspect of who and what a person is.
    c.   at birth, people do not possess culture.
    d.   culture becomes the lens through which we perceive and evaluate what is going on around us.

4. The disorientation that people experience when they come into contact with a fundamentally different culture and no longer can depend on their taken-for-granted assumptions about life is known as: (31)
    a.   cultural diffusion.
    b.   cultural leveling.
    c.   cultural relativism.
    d.   cultural shock.

5. An American who thinks citizens of another country are barbarians if they like to attend bullfights is demonstrating: (32)
    a.   cultural shock.
    b.   cultural relativism.
    c.   ethnocentrism.
    d.   ethnomethodology.

6.   Gestures: (34)
        a.   are studied by anthropologists but not sociologists.
        b.   are universal.
        c.   always facilitate communication between people.
        d.   can lead to misunderstandings and embarrassment.

7.   It is possible for human experiences to be cumulative and shared because of: (35)
        a.   language.
        b.   cultural universals.
        c.   gestures.
        d.   computers.

8.   The sociological theory that language creates a particular way of thinking and perceiving is: (38)
        a.   sociobiology.
        b.   the Davis-Moore theory.
        c.   the Sapir-Whorf hypothesis.
        d.   the Linguistic perspective.

9.   Sanctions: (38)
        a.   are always material.
        b.   can be either positive or negative.
        c.   have very little impact on most people today.
        d.   All of the above.

10.   Norms that are not strictly enforced are: (39)
        a.   taboos.
        b.   mores.
        c.   values.
        d.   folkways.

11.   Mores: (39)
        a.   are essential to our core values and require conformity.
        b.   are norms that are not strictly enforced.
        c.   state that a person should not try to pass you on the left side of the sidewalk.
        d.   are less important in contemporary societies.

12.   Subcultures: (39)
        a.   are a world within a world.
        b.   have values and related behaviors that set its members apart from the larger culture.
        c.   include ethnic groups.
        d.   All of the above.

13.   Heavy metal adherents who glorify Satanism, hatred, and sexism are examples of: (39-40)
        a.   ethnocentrists.
        b.   perverted people.
        c.   countercultures.
        d.   subcultures.

14. A pluralistic society: (40)
    a.   is made up of many different groups.
    b.   tends to discourage subcultures.
    c.   does not share core values.
    d.   no longer exists in the world.

15. Value contradictions occur when: (42)
    a.   a value, such as the one that stresses group superiority, comes into direct conflict with other values, such as democracy and equality.
    b.   societies have very little social change.
    c.   a series of interrelated values bind together to form a larger whole.
    d.   None of the above.

16. Ideal culture is: (45)
    a.   a value, norm, or other cultural trait that is found in every group.
    b.   the ideal values and norms of a people, the goals held out for them.
    c.   the norms and values that people follow when they know they are being watched.
    d.   not a sociological concept.

17. Zookeepers in Sacramento showed gorillas a movie of two adult gorillas mating because: (46)
    a.   the zookeepers were trying to learn how gorillas mate.
    b.   the gorillas were bored, and the zookeepers thought the movie might interest the gorillas.
    c.   the gorillas seemed to want to mate, but didn't seem to know how.
    d.   the gorillas requested the movie.

18. Studies of animals, such as those conducted by Goodall, have led to the conclusion that: (46)
    a.   animals do not have culture.
    b.   we will never know whether or not animals have culture because we cannot communicate effectively with them.
    c.   animal culture exists, but researchers are still studying to learn more about it.
    d.   animals not only have culture but also have an extensive capacity for language.

19. Copying aspects of another group's culture is: (48)
    a.   cultural diffusion.
    b.   ethnocentrism.
    c.   cultural relativism.
    d.   cultural filching.

20. The Golden Arches of McDonald's in Tokyo, Paris, and London are examples of: (48)
    a.   cultural shock.
    b.   cultural contradictions.
    c.   cultural universals.
    d.   cultural leveling.

TRUE-FALSE QUESTIONS

T F 1. Speech, gestures, beliefs and customs usually are taken for granted by people (31)
T F 2. Most people regularly question the basic assumptions of their daily lives. (31)
T F 3. Culture becomes the lens through which we perceive and evaluate what is going on around us. (31)
T F 4. No one can be entirely successful at practicing cultural relativism. (33)
T F 5. Gestures are the ways in which people use their bodies to communicate with one another. (34)
T F 6. The gesture of nodding the head up and down to indicate "yes" is universal. (35)
T F 7. Without language, human culture would be little more advanced than that of the lower primates. (35)
T F 8. Without language, humans could still successfully plan future events. (36)
T F 9. Sanctions are positive or negative reactions to the ways people follow norms. (38)
T F 10. Subcultures remain compatible with the dominant culture while countercultures are in opposition to the dominant culture. (39)
T F 11. Racism and group superiority are core values in U.S. society. (41)
T F 12. The value cluster surrounding success includes hard work, education, efficiency, and individualism. (42)
T F 13. Some values conflict with one another. (42)
T F 14. Concern for the environment has always been a core value in U.S. society. (44)
T F 15. Core values do not change without meeting strong resistance. (44)
T F 16. In studying chimpanzees, Goodall found that they made and used tools. (45)
T F 17. Animals living in zoos sometimes do not instinctively know how to reproduce. (46)
T F 18. Researchers who study primates have found that these animals are incapable of learning language. (47)
T F 19. Most "borrowing" between cultures has involved material culture. (48)
T F 20. Japan is no longer a purely Eastern culture because of cultural leveling. (48)

FILL-IN QUESTIONS

1. The material objects that distinguish a group of people, such as their art, buildings, weapons, utensils, machines, hairstyles, clothing, and jewelry are known as _____; their ways of thinking and doing are _____. (31)
2. The tendency to use our own group's way of doing things as a yardstick for judging others is known as _____. (32)
3. A _____ is something to which people attach meaning and then use to communicate with others. (34)
4. The ways in which people use their bodies to communicate with one another are _____. (34)
5. _____ is a system of symbols that can be combined in an infinite number of ways and can represent not only objects but also abstract thought. (35)
6. _____ are ideas of what is desirable in life. (38)
7. The expectations or rules or behavior that develop out of values are referred to as _____. (38)
8. A _____ is a norm so strongly ingrained that even the thought of its violation is greeted with revulsion. (39)

9. The United States is a _____ society, meaning that it is made up of many different groups. (40)
10. _____ are a series of interrelated values that together form a larger whole. (42)
11. Sociologists call the norms and values that people actually follow _____. (45)
12. Studies of chimpanzees indicate that they were able to make and use _____; they actually modified objects and used them for specific purposes. (45)
13. _____ is learned, shared behavior among animals. (46)
14. Air travel and rapid communications have contributed to _____. (48)
15. When Western industrial culture is imported and diffused into developing nations, the process is called _____. (48)

MATCHING QUESTIONS

___1. Edward Sapir and Benjamin Whorf   a. *studied animal culture*
___2. Robin Williams   b. *disorientation following contact with another culture*
___3. culture shock   c. *taught chimps a gestural language*
___4. Jane Goodall   d. *stated that language shapes perceptions of reality*
___5. instincts   e. *something to which people attach meaning*
___6. symbol   f. *inherited patterns of behavior common to a species*
___7. William Sumner   g. *noted core values of U.S. society*
___8. Allen and Beatrice Gardner   h. *developed the concept of ethnocentrism*

"DOWN-TO-EARTH SOCIOLOGY"

1. Many colleges and universities now teach courses about cultural differences -- such as those between Japan and the United States--for business majors and others who plan to conduct business with citizens of other countries. Why is it important to know how to communicate effectively across cultural boundaries? Why is it often difficult to cross cultural boundaries, even when you know the language?
2. When language is a big barrier--as in Miami today--why do many people stick with their own group and not try to talk to anyone else? Can you think of experiences of your own that are similar? Do you think it is important for Americans to learn another language?
3. Why do you think the image of the cowboy has been so positively portrayed, while Native Americans have been so negatively portrayed in U.S. books and movies? What would the reaction be if Native Americans were portrayed with the same traits as we generally associate with cowboys?
4. Critics argue that as Americans place more emphasis on leisure, the economy could ultimately be undermined. In Japan there is a contrary concern--too much work ethic. What do you think? Where do you think the balance between work and leisure should be?

☞ ANSWERS FOR CHAPTER 2

DEFINITIONS OF KEY TERMS

counterculture: a group whose values place its members in opposition to the values of the broader culture

cultural diffusion: the spread of cultural characteristics from one group to another

cultural leveling: the process by which cultures become similar to one another, and especially by which Western industrial culture is imported and diffused into developing nations

cultural relativism: understanding a people from the framework of their own culture

culture: the language, beliefs, values, norms, behaviors, and even material objects that are passed from one generation to the next

culture contact: when people from different cultures come in contact with one another

culture shock: the disorientation that people experience when they come in contact with a fundamentally different culture and can no longer depend on their taken-for-granted assumptions about life

ethnocentrism: the use of one's own culture as a yardstick for judging the ways of other individuals and societies, generally leading to a negative evaluation of their values, norms, and behaviors

folkways: norms which are not strictly enforced

gestures: the ways in which people use their bodies to communicate with one another

ideal culture: the ideal values and norms of a people, the goals held out for them

instincts: inherited patterns of behavior common to all normal members of a species

language: a system of symbols that can be combined in an infinite number of ways and can represent not only objects but also abstract thought

material culture: the material objects that distinguish a group of people, such as their art, buildings, weapons, utensils, machines, hairstyles, clothing, and jewelry

mores: norms strictly enforced because they are thought essential to core values

negative sanction: an expression of disapproval for breaking a norm; ranging from a mild, informal reaction such as a frown to a formal prison sentence, banishment, or death

nonmaterial culture: a group's ways of thinking (including its beliefs, values, and other assumptions about the world) and doing (its common patterns or behavior, including language and other forms of interaction)

norms: the expectations, or rules of behavior, that develop out of values

pluralistic society: a society made up of many different groups

positive sanction: a reward given for following norms, ranging from a smile to a prize

real culture: the norms and values that people actually follow

sanction: an expression of approval or disapproval given to people for upholding or violating norms

Sapir-Whorf hypothesis: Edward Sapir's and Benjamin Whorf's hypothesis that language itself creates a particular way of thinking and perceiving

subculture: the values and related behaviors of a group that distinguish its members from the larger culture; a world within a world

symbol: something to which people attach meaning and then use to communicate with others

symbolic culture: another term for nonmaterial culture

taboo: a norm so strong that it brings revulsion if it is violated

value cluster: a series of interrelated values that together form a larger whole

value contradiction: values that contradict one another; to follow the one means to come into conflict with the other

values: the standards by which people define what is desirable or undesirable, good or bad, beautiful or ugly

ANSWERS FOR MULTIPLE CHOICE QUESTIONS

1. b Sociologists refer to a group's ways of thinking and doing, including language and other forms of interaction as nonmaterial culture. (31)
2. d Material culture includes weapons and machines, eating utensils, jewelry, hairstyles, and clothing; thus all of the above is correct. (31)
3. a All of the statements are true regarding culture except "people generally are aware of the effects of their own culture." (31)
4. d The disorientation that people experience when they come into contact with a fundamentally different culture and can no longer depend on their taken-for-granted assumptions about life is known as cultural shock. (31)
5. c An American who thinks citizens of another country are barbarians if they like to attend bullfights is demonstrating ethnocentrism. (32)
6. d Gestures can lead to misunderstandings and embarrassment. (34)
7. a It is possible for human experience to be cumulative and for people to share memories because of language. (35)
8. c The sociological theory that language itself creates a particular way of thinking and perceiving is known as the Sapir-Whorf hypothesis. (38)
9. b Sanctions can be either positive or negative. (38)
10. d Norms that are not strictly enforced are folkways. (39)
11. a Mores are essential to our core values and require conformity. (39)
12. d Subcultures are a world within a world; are the values and related behaviors or a group that distinguish its members from the larger culture; and include ethnic groups. Therefore, all of the above are correct. (39)
13. c Sociologically speaking, heavy metal adherents who glorify Satanism, hatred, cruelty, and sexism are examples of countercultures. (39-40)
14. a A pluralistic society is made up of many different groups. (40)
15. a Value contradictions occur when a value, such as the one that stresses group superiority, comes into direct conflict with other values, such as democracy and equality. (42)
16. b Ideal culture is the ideal values and norms of a people, the goals held out for them. (45)
17. c Zookeepers in Sacramento showed gorillas a movie of two adult gorillas mating because the gorillas seemed to want to mate, but didn't seem to know how. (46)
18. c Studies of animals, such as those conducted by Goodall, have led to the conclusion that animal culture exists but researchers are still studying to learn more about it. (46)
19. a Copying aspects of another group's culture is cultural diffusion. (48)
20. d The Golden Arches of McDonald's in Tokyo, Paris, and London are examples of cultural leveling. (48)

ANSWERS FOR TRUE-FALSE QUESTIONS

1. *True* (31)
2. *False.* Most people usually do not question the basic assumptions of their daily lives because culture provides a taken-for-granted orientation to life. We assume our own culture is normal or natural, when in fact it is learned. (31)

3.   *True* (31)
4.   *True* (33)
5.   *True* (34)
6.   *False*. The gesture of nodding the head up and down to indicate "yes" is not universal. In some societies this gesture means "no." (35)
7.   *True* (35)
8.   *False*. Humans could not plan future events without language to convey meanings of past, present, and future points in time. (36)
9.   *True* (38)
10.   *True* (39)
11.   *True* (41)
12.   *True* (42)
13.   *True* (42)
14.   *False*. Concern for the environment has not always been a core value in U.S. society. It is one of the emergent values that is now increasing in importance. (44)
15.   *True* (44)
16.   *True* (45)
17.   *True* (46)
18.   *False*. While primates do not have the vocal apparatus necessary to utter the complex sounds that make up language, they are capable of learning language, as a series of experiments with chimpanzees have demonstrated. (47)
19.   *True* (48)
20.   *True* (48)

ANSWERS FOR FILL-IN QUESTIONS

1.   The material objects that distinguish a group of people, such as their art, buildings, weapons, utensils, machines, hairstyles, clothing, and jewelry are known as MATERIAL CULTURE; their ways of thinking and doing are NONMATERIAL CULTURE. (31)
2.   The tendency to use our own group's way of doing things as a yardstick for judging others is known as ETHNOCENTRISM. (32)
3.   A SYMBOL is something to which people attach meaning and then use to communicate with others. (34)
4.   The ways in which people use their bodies to communicate with one another are GESTURES. (34)
5.   LANGUAGE is a system of symbols that can be combined in an infinite number of ways and can represent not only objects but also abstract thought. (35)
6.   VALUES are ideas of what is desirable in life. (38)
7.   The expectations or rules or behavior that develop out of values are referred to as NORMS. (38)
8.   A TABOO is a norm so strongly ingrained that even the thought of its violation is greeted with revulsion. (39)
9.   The United States is a PLURALISTIC society, meaning that it is made up of many different groups. (40)
10.   VALUE CLUSTERS are a series of interrelated values that together form a larger whole. (42)
11.   Sociologists call the norms and values that people actually follow REAL CULTURE. (45)
12.   Studies of chimpanzees indicate that they were able to make and use TOOLS; they actually modified objects and used them for specific purposes. (45)

13. ANANI <u>ANIMAL CULTURE</u> is learned, shared behavior among animals. (46)
14. Air travel and rapid communications have contributed to <u>CULTURAL DIFFUSION</u>. (48)
15. When Western industrial culture is imported and diffused into developing nations, the process is called <u>CULTURAL LEVELING</u>. (48)

<u>ANSWERS TO THE MATCHING QUESTIONS</u>

1. d   Edward Sapir and Benjamin Whorf: *stated that language shapes reality*
2. g   Robin Williams: *noted core values in U.S. society*
3. b   culture shock: *disorientation following contact with another culture*
4. a   Jane Goodall: *studied animal culture*
5. f   instincts: *inherited patterns of behavior common to a species*
6. e   symbol: *something to which people attach meaning*
7. h   William Sumner: *developed the concept of ethnocentrism*
8. c   Allen and Beatrice Gardner: *taught chimps a gestural language*

CHAPTER 3
SOCIALIZATION

☞ CHAPTER SUMMARY

- Scientists have attempted to determine how much of people's characteristics come from heredity and how much from the social environment. Observations of isolated and institutionalized children help to answer this question. These studies have concluded that language and intimate interaction are essential to the development of human characteristics.

- Charles H. Cooley, George H. Mead, Jean Piaget, and Sigmund Freud provide insights into the social development of human beings. The work of Cooley and Mead demonstrate that the self is created through our interactions with others. Piaget identified four stages in the development of our ability to reason: (1) sensorimotor; (2) pre-operational; (3) concrete operational; and (4) formal operational. Freud defined the personality in terms of the id, ego, and superego; personality developed as the inborn desires (id) clashed with social constraints (superego).

- Gender socialization is a primary means of controlling human behavior, and a society's ideals of sex-linked behaviors are reinforced by its social institutions.

- The main agents of socialization--family, religion, school, peer groups, the mass media, and the workplace--each contribute to the socialization of people to become full-fledged members of society.

- Resocialization is the process of learning new norms, values, attitudes and behaviors. Intense resocialization takes place in total institutions. Most resocialization is voluntary, but some is involuntary.

- Socialization, which begins at birth, continues throughout the life course; at each stage the individual must adjust to a new set of social expectations.

- Although socialization lays down the basic self and is modified by our social location, humans are not robots but rational beings who consider options and make choices.

☞ LEARNING OBJECTIVES

As you read Chapter 3, use these learning objectives to organize your notes. After completing your reading, briefly state an answer to each of the objectives, and review the text pages in parentheses.

1. Discuss major studies of isolated and institutionalized children, as well as studies of deprived animals, and state what they demonstrate about the importance of early contact with other humans for the social development of children. (54-57)
2. Define socialization. (57)
3. Explain and distinguish between the theories of social development by Charles H. Cooley, George H. Mead, Jean Piaget, and Sigmund Freud. (57-61)
4. Explain what Henslin means when he says that we are socialized into emotions and analyze the relationship between socialization into emotions and social control in society. (61-62)
5. Describe ways in which gender socialization channels human behavior and reinforces cultural stereotypes of men and women. (62-63)
6. List and describe the influence of each agent of socialization on individuals. (63-67)
7. Define the term resocialization and discuss the process of resocialization that takes places within total institutions. (67-68)

8. Discuss socialization through the life course by summarizing each of its stages. (69-71)
9. Explain why human beings are not prisoners of socialization. (71-72)

☞ CHAPTER OUTLINE

I.   **What Is Human Nature?**
     A.   Isolated children show what humans might be like if secluded from society at an early age. Isabelle is an example.
          1.   Raised in isolation, Isabelle was unable to speak and appeared severely retarded. Without language and companionship, she had been unable to develop into an intelligent human.
          2.   Subsequent interaction with others at a fairly early age allowed her to reach normal intellectual levels.
     B.   Studies of institutionalized children show that characteristics we think of as human traits (intelligence, cooperative behavior, and friendliness) result from early close relations with other humans.
          1.   When infants in orphanages received little adult interaction, they appeared mentally retarded. When some were placed in the care of adult women--even though the women were mentally retarded--one-on-one relationships developed, and the infants gained intelligence.
          2.   Genie, who was locked in a small room from infancy until she was found at age 13, demonstrates the importance of early interaction. Intensive training was required for her to learn to walk, speak simple sentences, and chew correctly, yet even so she remained severely retarded.
     C.   Studies of monkeys raised in isolation have reached similar results. The longer and more severe the isolation, the more difficult adjustment becomes.
     D.   Babies do not "naturally" develop into human adults; although their bodies grow, human interaction is required for them to acquire the traits we consider normal for human beings.

II. **The Social Development of the Self, Mind, and Emotions**
     A.   Charles H. Cooley (1864-1929) concluded that human development is socially created--that our sense of self develops from interaction with others. He coined the term "looking-glass self" to describe this process.
          1.   According to Cooley, this process contains three steps: (1) we imagine how we look to others; (2) we interpret others' reactions (how they evaluate us); and (3) we develop a self-concept.
          2.   A favorable reflection in the "social mirror" leads to a positive self-concept, while a negative reflection leads to a negative self-concept.
          3.   Even if we misjudge others' reactions, the misjudgments become part of our self-concept.
          4.   This development process is an ongoing, lifelong process.
     B.   George H. Mead (1863-1931) agreed with Cooley, but added that play is critical to the development of a self. In play, we learn to take the role of others: to understand and anticipate how others feel and think.
          1.   Mead concluded that children are first able to take only the role of significant others (parents or siblings, for example); as the self develops, children internalize first the expectations of other people, and then eventually the entire group. Mead

referred to the norms, values, attitudes and expectations of people "in general" as the generalized other.

2. According to Mead, the development of the self goes through stages: (1) imitation (children initially can only mimic the gestures and words of others); (2) play (beginning at age three, children play the roles of specific people, such as a firefighter or the Lone Ranger); and (3) games (in the first years of school, children become involved in organized team games and must learn the role of each member of the team).

3. He distinguished between the "I" and the "me" in development of the self: The "I" component is the subjective, active, spontaneous, creative part of the social self (for instance, "I shoved him"), while the "me" component is the objective part--attitudes internalized from interactions with others (for instance, "He shoved me").

4. Mead concluded that not only the self but also the human mind is a social product. The symbols which we use in thinking originate in the language of our society.

C. Jean Piaget (1896-1980) noted that when young children take intelligence tests, they consistently give wrong answers while older children are able to give the expected answer. To understand why, he studied "cognitive development"--the four stages a child goes through in learning.

1. The sensorimotor stage (ages 0-2): Understanding is limited to direct contact with the environment (touching, listening, seeing).

2. The preoperational stage (ages 2-7): Children develop the ability to use symbols which allow them to experience things without direct contact.

3. The concrete operational stage (ages 7-12): Reasoning abilities become much more developed. Children now can understand numbers, causation, and speed, but have difficulty with abstract concepts such as truth.

4. The formal operational stage (ages 12+): Children become capable of abstract thinking, and can use rules to solve abstract problems ("If X is true, why doesn't Y follow?").

5. Although they pass through these stages at different speeds, children everywhere go through them in the same order. An individual's cognitive development can be limited by biological factors or enhanced by social experiences.

D. Sigmund Freud (1856-1939) believed that personality consists of three elements.

1. The id (inherited drives for self-gratification) demands fulfillment of basic needs such as attention, safety, food, and sex.

2. The ego balances between the needs of the id and the demands or society.

3. The superego (the social conscience we have internalized from social groups) gives us feelings of guilt or shame when we break rules, and feelings or pride and self-satisfaction when we follow them.

4. Sociologists object to Freud's view that inborn and unconscious motivations are the primary reasons for human behavior, for this view denies the central tenet of sociology that social factors shape people's behaviors.

E. Emotions are not simply the result of biology; they also depend on socialization within a particular society. We learn how to express emotions as well as what emotions to feel.

1. Americans may shake hands with each other to express pleasure in meeting someone, while Japanese may bow, and Arabs may kiss.

2. When a football player scores a touchdown, the response is quite physical: jumping up and down, and shouting. When a college professor gives a good lecture, the response is more subdued. Society has trained us to give the different reactions in the different settings.

F. Most socialization is meant to turn us into conforming members of society. We do some things and not others as a result of socialization. When we contemplate an action, we know the emotion (good or bad) that would result; thus, society sets up controls on our behavior.

III. **Socialization Into Gender**

A. By expecting different behaviors from people because they are male or female, society nudges boys and girls in separate directions from an early age, and this foundation carries over into adulthood.

B. Parents begin the process.
1. Studies conclude that in U.S. society, mothers unconsciously reward female children for being passive and dependent and male children for being active and independent.
2. In general parents teach their children gender roles is not by specific instruction, but by nonverbal cues.

C. The mass media reinforce society's expectations of gender in many ways.
1. On TV, male characters outnumber females, females are shown as passive, indecisive, and dominated by men. In commercials, women's voices are rarely used as the voice-over.
2. Music perpetuates sex role stereotypes: songs tell girls to be sexy, dependent, submissive, and boys to dominate male-female relationships. Ten percent of music videos showing females portray violence against them.

IV. **Agents of Socialization**

A. Our experiences in the family have a life-long impact on us, laying down a basic sense of self, motivation, values, and beliefs.
1. Research by Melvin Kohn suggests that there are social class differences in child-rearing. Often the main concern of working-class parents is their children's outward conformity (be neat and clean, and follow the rules); they are more likely to use physical punishment to encourage conformity. Middle-class parents show greater concern for the motivations for their children's behavior; they are less likely to use physical punishment and more likely to withdraw privileges and affection.
2. Kohn found that over and above social class, the type of job held by the parent is a factor: the more closely supervised the job is, the more likely the parent is to insist on outward conformity.

B. Religion plays a major role in the socialization of most Americans, even if they are not raised in a religious family. Religion especially influences morality, but also ideas about the dress, speech, and manners that are appropriate.

C. Schools serve many manifest (intended) functions for society, including teaching skills and values thought to be appropriate. Schools also have several latent (unintended) functions.
1. At school children are placed outside the direct control of friends/relatives and exposed to new values and ways of looking at the world. They learn to be part of a large group of people of similar age, and that the same rules apply to all.

Since their grades are recorded and become a permanent record, they learn the consequences of their own actions.

2. Schools also have a hidden curriculum: values not explicitly taught but inherent in school activities. For example, the wording of stories may carry messages about patriotism and democracy; by teaching that our economic system is just, schools may teach children to believe problems such as poverty are never caused by oppression and exploitation.

D. A peer group is a group of persons of roughly the same age who are linked by common interests. Next to the family, peer groups are the most powerful socializing force in society. In peer groups, children separate themselves by sex and develop their own worlds with unique norms.

1. For boys, norms that make them popular are athletic ability, coolness, and toughness.

2. For girls, the norms are family background, physical appearance, and interest in more mature concerns such as the ability to attract boys.

E. Sports are powerful socializing agents, teaching values and how to be a team player.

F. In contemporary societies, mass media such as television, newspapers, and magazines shape our attitudes, values, and other basic orientations to life. Television has a tremendous impact on the U.S. public.

1. Many parents use the medium as an electronic babysitter, although the values expressed may sharply conflict with their own. Due to such exposure, social analysts have become concerned over the content of what children see, especially violence.

2. Research indicates children with a heavy diet of TV violence are more likely to be aggressive.

V. Resocialization

A. Resocialization refers to the process of learning new norms, values, attitudes and behaviors. Resocialization in its most common form occurs each time we learn something contrary to our previous experiences, such as going to work in a new job. It can be voluntary or involuntary.

B. Erving Goffman coined the term total institution to refer to a place--such as boot camps, prisons, concentration camps, or some mental hospitals, religious cults, and boarding schools --in which people are cut off from the rest of society and are under almost total control of agents of the institution.

1. A person entering the institution is greeted with a degradation ceremony by which current identity is stripped away and replaced (e.g. fingerprinting, shaving the head, banning personal items, and being forced to strip and wear a uniform).

2. Total institutions are quite effective because they isolate people from outside influences and information; supervise their activities; suppress previous roles, statuses, and norms and replace them with new rules and values; and control rewards and punishments.

VI. Socialization Through the Life Course

A. Socialization occurs throughout a person's entire lifetime.

B. A general outline of the different stages in the life course would include:

1. Childhood (birth to age 12): In earlier times, children were considered miniature adults, who served an apprenticeship in which they learned and performed tasks. To keep them in line, they were beaten and subjected to psychological torture.

The current view is that children are tender and innocent, and parents should guide the physical, emotional, and social development of their children, while providing them with care, comfort, and protection.

2. Adolescence (ages 13 to 17): Economic changes resulting from the Industrial Revolution brought about material surpluses that allowed millions of teenagers to remain outside the labor force, while at the same time the demand for education increased. Biologically equipped for both work and marriage but denied both, adolescents suffer inner turmoil and develop their own standards of clothing, hairstyles, language, music, and other claims to separate identities.

3. Young Adulthood (ages 18-29): Adult responsibilities are postponed through extended education. During this period the self becomes more stable, and the period usually is one of high optimism.

4. The Middle Years (ages 30-65): People are surer of themselves and their goals in life than before, but severe jolts such as divorce or being fired can occur. For U.S. women, it can be a trying period due to trying to "have it all"--job, family, and everything. Later adulthood results in a different view of life--trying to evaluate the past and to come to terms with what lies ahead. Individuals may feel they are not likely to get much farther in life, while health and mortality become concerns. However, for most people it is the most comfortable period in their entire lives.

5. Older years (age 65 and beyond): People today live longer and there has been an improvement in general health. At the same time, people in this stage become more concerned with death--that their time is "closing in" on them.

VII. **Are We Prisoners of Socialization?**

A. Sociologists do not think of people as little robots who simply are the result of their exposure to socializing agents. Although socialization is powerful, and profoundly affects us all, we have a self, and the self is dynamic. Each of us uses his or her own mind to reason and make choices.

B. In this way, each of us is actively involved even in the social construction of the self. Our experiences have an impact on us, but we are not doomed to keep our orientations if we do not like them.

☞ GLOSSARY OF DIFFICULT-TO-UNDERSTAND WORDS

blindfolded: having something placed over the eyes so that a person cannot see (58)
cardinal rule: a basic rule (66)
circumvent: get around (62)
concrete: being solid or specific (60)
constraints: forced limits (60)
convergence: coming together; the place where that happens(70)
coronation: ceremony proclaiming a person as king or queen (70)
corroborate: confirm based on other evidence (57)
deaf-mute: a person who is deaf and unable to speak (54)
doting: seeming overly fond of someone (64)
embryos: in humans, the period from conception to about the eighth week (55)
enclave: small, almost completely surrounded, areas (65)
extrapolating: estimating a result based on known values (57)

floundering: acting in a clumsy or ineffective way (68)

fluttered: flapped, like a bird flaps its wings (54)

gringo: Latin American slang for Anglo-Americans (65)

gruesome: horrible, disgusting (70)

indelible: something that cannot be removed; permanent (68)

kibbutz: a type or settlement in Israel (55)

looking-glass: a mirror (57)

maladjusted: a person who does not fit in well (61)

mortality: relating to death and death rates (71)

orphanages: institutions where children without parents are sometimes cared for (54)

pervade: to exist everywhere; to be part of everything (64)

pinpointing: locating something very specifically (68)

siblings: brothers and sisters (58)

skittering gait: moving along quickly (54)

sniveling: falsely displaying a need for sympathy (63)

spontaneous: doing something without really thinking (58)

straitjacket: something that restrains a person (61)

subconscious: being aware of something without thinking about it (60)

toddler: a very small child (55)

touchdown: scoring points by crossing a goal line in football (62)

transmits: passing something from one person or place to another (61)

voice-over: the voice that speaks over the action, for instance in a TV commercial (63)

workaholic: a person addicted to work (55)

☞ KEY TERMS TO DEFINE

After studying the chapter, define each of the following terms. Then check your work by referring to the answers beginning at page 47 of this Study Guide.

agents of socialization	life course	significant other
degradation ceremony	looking-glass self	social environment
ego	manifest function	socialization
gender socialization	mass media	superego
generalized other	peer group	taking the role of the other
id	resocialization	total institutions
latent function	self	

☞ KEY PEOPLE

State the major theoretical contributions or findings of these people.

Patricia & Peter Adler	Susan Goldberg	George Herbert Mead
Charles H. Cooley	Harry & Margaret Harlow	Michael Messner
H.B. Dye	Steven Kless	Jean Piaget
Sigmund Freud	Melvin Kohn	H.M. Skeels
Erving Goffman	Michael Lewis	

☞ SELF-TEST

After completing this self-test, check your answers against the "Answer Key" beginning on page 47 of this Study Guide and against the text on page(s) indicated in parentheses.

MULTIPLE CHOICE QUESTIONS

1. From the case of Isabelle, it is possible to conclude that: (54)
    a. humans have no natural language.
    b. she was retarded.
    c. it is impossible for a person who has been isolated to progress through normal learning stages.
    d. All of the above.

2. Research by H. M. Skeels and H. B. Dye demonstrates: (56)
    a. the importance of institutional environment for the development of intelligence.
    b. the importance of the caregiver's intelligence for the development of intelligence in young children.
    c. the importance of human contact in the development of intelligence.
    d. the ability of an individual to rise above early deprivation and gain intelligence in later year.

3. Studies of isolated rhesus monkeys demonstrated that the monkeys: (57)
    a. were able to adjust to monkey life.
    b. instinctively knew how to enter into "monkey interaction" with other monkeys.
    c. knew how to engage in sexual intercourse.
    d. None of the above.

4. The term "looking-glass self" was coined by: (57-58)
    a. George H. Mead.
    b. Jean Piaget.
    c. Erving Goffman.
    d. Charles H. Cooley.

5. All of the following statements about the development of self are correct, except: (58)
    a. the development of self is an ongoing, lifelong process.
    b. we move beyond the looking-glass self as we mature.
    c. the process of the looking-glass self applies to old age.
    d. the self is always in process.

6. According to Mead's theory, children pretend to take the roles of specific people--such as the Lone Ranger, Supergirl, or Batman--during the _____ stage. (58)
    a. imitation
    b. game
    c. play
    d. generalized other

7. To George Mead, the "I" is the: (58)
    a. self as subject.
    b. self as object.
    c. same as the id.
    d. passive robot aspect of human behavior.

8. According to Jean Piaget, children develop the ability to use symbols during the _____ stage. (60)
    a. sensorimotor
    b. preoperational
    c. concrete operational
    d. formal operational

9. Freud's term for a balancing force between the inborn drives for self-gratification and the demands of society is the: (60)
    a. id.
    b. superego.
    c. ego.
    d. libido.

10. According to this chapter, society sets up effective controls over our behavior by: (62)
    a. hiring police officers and other law enforcement officials.
    b. defining those who do not abide by the rules as "deviants."
    c. socializing us into emotions.
    d. None of the above.

11. The ways in which society sets children onto different courses for life purely because they are male or female is called: (62)
    a. sex socialization.
    b. gender socialization
    c. masculinization and feminization.
    d. brainwashing.

12. We begin the lifelong process of defining ourselves as female or male in: (62)
    a. the family.
    b. school.
    c. the hospital where we are born
    d. church.

13. Psychologists Susan Goldberg and Michael Lewis observed mothers with their six-month-old infants in a laboratory setting and concluded that the mothers: (62)
    a. kept their male children closer to them.
    b. kept their male and female children about the same distance from them.
    c. touched and spoke more to their sons.
    d. unconsciously rewarded daughters for being passive and dependent.

14. According to sociologist Melvin Kohn, middle-class parents try to develop their children's: (64)
    a. outward conformity
    b. level of obedience, neatness, and cleanliness.
    c. curiosity, self-expression, and self-control.
    d. All of the above.

15. Melvin Kohn found that social class differences in childhood socialization were influenced by: (64)
    a. the educational level of the parents.
    b. the type of jobs the parents held.
    c. the age of the parents.
    d. the parents' income.

16. Participation in religious services teaches us: (64)
    a. beliefs about the hereafter.
    b. ideas about dress.
    c. speech and manners appropriate for formal occasions.
    d. All of the above.

17. A latent function of formal education is: (64)
    a. broadening students' social horizons.
    b. transmitting the skills needed in society.
    c. teaching values thought appropriate for a good citizen.
    d. teaching students how to manage money and vote.

18. A person's musical preferences, clothing styles, and dating standards typically are most influenced by: (64-65)
    a. one's parents.
    b. one's brothers and/or sisters.
    c. one's peers.
    d. mass media.

19. In a longitudinal study of the impact on behavior of watching TV, researchers found that: (66)
    a. at age 8, children who watched more TV were more violent.
    b. by age 19, those who had watched the most TV at age 8 were only slightly more likely to be violent than those who watched less TV.
    c. by age 30, the differences in violent behavior among participants had disappeared.
    d. all of the above.

20. The process of learning new norms, values, attitudes or behaviors to match new life situations is referred to as: (67)
    a. workplace socialization.
    b. resocialization.
    c. expectant socialization.
    d. mature socialization.

21.   Resocialization occurs when a person: (68)
      a.   takes a new job.
      b.   joins a cult.
      c.   goes to boot camp.
      d.   all of the above.

22.   Total institutions: (68)
      a.   is a term coined by Harold Garfinkel.
      b.   exist primarily in societies with totalitarian governments.
      c.   are places in which people are cut off from the rest of society and are almost totally
            controlled by the officials who run the place.
      d.   All of the above.

23.   As a consequence of the Industrial Revolution, the stage of the life course known as _____
      was invented. (70)
      a.   childhood
      b.   adolescence
      c.   adulthood
      d.   senior status

24.   Given recent social changes that have taken place within the United States, which of the following
      groups are particularly challenged by the early middle years stage of the life course? (71)
      a.   Generation X
      b.   women
      c.   Baby boomers
      d.   men

25.   What is it that prevents us from being prisoners of socialization? (71-72)
      a.   our culture
      b.   our education
      c.   our self
      d.   our families

TRUE-FALSE QUESTIONS

T F   1.   Studies of institutionalized children demonstrate that some of the characteristics that we
            take for granted as being "human" traits result from our basic instincts. (55-56)
T F   2.   Because monkeys and humans are so similar, it is possible to reach conclusions about
            human behavior from animal studies. (57)
T F   3.   Charles H. Cooley concluded that our sense of self develops out of our interaction with
            others. (57-58)
T F   4.   George H. Mead introduced the concept of the generalized other to sociology. (58)
T F   5.   Piaget used the term "operational" to mean abstract thought. (60)
T F   6.   Since emotions are natural human responses, socialization has very little to do with how
            we feel. (61-62)
T F   7.   Most socialization is intended to turn us into conforming members of society. (62)
T F   8.   Children's television shows overwhelmingly feature more males than females. (63)

T F 9. In commercials, women's voices are rarely used as the voice-over. (63)

T F 10. While TV may be biased towards males, music videos are not, showing an equal number of men and women. (63)

T F 11. Sociologist Melvin Kohn found that the main concern of middle-class parents is their children's outward conformity. (64)

T F 12. Participation in religious services teaches an individual about the dress, speech, and manners appropriate for formal occasions. (64)

T F 13. Next to the family, the peer group is the most powerful socializing force in society. (64-65)

T F 14. Studies indicate that a heavy diet of televised violence promotes aggressive behavior in children. (66)

T F 15. Resocialization always requires learning a radically different perspective. (67)

T F 16. Total institutions are very effective in stripping away people's personal freedom. (68)

T F 17. Adolescence is a social creation in industrialized societies. (70)

T F 18. In the middle years, some U.S. women find that "having it all" may be somewhat a myth. (71)

T F 19. Industrialization brought with it a delay in the onset of old age. (71)

T F 20. Most sociologists view humans as little robots: the socialization goes in and the expected behavior comes out. (71-72)

FILL-IN QUESTIONS

1. The entire human environment, including direct contact with others, is the _____. (54)

2. _____ is the process by which people learn the characteristics of their group--the attitudes, values, and actions thought appropriate for them. (57)

3. Charles H. Cooley coined the term _____ to describe the process by which a sense of self develops. (58)

4. According to George Herbert Mead, the development of the self through role-taking goes through three stages: (1) _____ ; (2) _____; and (3) _____. (58)

5. _____ is the term used to describe someone, such as a parent and/or a sibling, who plays a major role in our social development. (58)

6. The idea that personality consists of the id, ego, and superego was developed by _____. (60-61)

7. The different ways in which a society sets children onto different courses for life because they are male or female is _____. (62)

8. The _____ refers to values that form an inherent part of a school's message, even if not explicitly taught. (64)

9. _____ include the family, religion, schools, peers, sports, and mass media. (63-67)

10. Transmitting skills and values thought appropriate for earning a living and for being a "good citizen" are _____ of education. (64)

11. _____ are groups of individuals roughly the same age linked by common interests. (65)

12. Resocialization generally takes place in _____ such as boot camps, prisons, and concentration camps. (67)

13. _____ is a term coined by Harold Garfinkel to describe an attempt to remake the self by stripping away an individual's self-identity and stamping a new identity in its place. (68)

14.   The first stage in the life course, which takes place between birth and age twelve, is referred to by sociologists as _____ . (69)
15.   The stage of the life course which poses a special challenge for U.S. women is _____ . (71)

MATCH THESE SOCIAL SCIENTISTS WITH THEIR CONTRIBUTIONS

___1. Melvin Kohn   a. *coined the term "looking-glass self"*
___2. Erving Goffman   b. *conducted studies of isolated rhesus monkeys*
___3. George Herbert Mead   c. *coined the term "generalized other"*
___4. Charles H. Cooley   d. *studied total institutions*
___5. Jean Piaget   e. *found social class differences in child rearing*
___6. Harry and Margaret Harlow   f. *asserted that human behavior is based on unconscious drives*
___7. Sigmund Freud   g. *discovered that there are four stages in cognitive development*
___8. Michael Messner   h. *studied the role of sports for male socialization*

"DOWN-TO-EARTH SOCIOLOGY"

1.   What do studies like the one of identical twins Oskar and Jack, tell us about heredity and environment? Have you ever known a set of identical twins? If you are an identical twin, in what ways are you like your sibling? In what ways are you different?
2.   How is your concept of yourself based on the feedback that you have gotten from others? How does your understanding of yourself fit with Cooley's looking-glass self?
3.   Think about learning what emotions are appropriate for you because or your age, race or ethnicity, gender, and social class background. How were you socialized into emotions; for example, "little boys don't cry" and "little girls don't fight!"?
4.   Why is it problematic to be caught between two worlds like Richard Rodriguez was? Do you think many people today are in a similar situation? Do you consider yourself to be caught between two worlds?
5.   Do you agree that sports are an important part of male culture? As females get more involved in sports, what consequences will that have for female culture? Whether you are male or female, how important have sports been in your life?

☞ ANSWERS FOR CHAPTER 3

DEFINITIONS OF KEY TERMS

agents of socialization: people or groups that affect our self-concept, attitudes or orientation towards life
degradation ceremony: the term coined by Harold Garfinkel to describe rituals designed to strip an individual of his or her identity as a group member; for example, a court martial or the defrocking of a priest
ego: Freud's term for a balancing force between the id and the demands of society
gender socialization: the ways in which society sets children onto different courses for life because they are male or female

generalized other: taking the role of a large number of people

id: Freud's term for the individual's inborn basic drives

latent function: the unintended consequences of people's actions that help to keep a social system in equilibrium

life course: the stages of our life as we go from birth to death

looking-glass self: a term coined by Charles H. Cooley to refer to the process by which our self develops through internalizing others' reactions to us

manifest function: the intended consequences of people's actions designed to help some part of the social system

mass media: forms of communication directed to huge audiences

peer group: a group of individuals roughly the same age linked by common interests

resocialization: process of learning new norms, values, attitudes, and behaviors

self: the concept, unique to humans, of being able to see ourselves "from the outside;" to gain a picture of how others see us

significant other: an individual who significantly influences someone else's life

social environment: the entire human environment, including direct contact with others

socialization: the process by which people learn the characteristics of their group--the attitudes, values, and actions thought appropriate for them

superego: Freud's term for the conscience, which consists of the internalized norms and values of our social groups

taking the role of the other: putting oneself in someone else's shoes; understanding how someone else feels and thinks and thus anticipating how that person will act

total institution: a place in which people are cut off from the rest of society and are almost totally controlled by the officials who run the place

ANSWERS FOR MULTIPLE CHOICE QUESTIONS

1. a   From the case of Isabelle, we can conclude that humans have no natural language. (54)
2. c   Research by H. M. Skeels and H. B. Dye demonstrated that human contact, regardless of the intelligence level of the caregiver, was significant in the development of intelligence among young, institutionalized children. (56)
3. d   "None of the above" is the correct response because studies of isolated rhesus monkeys demonstrated that the monkeys were not able to adjust to monkey life, did not instinctively know how to enter into "monkey interaction" with other monkeys or how to engage in sexual intercourse. (57)
4. d   The term "looking-glass self" was coined by Charles H. Cooley. (57-58)
5. b   This statement "we move beyond the looking-glass self as we mature" is incorrect. All of the other statements about the development of self are correct: the development of self is an ongoing, lifelong process; the process of the looking-glass self applies to old age; and the self is always in process. (58)
6. c   According to Mead's theory, children pretend to take the roles or specific people--such as the Lone Ranger, Supergirl, or Batman--during the play stage. (58)
7. a   To George Mead, the "I" is the self as subject. (58)
8. b   According to Jean Piaget, children develop the ability to use symbols during the preoperational stage. (60)
9. c   Freud's term for a balancing force between the inborn drives for self-gratification and the demands of society is the ego. (60)

10. c   According to this chapter, society sets up effective controls over our behavior by socializing us into emotions. (62)

11. b   The ways in which society sets children onto different courses for life purely because they are male or female is called gender socialization. (62)

12. a   We begin the lifelong process of defining ourselves as female or male in the family. (61)

13. d   Psychologists Susan Goldberg and Michael Lewis observed mothers with their six-month-old infants in a laboratory setting and concluded that the mothers unconsciously rewarded daughters for being passive and dependent. (62)

14. c   According to Melvin Kohn, middle-class parents focus on developing their children's curiosity, self-expression, and self-control. (64)

15. b   Kohn found that the type of job the parent performed affected the pattern of childrearing; working-class parents employed in jobs characterized by individual autonomy were more likely to follow a middle-class pattern than a working-class one. (64)

16. d   "All of the above" is the correct response. Participation in religious services teaches us belief s about the hereafter; ideas about dress, and speech and manners appropriate for formal occasions. (64)

17. a   A latent function of formal education is broadening students' social horizons. (64)

18. c   A person's musical preferences, clothing styles, and dating standards typically are most influenced by one's peers. (64-65)

19. a   Researchers found that at age 8, those children who watched the most TV were the most violent. Among the group studied, this finding persisted, even when researchers measured the level of aggressiveness at age 30. (66)

20. b   The process of learning new norms, values and attitudes or behaviors when placed in new life situations is referred to as resocialization. (67)

21. d   Resocialization occurs when a person takes a new job, joins a cult, or goes to boot camp. (68)

22. c   Total institutions are places in which people are cut off from the rest of society and are almost totally controlled by the officials who run the place. "All of the above" is an incorrect response because the term was coined by Erving Goffman, not Harold Garfinkel, and these institutions exist in democracies as well as in societies with totalitarian governments. (68)

23. b   As a consequence of the Industrial Revolution, which produced new surpluses along with an increased demand for education, a new stage of the life course was invented--adolescence. (70)

24. b   As woman's role in U.S. society has changed in the past few decades, women have come to believe that they can "have it all"--a career, a marriage and a family. In the middle years, many women face challenges as they try to reconcile the often conflicting demands of multiple social roles. (71)

25. c   It is our self that provides each of us with the uniquely individual experience of socialization within the framework of society. Each of us acts on our environment, influencing the experiences we will have. (71-72)

ANSWERS FOR TRUE-FALSE QUESTIONS

1.   *False.* Studies of institutionalized children demonstrate that some of the characteristics that we take for granted as being "human" traits result not from basic instincts but rather from early close relations with other humans. (55-56)

2.   *False.* Because humans are not monkeys, we must always be careful about extrapolating from animal studies to human behavior. (57)

3.   *True.* (57-58)

4.   *True.* (58)
5.   *True.* (60)
6.   *False.* Socialization has a great deal to do with how we feel. Because different individuals' socialization differs, they will actually experience different emotions. (61-62)
7.   *True.* (62)
8.   *True.* (63)
9.   *True.* (63)
10.   *False.* On MTV, three-quarters of the music videos show only male performers. When women are portrayed, 10 percent show violence towards women and 74 percent either "put women down" or "put them in their place. (63)
11.   *False.* Melvin Kohn found that the main concern of middle-class parents was not their children's outward conformity but, rather, they focused on developing their children's curiosity, self-expression, and self-control. Working-class parents, on the other hand, did emphasize their children's outward conformity. (64)
12.   *True.* (64)
13.   *True.* (64-65)
14.   *True.* (66)
15.   *False.* Resocialization does not always require learning a radically different perspective; it usually only modifies existing orientations to life. (67)
16.   *True.* (68)
17.   *True.* (70)
18.   *True.* (71)
19.   *True.* (71)
20.   *False.* Sociologists do not think of people as little robots; they recognize that the self is dynamic and that people are actively involved in the social construction of the self. (71-72)

ANSWERS FOR FILL-IN QUESTIONS

1.   The entire human environment, including direct contact with others, is the SOCIAL ENVIRONMENT. (54)
2.   SOCIALIZATION is the process by which people learn the characteristics of their group--the attitudes, values, and actions thought appropriate for them. (57)
3.   Charles H. Cooley coined the term LOOKING-GLASS SELF to describe the process by which a sense of self develops. (58)
4.   According to George Herbert Mead, the development of the self through role-taking goes through three stages: (1) IMITATION; (2) PLAY; and (3) GAMES. (58)
5.   SIGNIFICANT OTHER is the term used to describe someone, such as a parent and/or a sibling, who plays a major role in our social development. (58)
6.   The idea that personality consists of the id, ego, and superego was developed by SIGMUND FREUD. (60-61)
7.   The different ways in which a society sets children onto different courses for life because they are male or female is GENDER SOCIALIZATION. (62)
8.   The HIDDEN CURRICULUM refers to values that form an inherent part of a school's message, even if not explicitly taught. (64)
9.   AGENTS OF SOCIALIZATION include the family, religion, schools, peers, sports, and mass media. (63-67)

10. Transmitting skills and values thought appropriate for earning a living and for being a "good citizen" are <u>MANIFEST FUNCTIONS</u> of education. (64)
11. <u>PEER GROUPS</u> are groups of individuals roughly the same age linked by common interests. (65)
12. Resocialization often takes place in <u>TOTAL INSTITUTIONS</u> such as boot camps, prisons, and concentration camps. (67)
13. <u>DEGRADATION CEREMONY</u> is a term coined by Harold Garfinkel to describe an attempt to remake the self by stripping away an individual's self-identity and stamping a new identity in its place. (68)
14. The first stage in the life course, which takes place between birth and age twelve, is referred to by sociologists as <u>CHILDHOOD</u>. (69)
15. The stage of the life course which poses a special challenge for U.S. women is <u>THE EARLY MIDDLE YEARS</u>. (71)

ANSWERS TO MATCH THESE SOCIAL SCIENTISTS WITH THEIR CONTRIBUTIONS

1. e Melvin Kohn: *found social class differences in child rearing*
2. d Erving Goffman: *studied total institutions*
3. c George Herbert Mead: *coined the term "generalized other"*
4. a Charles H. Cooley: *coined the term "looking-glass self"*
5. g Jean Piaget: *discovered that there are four stages in cognitive development*
6. b Harry and Margaret Harlow: *conducted studies of isolated rhesus monkeys*
7. f Sigmund Freud: *asserted that human behavior is based on unconscious drives*
8. h Michael Messner: *studied the role of sports for male socialization*

CHAPTER 4
SOCIAL STRUCTURE AND SOCIAL INTERACTION

☞ CHAPTER SUMMARY

- There are two levels of sociological analysis; macrosociology investigates the large-scale features of social structure, while microsociology focuses on social interaction. Functional and conflict theorists tend to use a macrosociological approach while symbolic interactionists are more likely to use a macrosociological approach.

- The term social structure refers to a society's framework. Culture, social class, social status, roles, groups, and institutions are the major components of the social structure. The individual's location in the social structure affects his or her perceptions, attitudes, and behaviors.

- Social institutions are the organized and standard means that a society develops to meet its basic needs. Functionalists view social institutions as established ways of meeting universal group needs; however, conflict theorists see social institutions as the primary means by which the elite maintains its privileged position.

- Over time, social structure undergoes changes; sweeping changes have followed each of the four social revolutions--the first is associated with the domestication of animals and plants, the second the invention of the plow, the third the invention of the steam engine, and the fourth the invention of the microchip. Both Durkheim's concepts of mechanical and organic solidarity, and Tönnies' constructs of *Gemeinschaft and Gesellschaft* focus on the social transformations of agricultural societies to industrial societies.

- In contrast to functionalist and conflict theorists, who as macrosociologists focus on the "big picture," symbolic interactionists tend to be microsociologists who look at social interaction in everyday life. They examine how people look at things and how that, in turn, affects their behavior. The dramaturgical analysis provided by Erving Goffman analyzes everyday life in terms of the stage while the ethnomethodologists try to uncover our background assumptions which provide the basic core of our reality.

- Both macrosociology and microsociology are needed to understand human behavior because we must grasp both social structure and social interaction.

☞ LEARNING OBJECTIVES

As you read Chapter 4, use these learning objectives to organize your notes. After completing your reading, briefly state an answer to each of the objectives, and review the text pages in parentheses.

1. Differentiate between macro- and microsociology and indicate which levels of analysis are most likely to be used by functionalists, conflict theorists, and symbolic interactionists. (76-77)

2. Discuss social structure and explain why one's location in this structure affects that person's perceptions, attitudes, and behaviors. (77)

3. Define the following concepts: culture, social class, social status, roles, groups, social institutions, and societies. (78-85)

4. Identify the nine social institutions common to all societies and summarize the basic features of each. (81-82)

5. Trace the transformation of societies through the five stages of development and note the degree of social inequality present in each stage. (83-85)

6.   Describe the characteristics of postindustrial society and indicate some of the major changes occurring in such societies. (85)
7.   Use Durkheim's concepts of mechanical and organic solidarity and Tönnies' typologies of *Gemeinschaft* and *Gesellschaft* to explain what holds societies together. (86-87)
8.   Explain the concepts of personal space and touching and discuss how they are used differently in different cultures. (89)
9.   Outline the key components of both the dramaturgical view of everyday life and ethnomethodology. (89-91)
10. Explain the Thomas theorem and the social construction of reality. (92)
11. Indicate why both macrosociology and microsociology are necessary for a full understanding of social life. (93-94)

☞ CHAPTER OUTLINE

I.   **Levels of Sociological Analysis**
   A.   Macrosociology places the focus on large-scale features of social structure. It investigates large-scale social forces and the effects they have on entire societies and the groups within them. It is utilized by functionalist and conflict theorists.
   B.   Microsociology places the emphasis on social interaction, or what people do when they come together. Symbolic interaction is an example.

II. **Social Structure: The Macrosociological Perspective**
   A.   Social structure is defined as the patterned relationships between people that persist over time.
      1.   Personal feelings and desires tend to be overridden by social structure. An individual's behaviors and attitudes are determined by that person's location in the social structure.
      2.   Major components or social structure are culture, social class, social status, roles, groups, social institutions, and societies.
   B.   Culture refers to a group's language, beliefs, values, behaviors, and gestures and the material objects used by a group. It determines what kind of people we will become.
   C.   Social class in U.S. society generally is based on income, education, and occupational prestige.
      1.   A large number of people who have similar amounts of income and education and who work at jobs that are roughly comparable in prestige make up a social class.
      2.   Social class influences our behavior, our ideas, and our attitudes.
   D.   Social status refers to the positions that an individual occupies. Each status provides guidelines for how people are to act and to feel.
      1.   Status set refers to all the statuses or positions that an individual occupies.
      2.   Ascribed statuses are positions an individual either inherits at birth or receives involuntarily later in life. Achieved statuses are positions that are earned, accomplished, or involve at least some effort or activity on the individual's part.
      3.   Status symbols are signs that identify a status.
      4.   A master status--such as being male or female--cuts across the other statuses that an individual occupies. Status inconsistency is a contradiction or mismatch between statuses.
   E.   Roles are the behaviors, obligations, and privileges attached to a status.

1. The individual occupies a status, but plays a role.
2. Roles are an essential component of culture because they lay out what is expected of people, and as individuals perform their roles, those roles mesh together to form the society.

F. A group consists of people who regularly and consciously interact with one another and typically share similar values, norms, and expectations.

G. Social institutions are society's organized means of meeting its basic needs.
1. The family, religion, law, politics, economics, education, science, medicine, and the military all are social institutions.
2. Each institution has its own set of roles, values, and norms that set limits and provide guidelines for behavior.

H. Society, which consists of people who share a culture and a territory, is the largest and most complex group that sociologists study. Contemporary industrial societies evolved over time, as social structures became larger and more complex.
1. The first societies were hunting and gathering societies; small in size and nomadic, the group moved elsewhere when the supply of food ran out. There were no opportunities to accumulate possessions; therefore these were the most egalitarian of all societies, with social divisions based primarily on the family.
2. Hunting and gathering societies were transformed into pastoral (characterized by the pasturing of animals) and horticultural (characterized by the growing of plants) societies as a result of the domestication revolution, called the first social revolution. Food surpluses emerged, which led to larger populations and some specialized division of labor. As trade developed, people began to accumulate objects they considered valuable, with leaders accumulating more of these possessions than others. Simple equality began to give way to inequality.
3. The agricultural revolution (the second social revolution) occurred with the invention of the plow and pastoral and horticultural societies were transformed. A much larger food surplus was produced and more people engaged in activities other than farming. Sometimes referred to as the dawn of civilization, this period also produced the wheel, writing, and numbers. Cities developed, and groups began to be distinguished by their greater or lesser possessions. An elite gained control of the surplus resources. Social inequalities became more complex, and females became subjugated to males.
4. The Industrial Revolution (the third social revolution) began in 1765, when the steam engine first was used to run machinery. Agricultural society gave way to industrial society. Initially social inequality increased greatly, as the individuals who first utilized the new technology accumulated great wealth, controlling the means of production and dictating the conditions under which people could work for them. A huge surplus of labor developed, as masses of people were thrown off the land their ancestors had farmed; these new industrial workers eventually won their demands for better living conditions. The consequence was that wealth spread to larger segments of society. As industrialization continued, the pattern of growing inequality was reversed.
5. Industrial societies are being transformed into postindustrial societies, suggesting a fourth social revolution, the information revolution, the basic component of which is information and the primary technological change involved is the microchip. Postindustrial societies are moving away from production and

manufacturing to service industries. The U.S. was the first country to have more than 50 percent of its work force employed in service industries. Australia, New Zealand, western Europe, and Japan soon followed.

I. Many sociologists have tried to find an answer to the question of what holds society together.

    1. Emile Durkheim used mechanical solidarity and organic solidarity to explain social cohesion, or the degree to which members of a society feel united by shared values and other social bonds.

        a. Mechanical solidarity is a collective consciousness that people experience as a result of performing the same or similar tasks.

        b. Organic solidarity is a collective consciousness based on the interdependence brought about by the division of labor--how people divide up tasks.

    2. Ferdinand Tönnies analyzed how intimate community *(Gemeinschaft)* was being replaced by impersonal associations *(Gesellschaft)*

        a. *Gemeinschaft* is a type of society in which life is intimate; a community in which everyone knows everyone else and people share a sense of togetherness

        b. *Gesellschaft* is a type of society dominated by impersonal relationships, individual accomplishments, and self interest.

III. **The Microsociological Perspective: Social Interaction in Everyday Life**

    A. The microsociological approach places its emphasis on face-to-face social interaction, or what people do when they are in the presence of one another.

    B. Symbolic interactionists are interested in the symbols that people use to define their worlds, how people look at things, and how that affects their behavior. They study personal space and how people surround themselves with a personal bubble.

        1. We regulate who we let in (intimates) and who we keep out (strangers).

        2. The amount or personal space people prefer varies from one culture to another.

        3. Anthropologist Edward Hall found that Americans use four different distance zones: (1) Intimate distance--about 18 inches from the body--for lovemaking, wrestling, comforting and protecting. (2) Personal distance--from 18 inches to 4 feet--for friends, acquaintances, and ordinary conversations. (3) Social distance--from 4 feet to 12 feet--for impersonal or formal relationships such as job interviews. (4) Public distance--beyond 12 feet--for even more formal relationships such as separating dignitaries and public speakers from the general public.

    C. Dramaturgy is an analysis of how we present ourselves in everyday life. Dramaturgy is the name given to an approach, pioneered by Erving Goffman, for analyzing social life in terms of drama or the stage.

        1. According to Goffman, socialization prepares people for learning to perform on the stage of everyday life.

        2. Impression management is the person's efforts to manage the impressions that others receive of her or him.

        3. Front stage is where performances are given (wherever a person delivers his or her lines). Back stage is where people rest from their performances, discuss their presentations, and plan future performances.

4. Role performance is the particular emphasis or interpretation that an individual gives a role, the person's "style". Role conflict occurs when the expectations attached to one role are incompatible with the expectations of another role--in other words, conflict between roles. Role strain refers to conflicts that someone feels within a role.

5. Teamwork, when two or more players work together to make sure a performance goes off as planned, show that we are adept players.

6. When a performance doesn't come off, we engage in face-saving behavior-- ignoring flaws in someone's performance.

D. Ethnomethodology involves the discovery of basic rules concerning our views of the world and how people ought to act.

1. Ethnomethodologists try to undercover people's background assumptions, which form the basic core of one's reality, and provide basic rules concerning our view of the world and of how people ought to act.

2. Harold Garfinkel founded the ethnomethodological approach.

E. The social construction of reality refers to what people define as real because of their background assumptions and life experiences.

1. The Thomas theorem (by sociologist W. I. Thomas) states, "If people define situations as real, they are real in their consequences."

2. Symbolic interactionists believe that people define their own reality and then live within those definitions.

IV. **The Need for Both Macrosociology and Microsociology**

A. To understand human behavior, it is necessary to grasp both social structure (macrosociology) and social interaction (microsociology).

B. Both are necessary for us to understand social life fully because each in its own way adds to our knowledge of human experience.

☞ GLOSSARY OF DIFFICULT-TO-UNDERSTAND WORDS

amorphous: not having a definite shape or structure (100)
bag lady: a street woman who carries her belongings in bag (79)
bewilderment: hopeless confusion (91)
defrocked rabbi, priest, or nun: a person who formerly was a priest (80)
dissociated: to have separated from your previous association with someone or something (92)
divine providence: care or guidance coming from God (88)
egalitarian: characterized by people having equal rights (83)
encrusted: coated over with (92)
euphoric: extremely happy (77)
face-saving: preserving a person's respect (91)
forefinger: finger closest to the thumb (76)
gynecological: relating to the female reproductive system (92)
hesitation: pausing because of uncertainty (76)
inherent: related to the essential character of something (91)
light years: a very long period of time (86)
menacing: threatening (76)
metamorphosis: process of a major change in something, as when a caterpillar turns into a butterfly (93)
microbes: really small living particles (92)

mused: thought over (here, I said to myself) (76)
nostalgic: looking back in time, fondly (78)
override: to dominate over; to prevail over (77)
pecking order: social hierarchy based on asserting rank or power (77)
pelvic: area of body where spinal column reaches legs (92)
perplexed: confused and concerned (86)
pervade: occur throughout (88)
prep school: school that prepares people for college (77)
reemergence: coming out again (93)
reminiscent: something similar from the past (88)
remnants: the small parts or portions that are left over (76)
segregating: setting apart (90)
semidarkness: almost, but not quite, dark (76)
split second: a really short period of time (76)
striptease: slowly removing clothes to excite someone (92)
subjugated: brought under the control of (85)
Thunderbird: a brand of cheap wine (76)

☞ KEY TERMS TO DEFINE

After studying the chapter, define each of the following terms. Then check your work by referring to the answers beginning at page 64 of this Study Guide.

achieved statuses	impression management	social cohesion
ascribed statuses	Industrial Revolution	social construction of reality
background assumptions	macrosociology	social institution
culture	master status	social interaction
dramaturgy	mechanical solidarity	social structure
ethnomethodology	microsociology	society
face-saving behavior	organic solidarity	status
Gemeinschaft	pastoral society	status inconsistency
Gesellschaft	role	status symbols
group	role conflict	teamwork
horticultural society	role strain	Thomas theorem
hunting & gathering society	social class	

☞ KEY PEOPLE

State the major theoretical contributions or findings of these people.

William Chambliss	Erving Goffman	Ferdinand Tönnies
Emile Durkheim	Edward Hall	
Harold Garfinkel	W. I. Thomas	

☞ **SELF-TEST**

After completing this self-test, check your answers against the Answer Key beginning on page 64 of this Study Guide and against the text on page(s) indicated in parentheses.

MULTIPLE CHOICE QUESTIONS

1.   Microsociology: (77)
       a.   places the focus on social interaction.
       b.   investigates large-scale social forces.
       c.   places the focus on broad features of social structure.
       d.   is used by functionalists and conflict theorists.

2.   Sociologists who study social class and how groups are related to one another are using: (77)
       a.   dramaturgy.
       b.   ethnomethodology.
       c.   macrosociology.
       d.   microsociology.

3.   According to sociologists, differences among individuals in behavior and attitudes is due to: (78)
       a.   biology.
       b.   location in the social structure.
       c.   conceptions of personal space.
       d.   different styles of impression management.

4.   Culture: (78)
       a.   is only the material objects used by a group.
       b.   is less important in modern societies.
       c.   is the social inheritance, learned from other people.
       d.   All of the above.

5.   One component of social structure which strongly influences our attitudes and behavior is: (78)
       a.   social class.
       b.   status sets.
       c.   normative clusters.
       d.   master status.

6.   Social class is based on: (79)
       a.   income.
       b.   education.
       c.   occupational prestige.
       d.   all of the above.

7.   A person is simultaneously a daughter, a lawyer, and a wife. Together these represent her: (79)
       a.   social status.
       b.   social class.
       c.   status position.
       d.   status set.

8.   One's race, sex, and the social class of his or her parents are examples of: (79)
        a.   ascribed statuses.
        b.   achieved statuses.
        c.   status inconsistencies.
        d.   status incongruities.

9.   All of the following are correct regarding status symbols, except: (80)
        a.   status symbols are signs that identify a status.
        b.   status symbols often are used to show that people have "made it."
        c.   status symbols are always positive signs or people would not wear them.
        d.   status symbols are used by people to announce their statuses to others.

10.   A master status is: (80)
        a.   always ascribed.
        b.   one that cuts across the other statuses that a person holds.
        c.   fairly easily changed.
        d.   All of the above.

11.   Status inconsistency is most likely to occur when: (81)
        a.   a contradiction or mismatch between statuses exists.
        b.   we know what to expect of other people.
        c.   a person wears too many status symbols at once.
        d.   a society has few clearly defined master statuses.

12.   The behaviors, obligations, and privileges attached to statuses are called: (81)
        a.   status sets.
        b.   master statuses.
        c.   status differentiations.
        d.   roles.

13.   Sociologically, roles are significant because: (81)
        a.   sociologists need something concrete to study.
        b.   they lay out what is expected of people by society.
        c.   most deviant behavior occurs in roles.
        d.   None of the above.

14.   People who regularly and consciously interact with one another: (81)
        a.   develop compatible roles.
        b.   are considered a group, according to the sociological definition.
        c.   make up a social institution.
        d.   all of the above.

15.   Religion, politics, education, and the military are examples of: (81)
        a.   involuntary groups.
        b.   voluntary associations.
        c.   social institutions.
        d.   social fixtures.

16.   The simplest societies are the: (83)
       a.   horticultural societies.
       b.   pastoral societies.
       c.   hunting and gathering societies.
       d.   primitive societies.

17.   Of all types of societies, the most egalitarian is: (83)
       a.   hunting and gathering societies.
       b.   horticultural societies.
       c.   agricultural societies.
       d.   industrial societies.

18.   Pastoral societies are based on: (84)
       a.   the cultivation of plants.
       b.   the pasturing of animals.
       c.   the invention of the plow.
       d.   large-scale agriculture.

19.   The domestication revolution led to: (84)
       a.   the human group becoming larger.
       b.   the creation of a food surplus.
       c.   a more specialized division of labor.
       d.   All of the above.

20.   A society based on large-scale agriculture, using plows drawn by animals is known as a(n): (85)
       a.   pastoral society.
       b.   farming society.
       c.   agricultural society.
       d.   horticultural society.

21.   In agricultural societies, social inequality: (85)
       a.   largely was non existent.
       b.   was developing slowly, but social stratification remained limited.
       c.   became more extensive than that found in earlier societies.
       d.   None of the above.

22.   Postindustrial society is based on: (85)
       a.   information, services, and high technology.
       b.   emphasis on raw materials.
       c.   the production of new products.
       d.   All of the above.

23.   Organic solidarity refers to a society: (86)
       a.   with a highly specialized division of labor.
       b.   whose members who are interdependent on one another.
       c.   with a high degree of impersonal relationships.
       d.   All of the above.

24.   Personal space might be a research topic for a sociologist using: (89)
      a.   macrolevel analysis.
      b.   functional analysis.
      c.   symbolic interactionism.
      d.   the conflict perspective.

25.   The Thomas theorem is based on: (92)
      a.   functionalism.
      b.   conflict theory.
      c.   symbolic interactionism.
      d.   exchange theory.

TRUE-FALSE QUESTIONS

T F   1.   Social structure has little impact on the typical individual. (77)
T F   2.   A person's ideas, attitudes, and behaviors largely depend on his or her social class. (79)
T F   3.   To sociologists, the terms "social class" and "social status" mean the same thing. (79)
T F   4.   Being a student is an example of an achieved status. (79)
T F   5.   Being male or female is a master status. (80)
T F   6.   You occupy a status, but you play a role. (81)
T F   7.   Sociologists have identified five basic social institutions in contemporary societies. (81)
T F   8.   Society is the largest and most complex group that sociologists study. (83)
T F   9.   The simplest societies are called horticultural societies. (83)
T F   10. Hunting-and-gathering societies have been called the "dawn of civilization." (84-85)
T F   11. The domestication of animals and plants was the first social revolution. (84)
T F   12. Industrial societies were brought about by the invention of the plow. (85)
T F   13. Japan was the first country to have more than 50 percent of its work force employed in service industries. (85)
T F   14. According to Emile Durkheim, with industrialization the basis for social cohesion shifts from organic to mechanical solidarity. (86)
T F   15. *Gemeinschaft* society is characterized by impersonal, short-term relationships. (87)
T F   16. The amount or personal space people prefer varies from one culture to another. (89)
T F   17. According to Erving Goffman, back stages are where we can let our hair down. (90)
T F   18. Role conflict is a conflict that someone feels within a role. (90)
T F   19. A face-saving technique, in which people give the impression that they are unaware of a flaw in someone's performance, is known as impression management. (91)
T F   20. Symbolic interactionists assume that reality has an objective existence, and people must deal with it. (92)

FILL-IN QUESTIONS

1.   _____ investigates such things as social class and how groups are related to one another. (77)
2.   The level of sociological analysis used by symbolic interactionists is _____. (77)
3.   _____ are signs used to identify a status. (80)
4.   Sociologists refer to the condition in which a person ranks high on some dimensions of social class but low on others as _____. (80)

5. The simplest societies are called _____ societies. (83)
6. The _____ revolution was brought about by the invention of the plow. (85)
7. A society based on information, services, and high technology is called the _____ society. (85)
8. The information revolution is the _____ revolution, based on technology that processes information. (85)
9. The degree to which members of a group or society feel united by shared values and other social bonds is referred to as _____. (86)
10. Durkheim referred to a collective consciousness that people experience due to performing the same or similar tasks as _____. (86)
11. Ferdinand Tönnies used the term _____ to refer to societies dominated by impersonal relationships, individual accomplishments, and self-interest. (87)
12. _____ focuses on fact-to-face social interactions. (87-88)
13. Goffman called the techniques that we use to try and salvage a performance that is going bad as _____. (91)
14. The _____ states, "If people define situations as real, they are real in their consequences." (92)
15. What people define as real because of their background assumptions and life experiences is the _____. (92)

MATCH THESE SOCIAL SCIENTISTS WITH THEIR CONTRIBUTIONS

___1. Emile Durkheim   a. *described **Gemeinschaft** and **Gesellschaft** societies*
___2. Ferdinand Tönnies   b. *wrote about mechanical and organic solidarity*
___3. Edward Hall   c. *analyzed everyday life in terms of dramaturgy*
___4. Erving Goffman   d. *found of ethnomethodolgy*
___5. W. I. Thomas   e. *studied the concept of personal space*
___6. Harold Garkinkel   f. *wrote a theorem about the nature of social reality*

"DOWN-TO-EARTH SOCIOLOGY"

1. Analyze the statuses and roles in your own life. How does when and where you were born affect your life? Have you ever experienced role conflict or role strain? Why?
2. Pretend that you were transplanted from the United States to the tribal society of the northeastern highlands of Laos when the United States forces withdrew from Vietnam. How would your experiences have compared with those of the Hmong people who were relocated to the United States?
3. Were you aware of the Amish before reading this chapter? Why are they concerned about social change? If you were given the opportunity to go and live in one of the Amish communities, would you be comfortable doing so? Why or why not?
4. Are you aware of your own sense of personal space? Have you ever encountered someone from a different culture, and thought that they stood too close, or perhaps too far from, you? How does our sense of space differ depending upon the social environment, e.g. at a party versus on public transportation?

☞ ANSWERS FOR CHAPTER 4

DEFINITIONS OF KEY TERMS

achieved statuses: positions that are earned, accomplished, or involve at least some effort or activity on the individual's part

ascribed statuses: positions an individual either inherits at birth or receives involuntarily later in life

background assumptions: deeply embedded common understandings, or basic rules, concerning our view of the world and how people ought to act

culture: the language, beliefs, values, norms, behaviors, and even material objects that are passed from one generation to the next

dramaturgy: an approach, pioneered by Erving Goffman, analyzing social life in terms of drama and the stage

ethnomethodology: the study of how people use background assumptions to make sense of life

face-saving behavior: techniques used to salvage a performance that is going sour

gemeinschaft: a type of society in which life is intimate; a community in which everyone knows everyone else and people share a sense of togetherness

gesellschaft: a type of society dominated by impersonal relationships, individual accomplishments, and self-interest

group: people who regularly and consciously interact with one another; in a general sense, people who have something in common and who believe that what they have in common is significant

horticultural society: a society based on the cultivation of plants by the use of hand tools

hunting and gathering society: a society dependent on hunting and gathering for survival

impression management: the term used by Erving Goffman to describe people's efforts to control the impressions that others receive of them

Industrial Revolution: the third social revolution, occurring when machines powered by fuels replaced most animal and human power

macrosociology: analysis of social life focusing on broad features or social structure, such as social class and the relationships of groups to one another; an approach usually used by functionalist and conflict theorists

master status: a status that cuts across the other statuses that an individual occupies

mechanical solidarity: Durkheim's term for the unity or shared consciousness that comes from being involved in similar occupations or activities

microsociology: analysis of social life focusing on social interaction; an approach usually used by symbolic interactionists

organic solidarity: Durkheim's term for the interdependence that results from people needing others to fulfill their jobs; the solidarity based on the division of labor

role: the behaviors, obligations, and privileges attached to a status

role conflict: conflict that someone feels *between* roles because the expectations attached to one role are incompatible with the expectations of another role

role strain: conflicts that someone feels *within* a role

social class: a large number of people with similar amounts of income and education who work at jobs that are roughly comparable in prestige

social cohesion: the degree to which members of a group or society feel united by shared values and other social bonds

social construction of reality: what people define as real because of their background assumptions and life experiences

social institutions: the organized usual or standard ways by which society meets its basic needs

social interaction: what people do when they are in the presence of one another

social structure: the relationship of people and groups to one another

society: a term used by sociologists to refer to a group of people who share a culture and a territory

status: the position that someone occupies in society or a social group; one's social ranking

status inconsistency: a contradiction or mismatch between statuses

status symbols: signs used to identify a status

teamwork: the collaboration of two or more persons interested in the success of a performance to manage impressions jointly

Thomas theorem: basically, that people live in socially constructed world; that is, that people jointly build their own realities; as summarized by W. I. Thomas's statement: "If people define situations as real, they are real in their consequences."

ANSWERS FOR MULTIPLE CHOICE QUESTIONS

1. a Microsociology places the focus on social interaction. Responses b, c, and d all describe macrosociology. (77)
2. c Sociologists who study social class and how groups are related to one another are using macrosociology. (77)
3. b Sociologists believe that people learn certain behaviors and attitudes because of their place in the social structure; in other words, whether they are privileged, deprived, or somewhere in between will affect their behavior and their attitudes. (78)
4. c Culture is the social inheritance, learned from other people. (78)
5. a One of the chief components of the social structure which strongly influences people's attitudes, ideas, and behavior is social class. (78)
6. d Income, education, and occupational prestige all define one's social class. (79)
7. d A person is simultaneously a daughter, a lawyer, a wife, and a mother; all of these together represent her status set. (79)
8. a One's race, sex, and the social class of his or her parents are examples of ascribed statuses. (79)
9. c The incorrect statement is: Status symbols are always positive signs or people would not wear them. Some social statuses are negative, and therefore, so are their status symbols (e.g.. prison clothing issued to inmates). (80)
10. b A master status is one that cuts across the other statuses that a person holds. (80)
11. a Status inconsistency is most likely to occur when a contradiction or mismatch between statuses exists. An example would be a wealthy African-American doctor who is denied membership in a prestigious country club. (81)
12. d The behaviors, obligations, and privileges attached to statuses are called roles. (81)
13. b Sociologically, roles are significant because they lay out what behaviors and attitudes are expected by society. (81)
14. b Sociologists define a group as people who regularly and consciously interact with one another. (81)
15. c Religion, politics, education, and the military are examples of social institutions. (81)
16. c The simplest societies are the hunting and gathering societies. (83)
17. a Of all types of societies, the most egalitarian is the hunting and gathering society. (83)
18. b Pastoral societies are based on the pasturing of animals. (84)
19. d "All of the above" is correct. The domestication revolution led to the human group becoming larger, the creation of a food surplus, and a more specialized division of labor. (84)

20. c A society based on large-scale agriculture, dependent on plows drawn by animals, is known as an agricultural society. (85)
21. c In agricultural societies, social inequality became more extensive than that found in earlier societies. (85)
22. a Postindustrial society is based on information, services, and high technology. (85)
23. d All of the above is correct. Organic solidarity refers to a society with a highly specialized division of labor; whose members who are interdependent on one another; and with a high degree of impersonal relationships. (86)
24. c Personal space might be a research topic for a sociologist using symbolic interactionism. (89)
25. c The Thomas theorem is based on symbolic interactionism. (92)

ANSWERS FOR TRUE-FALSE QUESTIONS

1. *False.* Social structure has a large impact on the typical individual because it gives direction to and establishes limits on a person's behavior. (77)
2. *True.* (79)
3. *False.* Social class is a large number of people with similar amounts of income and education who work at jobs that are roughly comparable in prestige. Social status refers to the social position that a person occupies (mother, teacher, daughter, or wife). Thus, sociologists use the two terms quite differently. (79)
4. *True.* (79)
5. *True.* (80)
6. *True.* (81)
7. *False.* Sociologists have identified at least nine basic social institutions in modern societies. (81)
8. *True.* (83)
9. *False.* The simplest societies are called hunting-and-gathering societies. (83)
10. *False.* It was not hunting-and-gathering societies, but rather agricultural societies that were recognized as the "dawn of civilization" because things popularly known as "culture," such as philosophy, art, literature, and architecture, emerged during this time. (84-85)
11. *True.* (84)
12. *False.* Industrial societies were brought about by the invention of the steam engine. (85)
13. *False.* The United States was the first country to have more than 50 percent of its work force employed in service industries. (85)
14. *False.* According to Durkheim, with industrialization the basis for social cohesion shifts from the mechanical solidarity that characterizes agricultural societies to organic solidarity. (86)
15. *False.* It is *Gesellschaft* society, not *Gemeinschaft* society, that is characterized by impersonal, short-term relationships. (87)
16. *True.* (89)
17. *True.* (90)
18. *False.* Role strain, not role conflict, is defined as a conflict someone feels within a role. Role conflict is when the expectations of one role are incompatible with those of another role. (90)
19. *False.* Studied nonobservance, not impression management, is a face-saving technique in which people give the impression that they are unaware of a flaw in someone's performance. Impression management describes people's efforts to control the impressions that others receive of them. (91)
20. *False.* Symbolic interactionists do not assume that reality has an independent existence, and people must deal with it. They believe that people define their own reality and then live within those definitions. (92)

ANSWERS FOR FILL-IN QUESTIONS

1. <u>MACROSOCIOLOGY</u> investigates such things as social class and how groups are related to one another. (77)
2. The level of sociological analysis used by symbolic interactionists is <u>MICROSOCIOLOGY</u>. (77)
3. <u>STATUS SYMBOLS</u> are signs used to identify a status. (80)
4. Sociologists refer to the condition in which a person ranks high on some dimensions of social class but low on others as <u>STATUS INCONSISTENCY</u>. (80)
5. The simplest societies are called <u>HUNTING-AND-GATHERING</u> societies. (83)
6. The <u>AGRICULTURAL</u> revolution was brought about by the invention of the plow. (85)
7. A society based on information, services, and high technology is called the <u>POSTINDUSTRIAL</u> society. (85)
8. The information revolution is the <u>FOURTH</u> revolution, based on technology that processes information. (85)
9. The degree to which members of a group or society feel united by shared values and other social bonds is referred to as <u>SOCIAL COHESION</u>. (86)
10. Durkheim referred to a collective consciousness that people experience due to performing the same or similar tasks as <u>MECHANICAL SOLIDARITY</u>. (86)
11. Ferdinand Tönnies used the term *GESELLSCHAFT* to refer to societies dominated by impersonal relationships, individual accomplishments, and self-interest. (87)
12. <u>SYMBOLIC INTERACTIONISM</u> focuses on fact-to-face social interactions. (87-88)
13. Goffman called the techniques that we use to try and salvage a performance that is going bad as <u>FACE-SAVING BEHAVIOR</u>. (91)
14. The <u>THOMAS THEOREM</u> states, "If people define situations as real, they are real in their consequences." (92)
15. What people define as real because of their background assumptions and life experiences is the <u>SOCIAL CONSTRUCTION OF REALITY</u>. (92)

ANSWERS TO MATCH THESE SOCIAL SCIENTISTS WITH THEIR CONTRIBUTIONS

1. b   Emile Durkheim: *wrote about mechanical/organic solidarity*
2. a   Ferdinand Tönnies: *described **Gemeinschaft** and **Gesellschaft** societies*
3. e   Edward Hall: *studied the concept of personal space*
4. c   Erving Goffman: *analyzed everyday life in terms of dramaturgy*
5. f   W. I. Thomas: *wrote the theorem about the nature of social reality*
6. d   Harold Garfinkel: *founder of ethnomethodology*

CHAPTER 5
SOCIAL GROUPS IN A SOCIALLY DIVERSE SOCIETY

☞ CHAPTER SUMMARY

- Groups are the essence of life in society. An essential feature of a group is that its members have something in common and that they believe what they have in common makes a difference. Society is the largest and most complex group that sociologists study.

- The following types of groups exist within society: primary groups, secondary groups, in-groups and out-groups, reference groups, and social networks.

- Robert Michels noted that formal organizations tend to be controlled by a small group; this elite bypasses members and limits leadership roles to its own inner circle. Michels called this tendency the "iron law of oligarchy."

- A bureaucracy is characterized as having a division of labor, written rules, written communications, and impersonality of positions. These allow bureaucracies to be efficient and enduring.

- The concept of corporate culture refers to the organization's traditions, values, and norms. Much of this culture is invisible. It can affect its members, either negatively or positively depending upon the members' available opportunities to achieve.

- The Japanese corporate model provides a contrast to the U.S. corporate model in terms of hiring and promotion practices, guarantees of lifetime security, worker involvement outside the work setting, the broad training of workers, and the collective decision-making.

- Group dynamics refers to the ways in which individuals and groups influence one another. Size affects the dynamics of a group. Different types of leaders serve different functions in the group; instrumental leaders are task-oriented, while expressive leaders focus on maintaining harmony. Authoritarian leaders give orders, democratic leaders lead by consensus, and laissez-faire leaders are highly permissive.

- The Asch experiment illustrates the power of peer pressure, while the Milgram experiment demonstrates the influence of authority. Both show how easily we succumb to "groupthink," a kind of collective tunnel vision.

☞ LEARNING OBJECTIVES

As you read Chapter 5, use these learning objectives to organize your notes. After completing your reading, briefly state an answer to each of the objectives, and review the text pages in parentheses.

1. Explain why groups are so important to individuals and to societies. (100)
2. Define primary groups and explain why these play a significant role in our lives. (100-101)
3. Compare secondary groups to primary groups in terms of the characteristics of each. (101)
4. Describe voluntary associations and explain why there is a tendency for an oligarchy to control these types of secondary groups, especially in socially diverse societies. (101-102)
5. Distinguish between in-groups and out-groups. (103)
6. Explain what the purpose of reference groups is and why, within a socially diverse society, we often receive contradictory messages from reference groups. (103-104)
7. Explain the relationship between cliques and social networks. Discuss how "networking" addresses some of the social barriers within a socially diverse society. (104-105)

8.   State the definition of bureaucracy, list its essential characteristics, and explain why it has a tendency to endure over time. (105-107)
9.   Explain what is meant by the "rationalization of society." (107)
10. Discuss the dark side of bureaucracies, and give examples of each type of problem. (108-109)
11. Identify the consequences of hidden values in the corporate culture, especially noting their impact on women and minority participants. (109)
12. Compare and contrast the Japanese and United States corporate organizational models. (111-112)
13. Explain the concept of group dynamics and indicate how group size affects interaction. (112-114)
14. Describe the two types of leaders in groups, and the three basic styles of leadership. (114-116)
15. Demonstrate the importance of peer pressure to conformity by analyzing the Asch and Milgram experiments. (116-118)
16. Discuss groupthink and explain how it can be dangerous for a society. (118-119)

☞ CHAPTER OUTLINE

I.   **Primary Groups**
     A.   Groups are the essence of life in society. An essential element of a social group is that its members have something in common and that they believe what they have in common makes a difference.
     B.   Primary groups refer to groups characterized by cooperative, intimate, long-term, face-to-face relationships.
          1.   The group becomes part of the individual's identity and the lens through which to view life.
          2.   They are essential to an individual's psychological well-being, since humans have an intense need for associations that provide feelings of self-esteem.

II. **Secondary Groups**
     A.   Secondary groups are larger, more anonymous, formal, and impersonal than are primary groups, and are based on some interest or activity.
          1.   Members are likely to interact on the basis of specific roles, such as president, manager, worker, or student.
          2.   Secondary groups tend to break down into primary groups, such as friendship cliques at school or work. The primary group serves as a buffer between the individual and the needs of the secondary group.
     B.   Voluntary associations are secondary groups made up of volunteers who have organized on the basis of some mutual interest.
     C.   Within voluntary associations is an inner core of individuals who stand firmly behind the group's goals and are firmly committed to maintaining the organization. Robert Michels used the term "iron law of oligarchy" to refer to the tendency of this inner core to dominate the organization by becoming a small, self-perpetuating elite.

III. **In-Groups and Out-Groups**
     A.   Groups toward which individuals feel loyalty are called in-groups, while those toward which they feel antagonisms are called out-groups.
     B.   The division is significant sociologically because in-groups provide a sense of identification or belonging, give feelings of superiority, and command loyalty, thus exercising a high degree of control over their members. The antagonisms that out-groups produce help reinforce the loyalty of members of the in-group.

C.   According to Robert K. Merton, the behaviors of an in-group's members are seen as virtues, while the same behaviors by members of an out-group are viewed as vices. This double standard can pose a danger for pluralistic societies, when out-groups come to symbolize some evil, arousing hatred and motivating members of the in-group to strike out against the out-group.

IV.   **Reference Groups**

A.   Reference groups are the groups we use as standards to evaluate ourselves, whether or not we actually belong to those groups. They exert great influence over our behavior; people may change their clothing, hair style, speech, and other characteristics to match what the reference group would expect of them.

B.   Having two reference groups that clearly conflict with each other can produce intense internal conflict.

V.   **Social Networks**

A.   Social networks consist of people linked by various social ties. Interaction takes place within social networks that connect us to the larger society.

B.   They tend to perpetuate social inequality since most jobs are secured through social networks; who you know may be more important than what you know. The "old boy" network, for instance, tends to keep the best positions available to men only, rather than women. The term networking refers to the conscious use or even cultivation of contacts people think will be helpful to them, for instance by joining and belonging to clubs.

VI.   **Bureaucracies**

A.   Almost 100 years ago, Max Weber noted the emergence of bureaucracies, a new type of organization whose goal was to maximize efficiency and results.

B.   The essential characteristics of bureaucracies are: (1) a hierarchy with assignments flowing downward and accountability flowing upward; (2) a division of labor; (3) written rules; (4) written communications and records; and (5) impersonality.

C.   Once bureaucracies come into existence, they tend to perpetuate themselves by replacing old goals for new ones.

D.   Weber predicted that bureaucracies would come to dominate social life because they were such a powerful form of social organization. He called this process the "rationalization of society."

E.   Bureaucracies also have a dark side.
1.   Sometimes the rules that govern bureaucratic activity can become too detailed or too cumbersome, such that procedures are no longer carried out efficiently.
2.   Bureaucratic alienation, a feeling of powerlessness and normlessness, occurs when workers are assigned to repetitive tasks in order for the corporation to achieve efficient production, thereby cutting them off from the product of one's labor. To resist alienation, workers form primary groups within the larger secondary organization.

F.   Rosabeth Moss Kanter's organizational research demonstrates that the corporate elite maintains hidden values--to keeps itself in power and also to provide better access to information, networking, and "fast tracks" for workers like themselves, usually white and male.
1.   Workers who fit in are given opportunities to advance; they outperform others and are more committed. Those who are judged outsiders and experience few opportunities think poorly of themselves, are less committed, and work below their potential.

2. Females and minorities do not match the hidden values of the corporate culture and may by treated differently. They may experience "showcasing"--being put in highly visible positions with little power so that the company is in compliance with affirmative action and "slow-track" positions--jobs where promotions are slow because accomplishments in these areas seldom come to the attention of top management.

G. The Japanese have become a giant in today's global economy because they developed a different form of corporate model.

1. The Japanese model features a team approach. A starting cohort of workers gets the same salary, is rotated through the organization, and develops intense loyalty to one another and to the organization. Lifetime security is taken for granted; the company is loyal to the employee, and expects the employee to be loyal to the company. Work is like a marriage in Japan in that the company and the employee are committed to each other. Workers move from one job to another within the corporation and decision-making occurs after lengthy deliberations in which each person to be affected by a decision is included in the process.

2. Research on Japanese corporations suggests that the Japanese corporate model fails to adequately reflect the reality of Japanese corporate life. The model probably reflects only a minority of Japanese firms. Japan has recently turned to the U.S. for insights into how to run more efficient corporations.

VII. **Group Dynamics**

A. How individuals affect groups and groups affect individuals is known as group dynamics.

B. The size of the group is significant for its dynamics.

1. Sociologist Georg Simmel (1858-1918) noted the significance of group size, making distinctions between a dyad, the smallest and most fragile of all human groupings containing only two members, and a triad, stronger than dyads because there are three members but still are extremely unstable. It is not uncommon for the bonds between two members to seem stronger, with the third person feeling hurt and excluded.

2. As more members are added to a group, intensity decreases and stability increases, for there are more linkages between more people within the group. The groups develop a more formal structure to accomplish their goals, for instance by having a president, treasurer, etc.

C. A leader may be defined as someone who influences the behavior of others.

1. There are two types of group leaders. Instrumental (task-oriented) leaders are those who try to keep the group moving toward its goals, reminding the members of what they are trying to accomplish. Expressive (socioemotional) leaders are those who are less likely to be recognized as leaders but help with the group's morale. These leaders may have to minimize the friction that instrumental leaders necessarily create.

2. There are three types of leadership styles. Authoritarian leaders are those who give orders and frequently do not explain why they praise or condemn a person's work. Democratic leaders are those who try to gain a consensus by explaining proposed actions, suggesting alternative approaches, and giving "facts" as the basis for their evaluation of the members' work. Laissez-faire leaders are those who are very passive and give the group almost total freedom to do as it wishes.

3. Psychologists Ronald Lippitt and Ralph White discovered that the leadership styles produced different results when used on small groups of young boys. Under authoritarian leaders the boys became either aggressive or apathetic; under democratic leaders they were more personal and friendly; and under laissez-faire leaders they asked more questions, made fewer decisions, and were notable for their lack of achievement.
4. People who become leaders are seen as strongly representing the group's values or as able to lead a group out of a crisis; they tend to be more talkative and to express determination and self-confidence.
D. A study by Dr. Solomon Asch indicates that people are strongly influenced by peer pressure. Asch was interested in seeing whether individuals would resist the temptation to change a correct response to an incorrect response because of peer pressure.
1. Asch held cards up in front of small groups of people and asked them which sets of cards matched; one at a time, they were supposed to respond aloud. All but one of the group members was a confederate, having been told in advance by the researcher how to answer the question.
2. After two trials in which everyone answered correctly, the confederates intentionally answered incorrectly, as they had been previously instructed to do.
3. Of the fifty people tested, 33 percent ended up giving the incorrect answers at least half of the time because of peer pressure, even though they knew the answers were wrong; only 25 percent always gave the right answer despite the peer pressure.
E. Sociologist Irving Janis coined the word "groupthink" to refer to situations in which a group of people think alike and any suggestion of alternatives becomes a sign of disloyalty. Even moral judgments are put aside for the perceived welfare of the group.
1. The Asch and Milgram experiments demonstrate how groupthink can develop.
2. U.S. history provides examples of governmental groupthink: presidents and their inner circles have committed themselves to a single course of action (refusal to believe the Japanese might attack Pearl Harbor; continuing and expanding the war in Vietnam) even when objective evidence showed the course to be wrong. The leaders became cut off from information that did not coincide with their own opinions.
3. Groupthink can be prevented only by insuring that leaders regularly are exposed to individuals who have views conflicting with those of the inner circle.

☞ GLOSSARY OF DIFFICULT-TO-UNDERSTAND WORDS

amenable: able to be influenced (110)
amorphous: not having a definite shape or structure (100)
boozers: heavy drinkers of alcoholic beverages (102)
cantankerous: bad-tempered (109)
cliques: small, tightly-knit groups (104)
cumbersome: awkward (105)
detention: being held after school because of misbehavior during school hours (100)
easel: three-legged structure to hold a chart, etc. (116)
electrodes: terminals that conduct electricity (117)

emblazoned: decorated (100)

epileptic seizures: type of physical and mental dysfunctions caused by nervous disorders (113)

estranged: removed; detached (109)

flying in the face: not conforming to the expected outcome (111)

hassle: a troubling situation (100)

mascot: animal or thing used by a group as a symbol (103)

mired: stuck in something, such as mud (119)

outlandish: very strange; bizarre (104)

pluralistic: composed of many different groups (103)

police cruiser: police car (100)

relinquish: giving something up to someone else (110)

repugnant: offensive to the senses (119)

scapegoating: blaming someone else for what is wrong (115)

sidetracked: diverted from the main issue (114)

stooges: people who play the role of the victim of another's pranks (116)

tunnel vision: the inability to consider a range of perspectives, preferring to keep attention focused in one direction only (118)

unabashed: obvious, and intended to be so (119)

☞ KEY TERMS TO DEFINE

After studying the chapter, define each of the following terms. Then check your work by referring to the answers beginning at page 80 of this Study Guide.

aggregate	goal displacement	out-groups
assimilation	group	primary group
authoritarian leader	group dynamics	(the) rationalization of society
bureaucracies	groupthink	reference group
category	in-groups	secondary group
clique	instrumental leader	small group
coalitions	iron law of oligarchy	social network
corporate culture	laissez-faire leaders	triad
democratic leader	leader	voluntary association
dyad	leadership styles	
expressive leader	networking	

☞ KEY PEOPLE

State the major theoretical contributions or findings of these people.

Solomon Asch	Bibb Latané	Georg Simmel
Charles H. Cooley	Ronald Lippitt	Max Weber
John Darley	Robert K. Merton	Ralph White
Irving Janis	Robert Michels	
Rosabeth Moss Kanter	Stanley Milgram	

☞ SELF-TEST

After completing this self-test, check your answers against the Answer Key beginning on page 80 of this Study Guide and against the text on page(s) indicated in parentheses.

MULTIPLE CHOICE QUESTIONS

1. People who have something in common and who believe that what they have in common is significant are called a(n): (100)
    a.   society.
    b.   aggregate.
    c.   category.
    d.   group.

2. _____ groups are essential to an individual's psychological well-being. (101)
    a.   Primary
    b.   Secondary
    c.   Therapy
    d.   Interpersonal

3. Secondary groups: (101)
    a.   have members who are likely to interact on the basis of specific roles.
    b.   are characteristic of industrial societies.
    c.   are essential to the functioning of contemporary societies.
    d.   All of the above.

4. Voluntary associations: (101)
    a.   are groups made up of volunteers who organize on the basis of some mutual interest.
    b.   include political parties, unions, professional associations, and churches.
    c.   have been an important part of American life.
    d.   All of the above.

5. The tendency for organizations to be dominated by a small, self-perpetuating elite is called: (102)
    a.   the Peter Principle.
    b.   bureaucratic engorgement.
    c.   the iron law of oligarchy.
    d.   the corporate power struggle.

6. Sociologists refer to groups which provide a sense of identification or belonging as: (103)
    a.   personal groups.
    b.   in-groups.
    c.   my-group.
    d.   homeboys' groups.

7. The groups we use as a standard to evaluate ourselves are: (103)
    a. primary groups.
    b. secondary groups.
    c. reference groups.
    d. evaluation groups.

8. Sociologically speaking, the social ties radiating outward from the self, that link people together are: (104)
    a. social networks.
    b. reference groups.
    c. cliques.
    d. inner-circles.

9. Sociologists refer to the process of using or cultivating networks for some gain as: (105)
    a. networking.
    b. group dynamics.
    c. social climbing.
    d. being a user.

10. All of the following are characteristics of bureaucracy, <u>except:</u> (105-106)
    a. a division of labor.
    b. a hierarchy with assignments flowing upward and accountability flowing downward.
    c. written rules, communications and records.
    d. impersonality.

11. Goal displacement occurs when: (106)
    a. a bureaucrat has the inability to see the goals of the organization and to function as a cooperative, integrated part of the whole.
    b. goals conflict with one another.
    c. an organization adopts new goals.
    d. members of an organization are promoted until they reach their level of incompetence.

12. The term "rationalization of society" was coined by: (107)
    a. Karl Marx.
    b. Emile Durkheim.
    c. Max Weber.
    d. Robert Michels.

13. George Ritzer used the term "the McDonaldization of society" to refer to: (108)
    a. the preference for McDonald's over Burger King.
    b. the spread of McDonald's world-wide.
    c. the increasing rationalization of daily living.
    d. All of the above.

14. The dark side of bureaucracies includes: (108-109)
    a. alienation.
    b. goal displacement.
    c. personal conflicts.
    d. All of the above.

15. Many of us have experienced frustration with the "correct procedures" of bureaucracies. We usually refer to these procedures as: (108)
    a. a pain in the neck.
    b. red tape.
    c. guidelines.
    d. goal displacement.

16. A feeling of powerlessness and normlessness is referred to as: (109)
    a. bureaucratic dysfunction.
    b. alienation.
    c. goal displacement.
    d. goal frustration.

17. Workers resist alienation by: (109)
    a. forming primary groups.
    b. praising each other and expressing sympathy when something goes wrong.
    c. putting pictures and personal items in their work areas.
    d. All of the above.

18. According to Rosabeth Moss Kanter, in a large corporation: (109)
    a. the corporate culture determines an individual's corporate fate.
    b. the people with the best qualifications typically will rise to the top of an organization.
    c. the employees who work the hardest and are the most cooperative have the greatest likelihood of being promoted.
    d. All of the above.

19. In which type of corporate model is lifetime security taken for granted? (111)
    a. the United States model.
    b. the Japanese model.
    c. both the United States and Japanese models.
    d. It is not taken for granted in either the United States or Japanese models.

20. Small groups: (112)
    a. are primary groups.
    b. are secondary groups.
    c. can be either primary or secondary groups.
    d. neither primary nor secondary groups, but fall somewhere between these two different types of groups.

21.   Dyads: (112)
        a.   are the most intense or intimate of human groups.
        b.   require continuing active participation and commitment of both members.
        c.   are the most unstable of social groups.
        d.   All of the above.

22.   An expressive leader: (114)
        a.   tries to keep the group moving toward its goals.
        b.   is also known as a task-oriented leader.
        c.   increases harmony and minimizes conflict in a group.
        d.   is the director of the drama club.

23.   According to sociologists, leaders tend to have certain characteristics which may include: (115)
        a.   they are more outgoing.
        b.   they tend to be taller and are judged better-looking than others.
        c.   where they sit in a group.
        d.   All of the above.

24.   In the Asch experiments, about _____ percent always gave the correct answer, even when that
        meant going against the sentiments of the groups. (116)
        a.   10
        b.   25
        c.   33
        d.   40

25.   The Milgram experiment demonstrates: (117)
        a.   that people who know they are being studied will behave differently as a result.
        b.   the awesome influence of peer groups over their members.
        c.   how strongly people are influenced by authority.
        d.   how isolated political leaders can become.

TRUE-FALSE QUESTIONS

T F   1.   Sociologists have concluded that the American family in general no longer provides the
                essential benefits of a primary group. (101)
T F   2.   Members of primary groups are likely to interact on the basis of specific roles. (101)
T F   3.   Voluntary associations are a special type of primary group. (101)
T F   4.   Voluntary associations are made up of volunteers who have organized on the basis of
                some mutual interest. (101)
T F   5.   The iron law of oligarchy was defined by Robert Michels. (102)
T F   6.   Tensions between in-groups and out-groups disappear in socially diverse societies. (103)
T F   7.   Reference groups are the groups we use as standards to evaluate ourselves. (103)
T F   8.   A person has to be a member of his or her reference groups in order to use them as a
                yardstick. (103)
T F   9.   Networks tend to limit social inequality by giving more people access to opportunities.
                (105)
T F   10.   Networking refers to the conscious use or even cultivation of networks. (105)

T F	11.	Weber identified five essential characteristics of bureaucracy. (105-106)
T F	12.	In a bureaucracy, each worker is a replaceable unit. (106)
T F	13.	Bureaucracies are likely to disappear as our dominant form of social organization in the near future. (106-107)
T F	14.	Marx coined the term alienation. (109)
T F	15.	Workers can prevent becoming alienated if they work at it. (109)
T F	16.	The Japanese corporate model emphasizes teamwork and lifetime security. (111)
T F	17.	As a small group grows larger, its intensity decreases and its stability increases. (113)
T F	18.	Sociologically speaking, a leader is one who is officially appointed or elected to be the "leader." (114)
T F	19.	The study of Lippitt and White regarding leadership style concluded that the authoritarian leader got the best results. (115)
T F	20.	The Asch Experiment used fake shocks to demonstrate that people would do anything for authority figures. (116-117)

FILL-IN QUESTIONS

1. People who have similar characteristics make up a _____. (100)
2. A _____ group is characterized by more anonymous, formal, and impersonal relationships. (101)
3. A group made up of volunteers who have organized on the basis of some mutual interest is called a(n) _____. (101)
4. _____ refers to the tendency of formal organizations to be dominated by a small, self-perpetuating elite. (102)
5. _____ provide a sense of identification or belonging while producing feelings of antagonisms towards _____. (103)
6. The groups we use as standards to evaluate ourselves are _____. (103)
7. The social ties radiating outward from the self, that link people together are known as _____. (104)
8. _____ occurs when new goals are adopted by an organization to replace previous goals which may have been fulfilled. (106)
9. The phrase _____ refers to the increasing influence of bureaucracies in society. (107)
10. _____ is a feeling of powerlessness and normlessness; the experience of being cut off from the product of one's labor. (109)
11. The smallest possible group is a(n) _____. (112)
12. A _____ is formed when some members of a group align themselves against other members. (113)
13. Someone who influences the behavior of others is a(n) _____. (114)
14. An individual who tries to keep the group moving toward its goals is a(n) _____ leader. An individual who increases harmony and minimizes conflict is a(n) _____ leader. (114)
15. _____ is a narrowing of thought by a group of people, which results in overconfidence and tunnel vision. (118)

MATCH THESE SOCIAL SCIENTISTS WITH THEIR CONTRIBUTIONS

___1. Irving Janis
___2. Georg Simmel
___3. Robert Michels
___4. Stanley Milgram
___5. Solomon Asch
___6. Charles H. Cooley

a. *primary groups*
b. *obedience to authority*
c. *dyads*
d. *the iron law of oligarchy*
e. *groupthink*
f. *conformity to peer pressure*

"DOWN-TO-EARTH SOCIOLOGY"

1. Acquire a copy of the organizational chart for your own college or university. Compare it with Figure 5.1 (p. 106) to determine ways in which the charts are similar and ways in which they differ. How effective do you think the organizational structure is at your institution? If you were able to do so, what would you change?

2. What was your reaction to the "Down-to-Earth Sociology" box on p. 108? Can you see evidence in your own life of McDonaldization? What do you see as the advantages of this trend? What do you see as the disadvantages?

3. Read "Managing Diversity in the Workplace" beginning on page 109. Do you think that such programs benefit workers or divide workers? Do you agree or disagree with Roosevelt Thomas that people can work together without assimilation?

4. Why did the female insurance executive say that women in her work organization have no other choice than to play corporate games in order to achieve their objectives? Do you agree or disagree? What has been your own experiences with the hidden culture in offices in which you have worked?

5. How do you feel about the "Mommy track" suggested by Felice Schwartz (p.111)? Does it solve the problem of combining career and family responsibilities? or does it just create another set of problems for women workers, as some critics of the proposal suggest? Thinking about your own life, how do, or will, you resolve the conflicting demands of work and family?

6. After reading about the Milgram experiments (pages 163-164), consider how you would have reacted if you had been selected to participate. Under what conditions would you have carried out the orders? Under what conditions would you have disobeyed? Did the fact that Milgram was able to discover an important aspect of human behavior justify the methods which he used?

☞ ANSWERS FOR CHAPTER 5

DEFINITIONS OF KEY TERMS

aggregate: individuals who temporarily share the same physical space but do not see themselves as belonging together

assimilation: the process of being absorbed into the mainstream culture

authoritarian leader: a leader who leads by giving orders

bureaucracies: a formal organization with a hierarchy of authority; a clear division of labor; emphasis on written rules, communications, and records; and impersonality of positions

category: people who have similar characteristics

clique: clusters of people within a larger group who choose to interact with one another; an internal faction

coalition: the alignment of some members of a group against others

corporate culture: the orientations that characterize corporate work settings

democratic leader: a leader who leads by trying to reach a consensus

dyad: the smallest possible group, consisting of two persons

expressive leader: an individual who increases harmony and minimizes conflict in a group; also known as a socioemotional leader

goal displacement: a goal displaced by another, such as the adoption of new goals by an organization

group: people who think of themselves as belonging together and who interact with one another

group dynamics: the ways in which individuals affect groups and the ways in which groups affect individuals

groupthink: Irving Janis's term for a narrowing of thought by a group of people, leading to the perception that there is only one correct answer, in which the suggestion of alternatives becomes a sign of disloyalty

in-groups: groups toward which one feels loyalty

instrumental leader: an individual who tries to keep the group moving toward its goals; also known as a task-oriented leader

the iron law of oligarchy: Robert Michels's phrase for the tendency of formal organizations to be dominated by a small, self-perpetuating elite

laissez-faire leader: an individual who leads by being highly permissive

leader: someone who influences other people

leadership styles: ways in which people express their leadership

networking: the process of consciously using or cultivating networks for some gain

out-groups: groups toward which one feels antagonisms

primary group: a group characterized by intimate, long-term, face-to-face association and cooperation

(the) rationalization of society: the increasing influence of bureaucracies in society, which makes the "bottom line" of results dominant in social life

reference group: Herbert Hyman's term for the groups we use as standards to evaluate ourselves

secondary group: compared with a primary group, a larger, relatively temporary, more anonymous, formal, and impersonal group based on some interest or activity, whose members are likely to interact on the basis of specific roles

small group: a group small enough so everyone can interact directly with all the other members

social networks: the social ties radiating outward from the self, that link people together

triad: a group of three persons

voluntary association: a group made up of volunteers who have organized on the basis of some mutual interest; the Girl Scouts, Baptists, and Alcoholics Anonymous are examples

ANSWERS FOR MULTIPLE CHOICE QUESTIONS

1. d   People who have something in common and who believe that what they have in common is significant are called a(n) group. (100)

2. a   Primary groups are essential to an individual's psychological well-being. (101)
3. d   "All of the above" is correct. Secondary groups have members who are likely to interact on the basis of specific roles; are characteristic of industrial societies; and are essential to the functioning of contemporary societies. (101)
4. d   All of the above is correct. Voluntary associations are groups made up of volunteers who organize on the basis of some mutual interest. They include political parties, unions, professional associations, and churches, and they have been an important part of American life. (101)
5. c   The tendency for organizations to be dominated by a small, self-perpetuating elite is called the iron law of oligarchy. (102)
6. b   Groups which provide a sense of identification or belonging are referred to as in-groups. (103)
7. c   The groups we use as a standard to evaluate ourselves are reference groups. (103)
8. a   Sociologically speaking, the social ties radiating outward from the self, that link people together are social networks. (104)
9. a   Sociologists refer to the process of consciously using or cultivating networks for some gain as networking. (105)
10. b   This choice is not a characteristic of bureaucracy because this type of organizational structure has a hierarchy with assignments flowing downward and accountability flowing upward. (105-106)
11. c   Goal displacement occurs when an organization adopts new goals. (106)
12. c   The term "rationalization of society" was coined by Max Weber. (107)
13. c   George Ritzer used the term "the McDonaldization of society" to refer to the increasing rationalization of daily living. (108)
14. a   The dark side of bureaucracies includes alienation. (108-109)
15. b   We usually refer to the "correct procedures" of bureaucracies as red tape. (108)
16. b   A feeling of powerlessness and normlessness is referred to as alienation (109)
17. d   All of the above is correct because workers resist alienation by forming primary groups, praising each other and expressing sympathy when something goes wrong, and putting pictures and personal items in their work areas. (109)
18. a   According to Rosabeth Moss Kanter, in a large corporation the corporate culture determines an individual's corporate fate. (109)
19. b   In the corporation, lifetime security is taken for granted in Japan. (111)
20. c   Small groups can be either primary or secondary groups. (112)
21. d   "All of the above" is correct. Dyads are the most intense or intimate of human groups; require continuing active participation and commitment of both members; and are the most unstable of social groups. (112)
22. c   An expressive leader increases harmony and minimizes conflict in a group. (114)
23. d   "All of the above" is correct. According to sociologists, leaders tend to have certain characteristics which may include: they are more outgoing; they tend to be taller and are judged better-looking than others; and where they sit in a group. (115)
24. b   In the Asch experiments, about 25 percent always gave the correct answer, even when that meant going against the sentiments of the groups. (116)
25. c   The Milgram experiment demonstrates how strongly people are influenced by authority. (117)

ANSWERS FOR TRUE-FALSE QUESTIONS

1.   *False.* Although the American family as an institution is experiencing vast changes, sociologists have not concluded that it no longer provides the essential benefits of a primary group. (101)

2. *False.* Members of secondary, not primary, groups are likely to interact on the basis of specific roles. (101)
3. *False.* Voluntary associations are a special type of secondary group. (101)
4. *True.* (101)
5. *True.* (102)
6. *False.* Rather than disappearing, tensions between in-groups and out-groups are heightened in socially diverse societies. (103)
7. *True.* (103)
8. *False.* A person does not have to belong to a group to use that group as a reference group. (103)
9. *False.* Networks tend to perpetuate social inequality because some people's networks are more important than others and because most jobs are secured through social networks. (105)
10. *True.* (105)
11. *True.* (105-106)
12. *True.* (106)
13. *False.* Bureaucracies are not likely to disappear as our dominant form of social organization in the near future because they generally are effective in getting the job done. Most people spend their working lives in such organizational environments. (106-107)
14. *True.* (109)
15. *False.* It is difficult for workers to prevent becoming alienated because of the nature of the organizational environment in which they work. According to Marx, alienation occurs because workers are cut off from the product of their own labor, which results in estrangement not only from the products but from their whole work environment. (109)
16. *True.* (111)
17. *True.* (113)
18. *False.* Sociologically speaking, a leader does not have to be officially appointed or elected to be the "leader." A leader is someone who influences the behaviors of others. (114)
19. *False.* The study concluded that the democratic leader got the best results. (115)
20. *False.* To study conformity the Asch experiment used cards with lines on them. To study obedience to authority the Milgram experiment used fake electrical shocks. (116-117)

ANSWERS FOR FILL-IN QUESTIONS

1. People who have similar characteristics make up a CATEGORY. (100)
2. A SECONDARY group is characterized by relatively temporary, more anonymous, formal, and impersonal relationships. (101)
3. A group made up of volunteers who have organized on the basis of some mutual interest is called a(n) VOLUNTARY ASSOCIATION. (101)
4. THE IRON LAW OF OLIGARCHY refers to the tendency of formal organizations to be dominated by a small, self-perpetuating elite. (102)
5. IN-GROUPS provide a sense of identification or belonging while producing feelings of antagonisms towards OUT-GROUPS. (103)
6. The groups we use as standards to evaluate ourselves are REFERENCE GROUPS. (103)
7. The social ties radiating outward from the self, that link people together are known as SOCIAL NETWORKS. (104)
8. GOAL DISPLACEMENT occurs when new goals are adopted by an organization to replace previous goals which may have been fulfilled. (106)

9.   The phrase <u>THE RATIONALIZATION OF SOCIETY</u> refers to the increasing influence of bureaucracies in society. (107)
10.   <u>ALIENATION</u> is a feeling of powerlessness and normlessness; the experience of being cut off from the product of one's labor. (109)
11.   The smallest possible group is a(n) <u>DYAD</u>. (112)
12.   A <u>COALITION</u> is formed when some members of a group align themselves against other members. (113)
13.   Someone who influences the behavior of others is a(n) <u>LEADER</u>. (114)
14.   An individual who tries to keep the group moving toward its goals is a(n) <u>INSTRUMENTAL</u> leader. An individual who increases harmony and minimizes conflict is a(n) <u>EXPRESSIVE</u> leader. (114)
15.   <u>GROUPTHINK</u> is a narrowing of thought by a group of people, which results in overconfidence and tunnel vision. (118)

<u>ANSWERS TO MATCH THESE SOCIAL SCIENTISTS WITH THEIR CONTRIBUTIONS</u>

1. e   Irving Janis: *groupthink*
2. c   Georg Simmel: *dyads*
3. d   Robert Michels: *the iron law of oligarchy*
4. b   Stanley Milgram: *obedience to authority*
5. f   Solomon Asch: *conformity to peer pressure*
6. a   Charles H. Cooley: *primary group*

CHAPTER 6
DEVIANCE AND SOCIAL CONTROL

☞ CHAPTER SUMMARY

- Deviance, which refers to violations of social norms, is relative; what people consider deviant varies from one culture to another and from group to group within a society. It is not the act itself, but the reaction to the act, that makes something deviant. To explain deviance, biologists and psychologists look for reasons within people, such as genetic predisposition's or personality disorders, while sociologists look for explanations in social relationships.

- Symbolic interactionists use differential association theory, control theory, and labeling theory to analyze the extent to which group membership influences people's behaviors and views of the world.

- People not only react to the deviant behavior of others; they also react to their own violation of the norms. Primary, secondary, and tertiary deviance refer to stages in people's reactions to their own disapproved behaviors. Many people succeed in neutralizing the norms of society and are able to commit deviant acts while thinking of themselves as conformists. Although most people resist being labeled deviant, there are those who embrace deviance.

- Functionalists state that deviance is functional, using strain theory and illegitimate opportunity structures to argue that widespread socialization into norms of material success accounts for much of the crime committed by the poor.

- Conflict theorists argue that the group in power imposes its definitions on other groups --the ruling class directs the criminal justice system against members of the working class, who commit highly visible property crimes, while it diverts its own criminal activities out of the criminal justice system.

- There is a growing tendency towards the medicalization of deviance; deviant acts are really external symptoms of internal disorders. Thomas Szasz argues that mental illnesses are neither mental nor illnesses, but are simply problem behaviors.

- With deviance inevitable, the larger issues are how to protect people from deviant behaviors that are harmful to their welfare, to tolerate those that are not, and to develop systems of fairer treatment for deviants.

☞ LEARNING OBJECTIVES

As you read Chapter 6, use these learning objectives to organize your notes. After completing your reading, briefly state an answer to each of the objectives, and review the text pages in parentheses.

1. Explain what sociologists mean when they say that deviance is relative. (124-125)
2. Compare and contrast biological, psychological, and sociological views on deviance. (126-128)
3. State the key components of the symbolic interaction perspective on deviance, and briefly explain differential association theory, control theory, and labeling theory. (128-133)
4. Distinguish between primary, secondary, and tertiary deviance. Give examples of each. (131-132)
5. Summarize these reactions by deviants: neutralizing deviance and embracing deviance. (132)
6. Discuss the major reasons why functionalists view deviance as functional for society. (133-134)
7. Describe Merton's strain theory, and list and briefly explain the five types of responses to anomie. (134-135)

8.   Identify the relationship between social class and crime by using the illegitimate opportunity theory and perspectives on white-collar crime. (135-137)
9.   Explain the conflict view of the relationship between class, crime, and the criminal justice system. (137-140)
10. Explain what is meant by the medicalization of deviance. (140-142)

☞ CHAPTER OUTLINE

I.   **Gaining a Sociological Perspective on Deviance**
    A.   Sociologists use the term deviance to refer to a violation of norms.
        1.   According to sociologist Howard S. Becker, it is not the act itself that makes an action deviant, but rather how society reacts to it.
        2.   Because different groups have different norms, what is deviant to some is not deviant to others.
        3.   Deviants are people who violate rules, whether the infraction is minor (jaywalking) or serious (murder). To sociologists, all people are deviants because everyone violates rules from time to time.
        4.   Erving Goffman used "stigma" to refer to attributes that discredit one's claim to a "normal" identity; a stigma (e.g. physical deformities, skin color) defines a person's master status, superseding all other statuses the person occupies.
    B.   Society's disapproval of deviance takes the form of negative sanctions and ranges from frowns and gossip to imprisonment and capital punishment, although most negative sanctions are informal.
    C.   Comparing Biological, Psychological, and Sociological Explanations
        1.   Psychologists and sociobiologists explain deviance by looking within individuals; sociologists look outside the individual.
        2.   Biological explanations focus on genetic predisposition--factors such as intelligence, "XYY" theory (an extra Y chromosome in men leads to crime), or body type (squarish, muscular persons more likely to commit street crimes).
        3.   Psychological explanations focus on personality disorders (e.g., "bad toilet training," "suffocating mothers," etc.). Yet these do not necessarily result in the presence or absence of specific forms of deviance in a person.
        4.   Sociological explanations search outside the individual: crime is a violation of norms written into law, and each society has its own laws against certain types of behavior, but social influences--such as socialization, subcultural group memberships, or social class (people's relative standing in terms of education, occupation, income and wealth)--may account for why some people break norms.
II. **The Symbolic Interaction Perspective: Learning, Controlling, and Labeling**
    A.   Differential association is Edwin Sutherland's term to indicate that those who associate with groups oriented toward deviant activities learn an "excess of definitions" of deviance and, thus, are more likely to engage in deviant activities.
        1.   The key to differential association is the learning of ideas and attitudes favorable to following the law or favorable to breaking it. Some groups teach members to violate norms (e.g. families involved in crime may set their children on a lawbreaking path; some neighborhoods tend to encourage deviant behavior).

2.   Symbolic interactionists stress that people are not mere pawns, because individuals help produce their own orientation to life and their choice of association helps to shape the self.

B.   According to control theory everyone is propelled towards deviance, but that two control systems work against these motivations to deviate.

1.   Inner controls are one's capacity to withstand temptations toward deviance, and include internalized morality, integrity, fear of punishment, and desire to be good; while outer controls involve groups (e.g. family, friends, the police) that influence a person to stay away from crime.

2.   Sociologist Travis Hirschi noted that strong bonds to society lead to more effective inner controls; bonds are based on attachments, commitments, involvements, and beliefs.

3.   The likelihood that we will deviate from social norms is related to the strength of our control systems--if the systems are strong we are less likely to deviate than if they are weak.

C.   Labeling theory is the view that the labels people are given affect their own and others' perceptions of them, thus channeling their behavior either into deviance or into conformity.

1.   There are three stages in the labeling process: (1) primary deviance refers to fleeting acts of deviance that do not become part of the self-concept; (2) secondary deviance is when the individual begins to incorporate a deviant identity into their self-concept, seeing themselves as deviant; and (3) tertiary deviance involves the relabeling of deviant behavior as non-deviant.

2.   Most people resist being labeled as deviant, even when engaging in deviant behavior. There are five different techniques of neutralization: (1) denial of responsibility ("I didn't do it"); (2) denial of injury ("Who really got hurt?"); (3) denial of a victim ("She deserved it"); (4) condemnation of the condemners ("Who are you to talk?"); and (5) appeal to higher loyalty ("I had to help my friends").

3.   Most people resist being labeled deviant, but some revel in a deviant identity (e.g. motorcycle gangs may pride themselves on getting into trouble, laughing at death, etc.).

4.   William J. Chambliss's study of law-breaking activities among two groups--the Saints (boys from respectable middle class families) and the Roughnecks (boys from working class families who hang out on the streets)--provides an excellent illustration of labeling theory. There were social class differences not only in terms of the visibility of the law-breaking behavior, but also the styles of interaction with those in authority. These influenced the ways in which teachers and the police saw them and treated them. The study showed how labels open and close door of opportunity for the individuals involved.

III. **The Functionalist Perspective: Functions, Strains, and Opportunity Structures**

A.   Emile Durkheim stated that deviance is functional, for it contributes to social order.

1.   Deviance clarifies moral boundaries (a group's ideas about how people should act and think) and affirms norms.

2.   Deviance promotes social unity.

3.   Deviance promotes social change (if boundary violations gain enough support, they become new, acceptable behaviors).

B.   Robert Merton developed strain theory to analyze what happens when people are socialized to desire a goal but denied the means to reach it.
  1.   Merton used "anomie" (Durkheim's term) to refer to the strain people experience when they are blocked in their attempts to achieve those goals. He identified five types of responses to anomie: conformity (using lawful means to seek goals society sets); innovation (using illegitimate means to achieve them); ritualism (giving up on achieving cultural goals but clinging to conventional rules of conduct); retreatism (rejecting cultural goals, dropping out); and rebellion (seeking to replace society's goals).
  2.   Merton's theory has held up under examination --anomie is highest among lower socioeconomic groups, which have less access to the institutionalized means to success.
  3.   According to strain theory, deviants are not pathogenic individuals but the products of society.

C.   According to illegitimate opportunity theory social classes have distinct styles of crime due to differential access to institutionalized means of achieving socially acceptable goals. Richard Cloward and Lloyd Ohlin suggest that opportunities for remunerative crime are woven into the texture of life and may result when legitimate structures fail. In this way the poor may be drawn into certain crimes in unequal numbers.
  1.   Illegal income-producing activities, such as robbery, drug dealing, prostitution, pimping, gambling, and other "hustles," are functional for those who want to make money, but whose access to legitimate activities is blocked.
  2.   Gangs offer disadvantaged youth an illegitimate opportunity structure. Research by Martín Sánchez Jankowski demonstrated that young men joined gangs because they provided them with access to steady money, recreation, anonymity in criminal activities, protection, and a way to help the neighborhood.
  3.   White-collar crime refers to crimes that people of respectable and high social status commit in the course of their occupations. Such crimes exist in greater numbers than commonly perceived, and can be very costly--may total about $200 billion a year. They can involve physical harm and sometimes death (concealing information that silicone breast implants might leak, for example).

IV.   **The Conflict Perspective: Power, Social Control, and Inequality**
  A.   Conflict theorists address the issue of why the legal system is inconsistent in terms of providing "justice for all." For them, the criminal justice system--the police, courts, and prisons--is a cultural device through which capitalists carry out self-protective and repressive policies.
  B.   According to conflict theory, the law is an instrument of repression, a tool designed to maintain the powerful in privileged positions and keep the powerless from rebelling and overthrowing the social order. When members of the working class get out of line, they are arrested, tried and imprisoned in the criminal justice system.
  C.   While the criminal justice system tends to overlook the harm done by the owners of corporations, flagrant violations are prosecuted. The publicity given to this level of white collar crime helps to stabilize the system by providing evidence of fairness.
  D.   Caution is needed in interpreting official statistics because the reactions of authorities are influenced by social class of the offender.
  E.   Imprisonment is an increasingly popular reaction to crime but fails to teach inmates to stay away from crime.

1.   The recidivism rate (the proportion of persons who are reasserted) in the United States runs as high as 85-90 percent, and those given probation do no better.

2.   There is disagreement within U.S. society as to why criminals should be imprisoned. Different reasons include retribution, deterrence, rehabilitation, and incapacitation.

V.   **The Medicalization of Deviance: Mental Illness**

A.   Medicalization of deviance is the view of deviance as a symptom of some underlying illness that needs to be treated by physicians.

1.   Thomas Szasz argues that mental illness is simply problem behaviors: some forms of "mental" illnesses have organic causes (e.g. depression caused by a chemical imbalance in the brain); while others are responses to troubles with various coping devices.

2.   Some sociologists find Szasz's analysis refreshing because it indicates that social experiences, and not some illness of the mind, underlie bizarre behaviors.

B.   Deinstitutionalization (release of mental patients into the community) occurred during the 1960s when counseling and other outpatient services were supposed to enable former patients to adjust to outside life; however, the network of outpatient services was not set up, and patients were released into the streets anyway.

VI.   **The Need for a More Humane Approach**

A.   With deviance inevitable, one measure of a society is how it treats its deviants

B.   The larger issues are how to protect people from deviant behaviors that are harmful to their welfare, to tolerate those that are not, and to develop systems of fairer treatment for deviants.

☞ GLOSSARY OF DIFFICULT-TO-UNDERSTAND WORDS

"burnout": condition of having become emotionally exhausted by a job, etc. (135)

aberration: something that deviates from norms (134)

avengers: people who get satisfaction from punishing a wrongdoer (132)

barrage: a massive amount of information given in a concentrated format (141)

collusion: acting together to cause something illegal or wrong to occur (138)

con artists: people who take advantage of others who are easily fooled (134)

conjugal rights: rights as a husband or wife (125)

deferential behavior: very respectful behavior (133)

exorbitant: very, very high (as with regard to price) (137)

felony: serious offense for which people frequently are imprisoned (139)

hallucinogenic: causing a person to see and hear things that don't exist (124)

hypocrites: people who say one thing, but do another (132)

inveterate conformists: people who always conform to a particular way of doing things (132)

jaywalker: person who crosses streets at improper places (125)

leeway: a margin of freedom or tolerance that is recognized as acceptable (127)

meted out: carried out the prescribed penalty (140)

mucus: slimy substance coming from the nasal passages (124)

outpatient services: medical services for which a person is not hospitalized (142)

remunerative: providing payment that is profitable (136)

sexual promiscuity: engaging in sex with many persons (131)

shoplift: steal something from a store that is open for business (129)
skid row: a place where bums hang out (142)
"squealing": informing on someone to the authorities (129)
supposition: something that is supposed to be true (127)
"turned ... tricks": engaged in prostitution (131)
typology: analysis based on symbols or meaning (134)

☞ KEY TERMS TO DEFINE

After studying the chapter, define each of the following terms. Then check your work by referring to the answers beginning at page 96 of this Study Guide.

capitalist class	illegitimate opportunity structure	recidivism rate
control theory	incapacitation	rehabilitation
crime	inner control	retribution
criminal justice system	institutionalized means	secondary deviance
cultural goals	labeling theory	social order
deinstitutionalization	marginal work class	stigma
deterrence	medicalization of deviance	strain theory
deviance	negative sanctions	street crime
differential association	outer control	techniques of neutralization
functional equivalent	personality disorders	tertiary deviance
genetic predispositions	positive sanctions	white-collar crime
halfway houses	primary deviance	working class

☞ KEY PEOPLE

State the major theoretical contributions or findings of these people.

Howard Becker	Erving Goffman	Lloyd Ohlin
William Chambliss	Travis Hirschi	Walter Reckless
Richard Cloward	Martín Sánchez Jankowski	Edwin Sutherland
Nanette Davis	David Matza	Gresham Sykes
Emile Durkheim	Robert Merton	Thomas Szasz

☞ SELF-TEST

After completing this self-test, check your answers against the Answer Key beginning on page 96 of this Study Guide and against the text on page(s) indicated in parentheses.

MULTIPLE CHOICE QUESTIONS

1.   In sociology, the term deviance: (124)
   a.   refers to behavior that is bad enough for those engaged in it to be punished by society.
   b.   refers to all violations of social rules.
   c.   refers to the violation of serious rules.
   d.   refers to crime.

2. Erving Goffman used the term _____ to refer to attributes, such as blindness, deafness, physical deformities and obesity, that society uses to discredit people. (125)
    a.   master status
    b.   mismanaged impression
    c.   stigma
    d.   deviance

3. Frowns, gossip, and crossing people off guest lists are examples of: (126)
    a.   retribution.
    b.   degradation ceremonies.
    c.   negative sanctions.
    d.   institutionalized means to achieve goals.

4. Which of the following attempts to understand deviance in terms of factors that lie outside the individual? (126)
    a.   psychological
    b.   biological
    c.   sociological
    d.   genetic

5. Differential association theory is based on the: (128)
    a.   functionalist perspective.
    b.   conflict perspective.
    c.   symbolic interactionist perspective.
    d.   psychological perspective.

6. The idea that two control systems--inner controls and outer controls--work against our tendencies toward deviance is called: (130)
    a.   conflict theory.
    b.   differential association theory.
    c.   control theory.
    d.   strain theory.

7. Incorporating a deviant identity into one's self-concept reflects: (131)
    a.   primary deviance.
    b.   secondary deviance.
    c.   tertiary deviance.
    d.   identity-based deviance.

8. All of the following are ways of neutralizing deviance, except: (132)
    a.   appeal to higher loyalties.
    b.   denial of responsibility.
    c.   denial of deviant labels.
    d.   denial of injury and of a victim.

9.   William Chambliss's study of the Saints and the Roughnecks suggests that: (132-133)
        a.   labels are easy to cast off once a person gets away from the group doing the labeling.
        b.   people often live up to the labels that a community gives them.
        c.   people often rebel against the labels given them and lead a completely different life.
        d.   sociological research on labeling has produced few conclusions.

10.   According to sociologist William Chambliss, factors which influence whether or not people will be seen as deviant include: (133)
        a.   social class.
        b.   the visibility of offenders.
        c.   styles of interaction.
        d.   All of the above.

11.   According to the _____ perspective, deviance promotes social unity and social change. (134)
        a.   functionalist
        b.   conflict
        c.   symbolic interactionist
        d.   differential association

12.   All of the following are responses to anomie as identified by Robert Merton, except: (134)
        a.   ritualism.
        b.   rebellion.
        c.   retreatism.
        d.   recidivism.

13.   According to Merton's strain theory, people who drop out of the pursuit of success by abusing alcohol or drug abuse: (134)
        a.   rebels.
        b.   retreatists.
        c.   neurotics.
        d.   ritualists.

14.   The illegitimate opportunity structures theory is based on: (135)
        a.   the conflict perspective.
        b.   the symbolic interactionist perspective.
        c.   the exchange perspective.
        d.   the functionalist perspective.

15.   According to Martín Sánchez Jankowski, who researched street gangs for more than ten years, the motive for joining a gang is: (136)
        a.   to escape from broken homes.
        b.   because gangs are seen as an economic alternative to the dead-end jobs held by parents.
        c.   to seek a substitute family.
        d.   to prove their masculinity not only to themselves but more importantly to other males in the community.

16.   Crimes committed by people of respectable and high social status in the course of their occupations are called: (136)
a.   upper-class crime.
b.   crimes of respectability.
c.   white-collar crime.
d.   tuxedo crime.

17.   The criminal justice system is made up of: (137)
a.   the police.
b.   the courts.
c.   the prisons.
d.   All of the above.

18.   The marginal working class: (137)
a.   includes people with few skills.
b.   holds low-paying, part-time, seasonal jobs.
c.   consists of the most desperate members of the working class.
d.   All of the above.

19.   According to Henslin, a severe problem associated with the policy of imprisonment is: (139)
a.   overcrowding.
b.   recidivism.
c.   violence in jails.
d.   being too soft on the prisoners.

20.   The purpose of deterrence is to: (139)
a.   right a wrong by making the offender suffer so he will become a conformist.
b.   resocialize the offender so he becomes a conformist.
c.   remove the offender from circulation.
d.   create fear in others.

21.   Halfway houses: (140)
a.   are community support facilities where ex-prisoners supervise aspects of their own lives.
b.   are examples of deterrence.
c.   do not require residents to report to authorities.
d.   All of the above.

22.   _____ switches the focus from punishing offenders to resocializing them so that they can become conforming citizens. (140)
a.   deterrence
b.   retribution
c.   rehabilitation
d.   incapacitation

23.   The removal of offenders from "normal" society, taking them "off the streets," is called: (140)
    a.   retribution.
    b.   incapacitation.
    c.   rehabilitation.
    d.   deterrence.

24.   The medicalization of deviance refers to: (142)
    a.   the castration of sex offenders.
    b.   use of lethal injections for the death penalty.
    c.   viewing deviance as a medical matter.
    d.   All of the above.

25.   The release of mental patients from institutions into the community pending treatment by a network of outpatient services is called: (142)
    a.   a pre-release program.
    b.   half-way institutionalization.
    c.   deinstitutionalization.
    d.   inhumane treatment.

TRUE-FALSE QUESTIONS

T F   1.   In sociology, the term deviance refers to all violations of social rules. (124)

T F   2.   Deviance is relative in societies. (125)

T F   3.   Across cultures, certain acts are considered to be deviant by everyone. (125)

T F   4.   Most negative sanctions are formal. (126)

T F   5.   According to differential association theory, the source of deviant behavior may be found in a person's socialization, or social learning. (128)

T F   6.   According to control theory, inner controls, such as your family, combined with outer controls, such as friends and the police, in combination represent a force keeping most of us from committing deviant acts. (130)

T F   7.   In tertiary deviance, the deviant behavior is normalized by relabeling it nondeviant. (131)

T F   8.   No one embraces deviance or wants to be labeled with a deviant identity. (132)

T F   9.   Outlaw bikers hold the conventional world in contempt and take pride in getting into trouble. (132)

T F   10.   In the study by Chambliss, the Saints and the Roughnecks both turned out largely as their labels would have predicted. (132)

T F   11.   The functionalist perspective states that deviance contributes to the social order. (134)

T F   12.   According to strain theory, everyone has a chance to get ahead in society, but some people prefer to use illegal means to achieve their goals. (134)

T F   13.   All of Merton's modes of adaptation involve illegal behavior. (135)

T F   14.   Illegitimate opportunity structures are readily available in urban slums. (136)

T F   15.   In his study of gangs, Martín Sánchez Jankowski found that more gang members came from broken homes than from stable homes. (136)

T F   16.   White-collar crime is not as costly as street crime. (136-137)

T F   17.   Both functionalists and conflict theorists agree that the criminal justice system functions for the well-being of all citizens. (137)

T F   18.   According to conflict theorists, most of those who are imprisoned in the United States come from the working class. (137)
T F   19.   Official statistics are accurate counts of the crimes committed in our society. (138)
T F   20.   According to official statistics, the number of Americans in prison doubled in the years between 1970 and 1994. (138)
T F   21.   Some researchers have found that the recidivism rate in the United States runs as high as 85 to 90 percent. (139)
T F   22.   The purpose of retribution is to create fear so that others won't break the law. (139)
T F   23.   According to Thomas Szasz, mental illness is a myth. (140)
T F   24.   The move to deinstitutionalize the mentally ill was largely successful. (142)
T F   25.   For Durkheim, deviance is inevitable, even among a group of saints. (142)

FILL-IN QUESTIONS

1.   _____ make social life possible by making behavior predictable. (124)
2.   _____ is a group's usual and customary social arrangements, on which its members depend and on which they base their lives. (124)
3.   _____ is the violation of rules or norms. (124)
4.   Erving Goffman used the term _____ to refer to attributes that discredit people. (125)
5.   _____ range from mild, informal reactions such as frowns to formal prison sentences or even capital punishment. (126)
6.   Inborn tendencies towards deviances such as juvenile delinquency and crime are called _____. (126)
7.   Crimes such as mugging, rape, and burglary are examples of _____. (127)
8.   _____ is the violation of norms that are written into law. (128)
9.   The term differential association was coined by _____. (128)
10.   _____ theory is the idea that two control systems--inner controls and outer controls--work against our pushes and pulls toward deviance. (130)
11.   By influencing a person to say away from crime, friends, family, and the police are all examples of _____ system. (130)
12.   Labeling theory is a based on the _____ perspective. (131)
13.   _____ occurs at the point when individuals incorporate a deviant identity into their self-concept. (131)
14.   When a deviant reacts by saying "Who are *you* to talk?" he/she is practicing one of the _____. (132)
15.   Strain theory is based on the idea that large number of people are socialized into desiring _____ (the legitimate objects held out to everyone) but many do not have access to _____ in order to achieve those goals. (134)
16.   Embezzlers, robbers, and con artists are all examples of what Robert Merton called _____. (134)
17.   The most desperate members of the working class, who have few skills, little job security, and are often unemployed, are referred to as the _____. (137)
18.   The _____ refers to the proportion of people who are rearrested. (139)
19.   Creating fear so people will refrain from committing a deviant act is the goal of _____. (139)
20.   The view that deviance, including crime, is the product of mental illness is referred to as _____. (140)

MATCH THESE SOCIAL SCIENTISTS WITH THEIR CONTRIBUTIONS

___1. Edwin Sutherland   a. *strain theory*
___2. Robert Merton   b. *control theory*
___3. Erving Goffman   c. *primary, secondary, tertiary deviance*
___4. Thomas Szasz   d. *white-collar crime*
___5. Emile Durkheim   e. *functions of deviance*
___6. William Chambliss   f. *effects of labeling*
___7. Gresham Sykes & David Matza   g. *importance of stigma*
___8. Walter Reckless   h. *techniques of neutralization*
___9. Edwin Lemert   i. *myth of mental illness*

"DOWN-TO-EARTH SOCIOLOGY"

1. What can we learn about deviance by looking at it from a cross-cultural perspective? (p. 125) What would happen in the United States if a wife gathered her friends around her husband's bed to beat him because he had not satisfied her sexually? As the example of the Zapotec Indians demonstrates, societies often have covert norms, which contradict the real ones but which should be followed anyway. Can you think of some examples of covert norms that represent the "real" norms in our own society?
2. After reading "When Cultures Clash: Problems in Defining Deviance" (p. 127) think what the proper reaction should be when cultural values collide. How would you have voted if you had been on a jury in the trial of Kong Moua? Should the full force of the law be applied in such cases?
3. What kinds of things have you done that are considered deviant? What kinds of techniques of neutralization did you use in order to help deflect being labeled deviant?

☞ ANSWERS FOR CHAPTER 6

DEFINITIONS OF KEY TERMS

capitalist class: the wealthy who own the means of production and buy the labor of the working class
control theory: the idea that two control systems--inner controls and outer controls--work against our tendencies to deviate
crime: the violation of norms that are written into law
criminal justice system: the system of police, courts, and prisons set up to deal with people who are accused of having committed a crime
cultural goals: the legitimate objectives held out to the members of a society
deinstitutionalization: the release of mental patients from institutions into the community pending treatment by a network of outpatient services

deterrence: creating fear so people will refrain from breaking the law

deviance: the violation of rules or norms

differential association: Edwin Sutherland's term to indicate that associating with some groups results in learning an "excess of definitions" of deviance (attitudes favorable to committing deviant acts), and, by extension, in a greater likelihood that their members will become deviant

functional equivalent: one item or activity that serves the same function as another

genetic predispositions: inborn tendencies, in this context, to commit deviant acts

halfway house: community support facilities where ex-prisoners supervise many aspects of their own lives, such as household tasks, but continue to report to authorities

illegitimate opportunity structures: opportunities for crimes woven into the texture of life

incapacitation: the removal of offenders from "normal" society; taking them "off the streets," thereby removing their capacity to commit crimes against the public

inner control: capacity to withstand pressures and tendencies to deviate

institutionalized means: approved ways of reaching cultural goals

labeling theory: the view, developed by symbolic interactionists, that the labels people are given affect their own and others' perceptions of them, thus channeling their behavior either into deviance or into conformity

marginal working class: the most desperate members of the working class, who have few skills, little job security, and are often unemployed

medicalization of deviance: to make some deviance a medical matter, a symptom of some underlying illness that needs to be treated by physicians

negative sanction: an expression of disapproval for breaking a norm; ranging from a mild, informal reaction such as a frown to a formal prison sentence or even capital punishment

outer control: groups and individuals, such as family friends, and police, that influence us to avoid deviance

personality disorders: as a theory of deviance, the view that a personality disturbance of some sort causes an individual to violate social norms

positive sanction: reward or positive reaction for following norms, ranging from a smile to a prize

primary deviance: Edwin Lemert's term for acts of deviance that have little effect on the self-concept

recidivism rate: the proportion of persons who are rearrested

rehabilitation: the resocialization of offenders so that they can become conforming members

retribution: the punishment of offenders in order to restore the moral balance upset by the offense

secondary deviance: Edwin Lemert's term for acts of deviance incorporated into the self-concept, around which an individual orients his or her behavior

social order: a group's usual and customary social arrangements

stigma: "blemishes" that discredit a person's claim to a "normal" identity

strain theory: Robert Merton's term for the strain engendered when a society socializes large numbers of people to desire a cultural goal (such as success) but withholds from many the approved means to reach that goal; one adaptation to the strain is deviance, including crime, the choice of an innovative means (one outside the approved system) to attain the cultural goal

street crime: crimes such as mugging, rape, and burglary

techniques of neutralization: ways of thinking or rationalizing that help people deflect society's norms

tertiary deviance: "normalizing" behavior considered deviant by mainstream society; relabeling behavior as nondeviant, even as good

white-collar crime: Edwin Sutherland's term for crimes committed by people of respectable and high social status in the course of their occupations

working class: those who sell their labor to the capitalist class

ANSWERS FOR MULTIPLE CHOICE QUESTIONS

1. b   In sociology, the term deviance refers to all violations of social rules. (124)
2. c   Erving Goffman used the term sigma to refer to attributes, such as blindness, deafness, physical deformities and obesity, that society uses to discredit people. (125)
3. c   Frowns, gossip, and crossing people off guest lists are examples of negative sanctions. (126)
4. c   The sociological perspective attempts to understand deviance in terms of factors that lie outside the individual. They assume that there is something in the individual's environment that is influencing him or her to become deviant. (126)
5. c   Differential association theory is based on the symbolic interactionist perspective. (128)
6. c   The idea that two control systems--inner controls and outer controls--work against our pushes and pulls toward deviance is called control theory. (130)
7. b   Incorporating a deviant identity into one's self-concept reflects secondary deviant. (131)
8. c   All of the following are ways of neutralizing deviance: appeal to higher loyalties, denial of responsibility, and denial of injury and of a victim. Denial of deviant labels is not one of the ways of neutralizing such behavior. (132)
9. b   William Chambliss's study of the Saints and the Roughnecks suggests that people often live up to the labels that a community gives them. (132-133)
10. d   All of the above is correct. William Chambliss states that all of these are factors which influence whether or not people will be seen as deviant: social class, the visibility of offenders, and their styles of interaction. (133)
11. a   According to the functionalist perspective, deviance promotes social unity and social change. (134)
12. d   Recidivism is not one of the responses to anomie identified by Merton. (134)
13. b   According to Merton's strain theory, people who drop out of the pursuit of success by abusing alcohol or drugs are retreatists. (134)
14. d   The illegitimate opportunity structures theory is based on the functionalist perspective. (135)
15. b   Contrary to what many people believe, the motive for joining a gang was not to escape a broken home or to find a substitute family or to prove one's masculinity. After studying a number of street gangs in different cities around the U.S. for more than ten years, Martín Sánchez Jankowski concluded that young men joined a gang because it was seen as an economic alternative to the dead-end jobs held by parents. (136)
16. c   Crimes committed by people of respectable and high social status in the course of their occupations are called white-collar crime. (136)
17. d   All of the above is correct. The criminal justice system is made up of the police, the courts, and the prisons. (137)
18. d   All of the above is correct. The marginal working class includes people with few skills, who hold low-paying, part-time, seasonal jobs, and who are the most desperate members of the working class. (137)
19. b   According to Henslin, a severe problem associated with the policy of imprisonment is the rate of recidivism. (139)
20. d   The purpose of deterrence is to create fear in others, with the idea that they will not commit the crimes. (139)
21. a   Halfway houses are community support facilities where ex-prisoners supervise aspects of their own lives. (140)
22. c   Rehabilitation switches the focus from punishing offenders to resocializing them so that they can become conforming citizens. (140)

23. b Incapacitation is the removal of offenders from "normal" society, taking them "off the streets." (140)
24. c The medicalization of deviance refers to viewing deviance as a medical matter. (142)
25. c The release of mental patients from institutions into the community pending treatment by a network of outpatient services is called deinstitutionalization. (142)

ANSWERS FOR TRUE-FALSE QUESTIONS

1. *True.* (124)
2. *True.* (125)
3. *False.* What is deviant to some is not deviant to others. This principle holds true within a society as well as across cultures. Thus, acts perfectly acceptable in one culture may be considered deviant in another culture. (125)
4. *False.* Most negative sanctions are informal, not formal. (126)
5. *True.* (128)
6. *False.* According to control theory, inner controls, such as your conscience, ideas of right and wrong, and your reluctance to violate religious principles, combined with outer controls, such as family, friends and the police, in combination represent a force keeping most of us from committing deviant acts. (130)
7. *True.* (131)
8. *False.* Some people and groups do embrace deviance and want to be labeled with a deviant identity. Examples include teenagers who make certain that their clothing, music, and hairstyles are outside adult norms, and outlaw bikers. (132)
9. *True.* (132)
10. *True.* (132)
11. *True.* (134)
12. *False.* According to strain theory, everyone does not have an equal chance to get ahead in society because of structural factors in the society (e.g. racism, sexism, and social class) which may deny them access to the approved ways of achieving cultural goals. (134)
13. *False.* Not all of Merton's modes of adaptation involve illegal behavior. One mode is conformity. Behavior arising out of such modes as ritualism or retreatism may not be in violation of the law. (135)
14. *True.* (136)
15. *False.* In his study of gangs, Martín Sánchez Jankowski found that as many gang members came from intact homes as came from broken homes. (136)
16. *False.* White-collar crime often is more costly than street crime. Examples include the plundering of the U.S. savings and loan industry and other "crimes in the suites." (136-137)
17. *False.* Conflict theorists believe that the criminal justice system functions for the well-being of the capitalist class. (137)
18. *False.* According to conflict theorists, most of those who are imprisoned in the United States come from the *marginal* working class. (137)
19. *False.* Official statistics are not always accurate counts of the crimes committed in our society. Both conflict theorists and symbolic interactionists believe that these statistics have bias built into them because of police discretion in arresting people, as well as many other factors. (138)
20. *False.* According to official statistics, the number of Americans in prison quintupled in the years between 1970 and 1994. (138)
21. *True.* (139)

22. *False.* The purpose of retribution is to right a wrong by making offenders suffer or pay back what they have stolen. The purpose of deterrence is to create fear so that others won't break the law. (139)
23. *True.* (140)
24. *False.* The move to deinstitutionalize the mentally ill was largely unsuccessful. The original plan called for a network of community-based, out-patient clinics to serve their medical needs; however, the government failed to provide the adequate funding with which to build the necessary services. (142)
25. *True.* (142)

ANSWERS FOR FILL-IN QUESTIONS

1. NORMS make social life possible by making behavior predictable. (124)
2. SOCIAL ORDER is a group's usual and customary social arrangements, on which its members depend and on which they base their lives. (124)
3. DEVIANCE is the violation of rules or norms. (124)
4. Erving Goffman used the term STIGMA to refer to attributes that discredit people. (125)
5. NEGATIVE SANCTIONS range from mild, informal reactions such as frowns to formal prison sentences or even capital punishment. (126)
6. Inborn tendencies towards deviances such as juvenile delinquency and crime are called GENETIC PREDISPOSITIONS. (126)
7. Crimes such as mugging, rape, and burglary are examples of STREET CRIME. (127)
8. CRIME is the violation of norms that are written into law. (128)
9. The term differential association was coined by EDWIN SUTHERLAND. (128)
10. CONTROL theory is the idea that two control systems--inner controls and outer controls-- work against our pushes and pulls toward deviance. (130)
11. By influencing a person to say away from crime, friends, family, and the police are all examples of OUTER CONTROL system. (130)
12. Labeling theory is a based on the SYMBOLIC INTERACTIONIST perspective. (131)
13. SECONDARY DEVIANCE occurs at the point when individuals incorporate a deviant identity into their self-concept. (131)
14. When a deviant reacts by saying "Who are *you* to talk?" he/she is practicing one of the TECHNIQUES OF NEUTRALIZATION. (132)
15. Strain theory is based on the idea that large number of people are socialized into desiring CULTURAL GOALS (the legitimate objects held out to everyone) but many do not have access to INSTITUTIONALIZED MEANS in order to achieve those goals. (134)
16. Embezzlers, robbers, and con artists are all examples of what Robert Merton called INNOVATORS. (134)
17. The most desperate members of the working class, who have few skills, little job security, and are often unemployed, are referred to as the MARGINAL WORKING CLASS. (137)
18. The RECIDIVISM RATE refers to the proportion of people who are rearrested. (139)
19. Creating fear so people will refrain from committing a deviant act is the goal of DETERRENCE. (139)
20. The view that deviance, including crime, is the product of mental illness is referred to as MEDICALIZATION OF DEVIANCE. (140)

ANSWERS TO MATCH THESE SOCIAL SCIENTISTS WITH THEIR CONTRIBUTIONS

1. d   Edwin Sutherland: *white collar crime*
2. a   Robert Merton: *strain theory*
3. g   Erving Goffman: *importance of stigma*
4. i   Thomas Szasz: *myth of mental illness*
5. e   Emile Durkheim: *functions of deviance*
6. f   William Chambliss: *effects of labeling*
7. h   Gresham Sykes and David Matza: *techniques of neutralization*
8. b   Walter Reckless: *control theory*
9. c   Edwin Lemert: *primary, secondary, tertiary deviance*

CHAPTER 7
SOCIAL STRATIFICATION IN GLOBAL PERSPECTIVE

☞ CHAPTER SUMMARY

- Social stratification is a system in which people are divided into layers according to their relative power, property, and prestige.

- The major systems of social stratification include: (1) slavery--owning other people; (2) caste-- lifelong status determined by birth; and (3) class--based on possession of money or material possessions. Class systems are characteristic of industrialized societies. Gender discrimination cuts across all systems of social stratification.

- Early sociologists disagreed about the meaning of social class in industrialized nations. Karl Marx argued that a person's relationship to the means of production was the only factor determining social class. Max Weber argued that three elements--property, prestige, and power--dictate an individual's standing in society.

- Various arguments have been developed to explain the universal presence of stratification. Kingsley Davis and Wilbert Moore argued that society must offer rewards in order to assure that important social positions are filled by the most competent people. Gaetano Mosca believed that leadership perpetuates inequality. Conflict theorists saw that stratification was the consequence of group struggles for scarce resources. Gerhard Lenski combined different views to explain the historical evolution of stratification systems.

- To maintain stratification within a nation, the ruling class controls ideas and information, depends on social networks, and relies on force. The social networks of the rich and poor also perpetuate social inequality.

- In Britain, the most striking features of the class system are differences in speech and accent, and differences in education. In the former Soviet Union, the 1917 Revolution resulted in one set of social classes being replaced by another.

- The most common model of global stratification divides nations into three groups: First, Second, and Third Worlds.

- Four theories explaining the origins of global stratification are imperialism and colonialism, world system theory, dependency theory, and a culture of poverty. International stratification is maintained both through neocolonialism, the ongoing dominance of Third World nations by First World nations, and multinational corporations, which operate across national boundaries.

☞ LEARNING OBJECTIVES

As you read Chapter 7, use these learning objectives to organize your notes. After completing your reading, briefly state an answer to each of the objectives, and review the text pages in parentheses.

1. Define social stratification and social class. (148-149)
2. Describe the characteristics of slavery and note the uses of slavery in the New World. (149-151)
3. Identify the features of caste systems. Give examples of different ones. (151-152)
4. List the characteristics of a class system. (152)
5. State the relationship between gender and social stratification. (152)
6. Identify the basic assumptions of Karl Marx regarding what determines social class. (153)

7.   Explain why Max Weber was critical of Marx's perspective, and summarize Weber's views regarding social class position. (153-154)
8.   State the basic assumptions of functionalists like Davis and Moore, and present Tumin's criticisms of this viewpoint. (154-155)
9.   Discuss Mosca's perspective on the universality of social stratification and explain why he is considered to be a forerunner of the conflict view. (155)
10.   Compare Marx's early conflict-oriented perspective with that or later conflict theorists. (155)
11.   Explain the mechanisms by which the elite maintains stratification. (156-157)
12.   Compare and contrast social stratification in Great Britain and the former Soviet Union. (157-158)
13.   Describe the major characteristics of First World, Second World, and Third World nations, and name at least three countries which fit in each category. (159-163)
14.   Outline the major theories of how the world's nations became stratified. (163-165)
15.   Explain how global stratification has been maintained. (165-167)

☞ CHAPTER OUTLINE

I.   **What is Social Stratification?**
A.   Social stratification is a system in which people are divided into layers according to their relative power, property, and prestige.
B.   Social class is the layer of society into which a person is born, and this position vitally affects his or her life.

II.   **Systems of Social Stratification**
A.   Slavery is a form of social stratification in which some people own other people.
1.   Initially, slavery was based on debt, punishment for violation of the law, or defeat in battle. Given this last practice, many of the first slaves were women, captured after the defeat of their village.
2.   Slavery could be temporary or permanent and was not necessarily passed on to one's children. Typically, slaves owned no property and had no power; however, this was not universally true.
3.   American colonists first tried to enslave Indians and then turned to Africans, who were being brought to North and South America by the British, Dutch, English, Portuguese, and Spanish. When American slave owners found it was profitable to own slaves for life, they developed beliefs to justify what they wanted and to make slavery inheritable.
B.   In a caste system, status is determined by birth and is lifelong.
1.   Ascribed status is the basis of a caste system. Societies with caste systems try to make certain that boundaries between castes remain firm by practicing endogamy (marriage within their own group) and developing rules about ritual pollution-- teaching that contact with inferior castes contaminates the superior caste.
2.   Although abolished by the Indian government in 1949, the caste system remains part of everyday life, as it has for almost three thousand years. Based on religion, it is made up of four main castes, or varnas, which are subdivided into thousands of specialized subcastes or *jati*. The lowest caste is considered to be "untouchable," and ablution--washing rituals--are required to restore purity for those contaminated by individuals from this group. India's caste system is finally breaking down because of industrialization and urbanization.

3. An American racial caste system developed in the United States when slavery ended. Even in the earlier parts of this century, all whites were considered higher than all African Americans and separate accommodations were maintained for the races in the South.

C. A class system is a form of social stratification based primarily on the possession of money or material possessions.
   1. An individual's initial social class position is based on that of her or his parents (ascribed status).
   2. A class system allows for social mobility--movement up or down the social class ladder--based on achieved status.

D. No matter what system a society may use to divide people into different layers, gender is always an essential part of those distinctions within each layer. On the basis of gender, people are sorted into categories and given differential access to rewards. Social distinctions have always favored males.

III. **What Determines Social Class?**
A. According to Karl Marx, social class is determined by one's relationship to the means of production--the tools, factories, land, and investment capital used to produce wealth.
   1. The bourgeoisie (capitalists) own the means of production; the proletariat (workers) are the people who work for those who own the means of production.
   2. As capital becomes more concentrated, the two classes will become increasingly more hostile to one another.
   3. Class consciousness--awareness of a common identity based on position in the means of production--will develop; it is the essential basis of the unity of workers, according to Marx.
   4. Marx believed that the workers would revolt against the capitalists, take control of the means of production, and usher in a classless society. However, the workers' unity and revolution are held back by false consciousness--the mistaken identification of workers with the interests of capitalists.

B. Unlike Marx, Max Weber did not believe that property was the sole basis of a person's position in the stratification system, but rather that property, prestige, and power determine social class.
   1. Property is an essential element; however, powerful people, like managers of corporations, control the means of production although they do not own them.
   2. Prestige may be derived from ownership of property; however, it also may be based on other factors such as athletic skills.
   3. Power is the ability to control others, even over their objections.

IV. **Why is Social Stratification Universal?**
A. According to the functionalist view expressed by Kingsley Davis and Wilbert Moore, stratification is inevitable.
   1. Society must make certain that its important positions are filled; to guarantee that the more important positions are filled by the more qualified people, society must offer them greater rewards.
   2. Davis and Moore argued that society offers greater rewards for its more responsible, demanding, and accountable positions.

B. In his critique Melvin Tumin asked how the importance of a position is measured (e.g. "Is a surgeon really more important to society than a garbage collector?").

1.   He noted that if stratification worked as Davis and Moore describe it, society would be a meritocracy--a form of social stratification in which all positions are awarded on the basis of merit--but it does not work this way (e.g. the best predictor of college entrance is family income, not ability).

2.   He also argued that money and fringe benefits are not the only reasons people take jobs.

3.   Finally, he noted that stratification is dysfunctional to many people, not functional.

C.   Gaetano Mosca argued that every society will be stratified by power. According to Mosca, stratification is inevitable; the ruling class is well organized and enjoys easy communication among its relatively few members; it is extremely difficult for the majority they govern to resist.

1.   Society cannot exist unless it is organized, thus, there must be politics to get the work of society done.

2.   Politics results in inequalities of power because some people take leadership positions and others follow.

3.   It is human nature to be self-centered, thus, people in positions of power use their positions to bring greater rewards to themselves.

D.   Conflict theorists stress that conflict, not function, is the basis of social stratification.

1.   Every society has only limited resources to go around, and in every society groups struggle with one another for those resources.

2.   Whenever a group gains power, it uses that power to extract what it can from the groups beneath it. The dominant group takes control of the social institutions, using them to keep other groups weak and to preserve the best resources for itself. Ruling classes develop an ideology to justify people's relative positions.

3.   Modern conflict theorists such as C. Wright Mills, Ralf Dahrendorf, and Randall Collins stress that conflict between capitalists and workers is not the only important conflict in contemporary society; the competition for scarce resources results in conflict not only between groups from different classes but also between groups within the same social class (e.g. young vs. old; women vs. men).

E.   Gerhard Lenski offered a synthesis between functionalist and conflict theories.

1.   Functionalists are right when it comes to societies that have only basic resources and do not accumulate wealth, such as hunting and gathering societies.

2.   Conflict theorists are right when it comes to societies with a surplus. In such societies humans pursue self-interests and struggle to control those surpluses. This leads to the emergence of a small elite who then builds inequality into the society, resulting in a full-blown system of social stratification.

V.   **Maintaining National Stratification**

A.   Social stratification is maintained within a nation because elites control ideas and information, maintain social networks, and use force.

1.   The control of ideas can be remarkably more effective than the use of brute force. The control of ideas is used by elites everywhere to maintain their positions of power--whether in dictatorships or in democracies.

2.   Elites also try to control information through the threat of force, as in a dictatorship, or through the manipulation of the media by the selective release of information, as in a democracy.

        3.   Social networks provide valuable information and tend to perpetuate social inequality.

   B.   Underlying the maintenance is control of social institutions--the legal establishment, the police, and the military.

VI.   Comparative Social Stratification

   A.   Great Britain's class system can be divided into upper, middle, and lower classes.

        1.   A little over half of the population is in the lower or working class. Half of the population is in the middle class. About 1 percent is in the upper class.

        2.   The British are extremely class conscious. Language and speech patterns are important class indicators. Education is the primary way the class system is perpetuated from one generation to the next.

   B.   The ideal of communism--a classless society--was never realized in the former Soviet Union.

        1.   Before the Communist revolution the elite was based on inherited wealth; afterwards, the major basis for stratification was membership in the Communist Party, which consisted of top party officials, a relatively small middle class, and a massive lower class of peasants and unskilled workers.

        2.   How recent reforms will impact the stratification system is yet to be seen, but a class of newly-rich individuals is emerging. Some of these had political connections, others had the foresight and initiative to take advantage of the changes.

VII.   Global Stratification: The Three Worlds of Development

   A.   The First World is the heavily industrialized nations (U.S., Canada, Great Britain, France, Germany, Switzerland, Japan, Australia, New Zealand), which are capitalistic, although variations exist in economic systems. The poor in these countries live better/longer than the average citizens in the Third World.

   B.   The Second World is the more or less industrialized nations (former Soviet Union, Poland, Czechoslovakia, Hungary). People living in these countries have considerably lower income and a poorer standard of living than people in the First World, but better than those living in the Third World. A higher proportion of people lives on farms with limited access to electricity, indoor plumbing, and other material goods.

   C.   The Third World is nations with little industrialization--such as Greece, Portugal, Mexico, Indonesia, and Ethiopia. Most people live on farms or in villages with low standards of living. The Third World is characterized by high birth rates and rapidly growing populations (placing even greater burdens on limited facilities).

VIII. What Caused Global Stratification?

   A.   The explanation of how the world became stratified focuses on how European nations exploited weaker nations.

        1.   Colonialism occurred when industrialized nations made colonies of weaker nations and exploited their labor/natural resources. European nations tended to focus on Africa, while the U.S. concentrated on Central and South America.

        2.   Imperialism (the pursuit of unlimited geographic expansion) was practiced by First World powers over the centuries. The U.S. has practiced "economic imperialism"--planting corporate flags in the particular colony and letting corporations dominate the territory's government.

   B.   According to world system theory (as espoused by Immanuel Wallerstein) countries are politically and economically tied together.

1.   There are four groups of interconnected nations: (1) core nations, where capitalism first developed; (2) semi-periphery (Mediterranean area), highly dependent on trade with core nations; (3) periphery (eastern Europe), mainly limited to selling cash crops to core nations, with limited economic development; (4) external area (most of Africa/Asia) left out of growth of capitalism, with few economic ties to core nations.

2.   A capitalist world economy (capitalist dominance) results from relentless expansion; even external area nations are drawn into commercial web.

3.   Globalization (the extensive interconnections among nations resulting from the expansion of capitalism) has speeded up because of new forms of communication and transportation. The consequence is that no nation is able to live in isolation.

C.   Dependence theory attributes lack of economic development in Third World to dominance of world economy by industrialized nations. It asserts that First World nations turned less developed nations into their plantations and mines, taking whatever they needed; as a result, many Third World nations began to specialize in a single cash crop.

D.   John Kenneth Galbraith argued that some nations remain poor because they are crippled by a culture of poverty, a way of life based on traditional values and religious beliefs that perpetuates poverty from one generation to the next and keeps some Third World from developing.

E.   Most sociologists find imperialism/world system/dependency theory explanations preferable to the culture of poverty theory because the last places the blame on the victim, but each theory only partially explains global stratification.

IX.   **Maintaining Global Stratification**

A.   Neocolonialism is the economic and political dominance of Third World nations by First World nations. Michael Harrington assets that the First World controls the Third World because it controls markets, sets prices, etc. The First World moves hazardous industries to the Third World. It sells weapons and manufactured goods to the Third World, preventing it from developing its own industrial capacity.

B.   Multinational corporations contribute to exploitation of Third World.

1.   Some exploit Third World nations directly by controlling national and local politics, running them as a fiefdom. Multinational corporations work closely with Third World elites, funneling investments to this small circle of power in exchange for their cooperation.

2.   First World nations are primary beneficiaries of profits made in Third World nations.

3.   In some situations, multinational corporations may bring prosperity to Third World nations because new factories provide salaries and opportunities which otherwise would not exist for workers in those countries.

☞ GLOSSARY OF DIFFICULT-TO-UNDERSTAND WORDS

armaments: weapons (163)
bartered: traded for something else (151)
benevolently: kindly, without other motives (155)
bondage: held in chains; slavery (166)
death squads: military squadrons that engage in the clandestine murder of civilians (162)

food stamps: government-issued stamps that are used by poorer people to purchase food (148)
free-for-all: chaotic situation (163)
full-blown: to be fully developed (156)
lap of luxury: living in grand style (153)
Pacific Rim: a term used to refer to countries whose boundaries are on the Pacific Ocean; it includes countries in both North and South America as well as Asia (167)
perks: benefits of a particular position or job (153)
pittance: a very small (pitiful) amount (153)
plight: bad situation (153)
prey: to seize and devour someone who is weak and defenseless (163)
projects (the): housing developments, owned and managed by the government, in which poorer people live because the rents are low (148)
stagnated: changing very little (163)
tried-and-true: proven arrangements (165)
tweak the nose: irritate (literally, flick a finger on the nose) (158)
vagrants: people with no home or job (153)
vanquished: the people who were conquered (150)
veneer: a thin outer layer (162)

☞ KEY TERMS TO DEFINE

After studying the chapter, define each of the following terms. Then check your work by referring to the answers beginning at page 115 of this Study Guide.

bourgeoisie	divine right of kings	neocolonialism
capitalist world economy	endogamy	proletariat
caste system	false consciousness	slavery
class consciousness	globalization	social class
class system	ideology	social mobility
colonialism	Information Superhighway	social stratification
culture of poverty	means of production	world system
cyberspace	meritocracy	
dependency theory	multinational corporation	

☞ KEY PEOPLE

State the major theoretical contributions or findings of these people.

Randall Collins	Irving L. Horowitz	Wilbert Moore
Ralf Dahrendorf	Gerhard Lenski	Melvin Tumin
William Domhoff	Michael Lipton	Immanuel Wallerstein
Kingsley Davis	Karl Marx	Max Weber
John Kenneth Galbraith	C. Wright Mills	
Michael Harrington	Gaetano Mosca	

☞ SELF-TEST

After completing this self-test, check your answers against the Answer Key beginning on page 115 of this Study Guide and against the text on page(s) indicated in parentheses.

MULTIPLE CHOICE QUESTIONS

1.   The division of people into layers according to their relative power, property, and prestige is: (148-149)
      a.   social distinction.
      b.   social stratification.
      c.   social distance
      d.   social diversification.

2.   A form of social stratification in which some people own other people is: (149)
      a.   a caste system.
      b.   slavery.
      c.   a class system.
      d.   apartheid.

3.   All of the following were initial bases for slavery <u>except</u>: (149)
      a.   racism.
      b.   debt.
      c.   violation of the law.
      d.   war and conquest.

4.   Slavery in the United States: (150)
      a.   was attempted with Native Americans before turning to Africans.
      b.   was based on the ideology of racism that justified importing slaves from Africa by asserting that they were inferior, and perhaps not even full human.
      c.   became inheritable.
      d.   All of the above.

5.   The practice of endogamy is most likely to found in: (151)
      a.   class system.
      b.   caste system.
      c.   meritocracy.
      d.   socialist system.

6.   The best example of a caste system is: (152)
      a.   the United States.
      b.   South America.
      c.   India.
      d.   none or the above.

7.   Class systems are characterized by: (152)
    a.   social mobility
    b.   geographic mobility
    c.   distribution of social standings belonging to an extended network of relatives
    d.   all of the above

8.   Marx concluded that social class depends on: (153)
    a.   wealth, power, and prestige.
    b.   the means of production.
    c.   where one is born in the social stratification system.
    d.   what a person achieves during his or her lifetime.

9.   According to Max Weber, social class is determined by: (153-154)
    a.   one's property, prestige, and power.
    b.   one's relationship to the means of production.
    c.   one's tasks and how important they are to society.
    d.   one's political power.

10.   The functionalist view of social stratification was developed by: (154)
    a.   Gaetano Mosca.
    b.   John Kenneth Galbraith.
    c.   Melvin Tumin.
    d.   Kingsley Davis and Wilbert Moore.

11.   Melvin Tumin was the first sociologist to: (155)
    a.   explain the how social inequality is functional for society.
    b.   point out major flaws in the functionalist position.
    c.   point out major flaws in the conflict perspective.
    d.   study global stratification.

12.   A form of social stratification in which positions are awarded based on merit is called a(n): (155)
    a.   meritocratic system.
    b.   egalitarian system.
    c.   socialistic system.
    d.   democratic system.

13.   Gaetano Mosca argued that every society will be stratified by: (155)
    a.   wealth.
    b.   class.
    c.   individuals' relation to the mean of production.
    d.   power.

14.   According to conflict theorists, the basis of social stratification is: (155)
    a.   functional necessity in society.
    b.   conflict over limited resources.
    c.   ascribed statuses.
    d.   the way in which individuals perceive their social class position.

15. The key to maintaining national stratification is: (156-157)
    a. having a strong police force and military to demand compliance.
    b. control of social institutions.
    c. control of information.
    d. All of the above.

16. The British perpetuate their class system between generations by: (157)
    a. emphasis on material possessions such as clothes and cars.
    b. religion.
    c. education.
    d. encouraging persons in all class to marry others within their own class.

17. In the former Soviet Union, the system of stratification was based on: (158)
    a. occupation.
    b. trade union membership.
    c. Communist party membership.
    d. education.

18. The United States, Canada, Great Britain, and France are examples of: (159)
    a. First World nations.
    b. Second World nations.
    c. Third World nations.
    d. None of the above.

19. Most people in the Third World live on less than _____ a year. (159)
    a. $1,0000
    b. $5,000
    c. $8,000
    d. $10,000

20. An arrangement in which a more powerful nation first invades and subdues a less powerful nation, and then establishes a controlling force to exploit the labor and natural resources of the defeated nation is: (163)
    a. communism.
    b. colonialism.
    c. globalism.
    d. a banana republic.

21. According to world system theory, all of the following are groups of interconnected nations, except: (163)
    a. core nations.
    b. nations on the semiperiphery.
    c. nations on the periphery.
    d. nations on the internal area which have extensive connections with the core nations.

22.   According to Henslin, today was is a key to the continued global dominance by First World nations? (164)
    a.   military strength
    b.   atomic weapons
    c.   control of cyberspace
    d.   all of the above

23.   The term "banana republic" reflects which of the following theories about global stratification? (164)
    a.   world system theory
    b.   dependency theory
    c.   culture of poverty theory
    d.   neocolonialism

24.   The culture of poverty theory was used to analyze global stratification by: (165)
    a.   Immanuel Wallerstein.
    b.   Max Weber.
    c.   John Kenneth Galbraith.
    d.   Karl Marx.

25.   Multinational corporations: (165-166)
    a.   are companies that operate across many national boundaries.
    b.   always exploit Third World nations directly.
    c.   benefit Third World nations as much as they do First World nations.
    d.   All of the above.

TRUE-FALSE QUESTIONS

T F   1.   According to sociologists, the social class to which you were born has a vital effect on your life. (149)
T F   2.   Throughout history, slavery has always been based on racism. (149)
T F   3.   One of the first groups in the New World to be enslaved were Native Americans. (150)
T F   4.   A caste system is a form of social stratification in which individual status is determined by birth and is lifelong. (151)
T F   5.   A class system is based primarily on money or material possessions. (152)
T F   6.   Gender discrimination cuts across all systems of social stratification. (152)
T F   7.   According to Karl Marx, the means of production is the only factor in determining social class. (153)
T F   8.   According to Weber, class standing is a combination of power, prestige, and property. (153-154)
T F   9.   J.Edgar Hoover's power derived from his position as the head of a powerful government agency, the F.B.I. (154)
T F   10.   Functionalists believe that people should be rewarded for their unique abilities and the type of position they hold in society is not important. (154)
T F   11.   Most people view meritocracy as bad for societies. (155)
T F   12.   According to conflict theorists, the oppressed often support laws which operate against their own interests. (155)

T F   13.   Gerhard Lenski said that the functionalist view of stratification was most appropriate when studying societies with a surplus of wealth. (156)

T F   14.   In maintaining stratification, elites find that brute force is more effective than the control of ideas. (156)

T F   15.   The idea of the divine right of kings is an example of how the ruling elite uses ideas to maintain stratification. (156)

T F   16.   The term "First World" means that nations in this category are better than nations in the "Second World" and "Third World." (159)

T F   17.   The U.S. has generally practiced "economic imperialism." (163)

T F   18.   The expansion of capitalism resulted in a capitalist world economy dominated by the core nations. (163)

T F   19.   The culture of poverty thesis is generally preferred by sociologists as an explanation of global stratification. (165)

T F   20.   Neocolonialism is the economic and political dominance of Third World nations by First World nations. (165)

FILL-IN QUESTIONS

1.   _____ is a system in which people are divided into layers according to their relative power, property, and prestige. (148)

2.   A form of social stratification in which some people own other people is _____. (149)

3.   A(n) _____ system is a form of social stratification in which individual status is determined by birth and is lifelong. (151)

4.   Caste societies use the practice of _____ to make certain that boundaries between castes remain firm. (151)

5.   According to Marx, the tools, factories, land, and investment capital used to produce wealth is _____. (153)

6.   According to Marx, the awareness of a common identity based on one's position in the means of production is _____. (153)

7.   Karl Marx's term for the mistaken identification of workers with the interests of capitalists was _____. (153)

8.   _____ was the first sociologist to point out what he saw as major flaws in the functionalist position on stratification. (155)

9.   _____ was the forerunner of the contemporary conflict view regarding social stratification. (155)

10.   The _____ is the idea that the king's authority comes directly from God. (156)

11.   _____ is the process in which one nation takes over another nation, usually for the purpose of exploiting its labor and natural resources. (163)

12.   World system theory was developed by _____. (163)

13.   _____ is the extensive interconnections among world nations resulting from the expansion of capitalism. (163)

14.   _____ is a culture that perpetuates poverty from one generation to the next. (165)

15.   Companies that operate across many national boundaries are _____. (165)

MATCH THESE SOCIAL SCIENTISTS WITH THEIR CONTRIBUTIONS

___1. Karl Marx
___2. Kingsley Davis & Wilbert Moore
___3. Gaetano Mosca
___4. Immanuel Wallerstein
___5. Michael Harrington
___6. John Kenneth Galbraith
___7. Max Weber
___8. Melvin Tumin

a. *world system theory*
b. *criticism of functional view of stratification*
c. *stressed culture of poverty*
d. *false consciousness*
e. *stated functionalist view of stratification*
f. *forerunner of conflict view of stratification*
g. *neocolonialism*
h. *class based on property, prestige and power*

"DOWN-TO-EARTH SOCIOLOGY"

1. Look at the maps and accompanying tables on pages 160-161. Why do you think the income per person is so much higher in First World nations? Does money just "go a lot farther" in Second and Third World nations or do people in these countries have much lower standards of living than people in First World nations? Could you live on $1,000 a year?

2. What was your reaction after reading about Third World children who are growing up in poverty? (p. 162) How does the image of life in the slums compare with your image of life in U.S. inner-city ghettos? What do you think that First World countries should do about this situation in the Third World?

3. Read "The Patriotic Prostitute" on page 166. What do you think would happen if the United States government encouraged prostitution as a service to one's country? What would happen if the President of the United States suggested that a way to cut the federal debt would be for young women to prostitute themselves to earn money and contribute to the country to cut this nation's debt? Why do women's groups protest the international sex trade such as that described in this article?

☞ **ANSWERS FOR CHAPTER 7**

DEFINITIONS OF KEY TERMS

bourgeoisie: Karl Marx's term for capitalists, those who own the means of production
capitalist world economy: the dominance of capitalism in the world, along with the interdependence of the world's nations capitalism has created
caste system: a form of social stratification in which one's status is determined by birth and is lifelong
class consciousness: Karl Marx's term for awareness of a common identity based on one's position in the means of production
class system: a form of social stratification based primarily on the possession of money or material possessions

colonialism: the process by which one nation takes over another nation, usually for the purpose of exploiting its labor and natural resources

culture of poverty: the values and behaviors of the poor that are assumed to make them fundamentally different from other people

cyberspace: the worldwide network of telecommunications; computer-linked communications that transcend national, regional, and cultural boundaries

dependency theory: the belief that lack of industrial development in Third World nations is caused by the industrialized nations dominating the world economy

divine right of kings: the idea that the king's authority comes directly from God

endogamy: the practice of marrying within one's own group

false consciousness: Karl Marx's term to refer to workers identifying with the interests of capitalists

globalization: the extensive interconnections among world nations due to the expansion of capitalism

ideology: beliefs about the way things ought to be that justify social arrangements

Information Superhighway: another term for *cyberspace*

means of production: the tools, factories, land, and investment capital used to produce wealth

meritocracy: a form of social stratification in which all positions are awarded on the basis of merit

multinational corporations: companies that operate across many national boundaries

neocolonialism: the economic and political dominance of Third World nations by First World nations

proletariat: Karl Marx's term for the people who work for those who own the means of production

slavery: a form of social stratification in which some people own other people

social class: a large number of people with similar amounts of income and education who work at jobs that are roughly comparable in prestige

social mobility: movement up or down the social class ladder

social stratification: the division of people into layers according to their relative power, property, and prestige; applies to both a society or to nations

world system: economic and political connections that tie the world's countries together

ANSWERS FOR MULTIPLE CHOICE QUESTIONS

1. b   The division of people into layers according to their relative power, property, and prestige is social stratification. (148-149)
2. b   Slavery is a form of social stratification in which some people own other people. (149)
3. a   Initially in antiquity, violation of the law, debt, and war and conquest were all ways in which a society justified the enslavement of individuals. It was only later, in the United States, that racism became a justification for the enslavement of Africans. (149)
4. d   All of the above is correct. In the United States the colonists initially tried to enslave Native Americans; when this practice proved to be unworkable, they turned to Africa for a supply of slave labor. An ideology of racism justified these actions by asserting that the slaves were inferior, and perhaps not even fully human. Slavery became inheritable because if one's parents were slaves, the child also was considered to be a slave. (150)
5. b   Caste systems practice endogamy, marriage within the group, and prohibit intermarriage. (151)
6. c   India is the best example of a caste system, although industrialization and other global factors are contributing to the gradual demise of that system. (152)
7. a   Class systems are characterized by social mobility--either upward or downward. (152)
8. b   Marx concluded that social class depends on the means of production. (153)
9. a   According to Max Weber, social class is determined by one's property, prestige, and power. (153-154)

10. d   The functionalist view of social stratification was developed by Kingsley Davis and Wilbert Moore. (154)
11. b   Melvin Tumin was the first sociologist to point out major flaws in the functionalist position. (155)
12. a   A form or social stratification in which all positions are awarded on the basis of merit is called a meritocratic system. (155)
13. d   Gaetano Mosca argued that every society will be stratified by power. (155)
14. b   According to conflict theorists, the basis of stratification is conflict over limited resources. (155)
15. d   All of the above is correct. The key to maintaining national stratification is having a strong police force and military to demand compliance, control of social institutions, and control of information. (156-157)
16. c   The British perpetuate their class system from one generation to the next by education. (157)
17. c   The system of stratification in the former Soviet Union was based on membership in the Communist Party; within the party there was also stratification, with most members at the bottom, some bureaucrats in the middle, and a small elite at the top. (158)
18. a   The United States, Canada, Great Britain, and France are examples of First World nations. (159)
19. a   Most people in the Third World live on less than $1,000 a year. (159)
20. b   Colonialism occurs when a more powerful nation first invades and subdues a less powerful nation, and then establishes a controlling force to exploit the labor and natural resources of the defeated nation. (163)
21. d   According to Wallerstein these groups of interconnected nations exist: core nations--which are rich and powerful; nations on the semiperiphery which have become highly dependent on trade with core nations; nations on the periphery which sell cash crops to the core nations; and the external area--including most of Africa and Asia--which have been left out of the development of capitalism and had few, if any, economic connections with the core nations. (163)
22. c   According to Henslin, control of cyberspace is a key to the continued global dominance by First World nations. (164)
23. b   Banana republics are Central American countries that developed a single cash crop for export to the United States, thereby becoming economically dependent upon the U.S. (164)
24. c   John Kenneth Galbraith used the culture of poverty theory to analyze global stratification. (165)
25. a   Multinational corporations are companies that operate across many national boundaries. According to the text, they do not always exploit Third World nations directly, but they do not benefit Third World nations as much as they do First World nations. (165-166)

ANSWERS FOR TRUE-FALSE QUESTIONS

1.   *True.* (149)
2.   *False.* Historically, slavery was based on defeat in battle, a criminal act, or a debt, but not some supposedly inherently inferior status such as race. (149)
3.   *True.* (150)
4.   *True.* (151)
5.   *True.* (152)
6.   *True.* (152)
7.   *True.* (153)
8.   *True.* (153-154)
9.   *True.* (154)

10.   *False*. Functionalists believe that society offers greater rewards for its more responsible, demanding, and accountable positions because society works better if its most qualified people hold its most important positions. From this standpoint, unique abilities would not be more important than the type of position held by the individual. (154)

11.   *False*. In American society, most people view meritocracy positively because they like to believe that positions are awarded on the basis of merit. (e.g. "May the best person/team win!") (155)

12.   *True*. (155)

13.   *False*. Gerhard Lenski felt that the functional view of stratification was most appropriate when studying societies that did not accumulate wealth. (156)

14.   *False*. In maintaining stratification, the elite finds the control of ideas more effective than brute force. (156)

15.   *True*. (156)

16.   *False*. As used by sociologists, the term "First World" does not mean that nations in this category are better than nations in the "Second World" and "Third World." The term refers to the most heavily industrialized nations. (159)

17.   **True.** (163)

18.   *True*. (163)

19.   *False*. Most sociologists find imperialism, world systems and dependency theory preferable to an explanation based on the culture of poverty. (165)

20.   *True*. (165)

ANSWERS FOR FILL-IN QUESTIONS

1.   SOCIAL STRATIFICATION is a system in which people are divided into layers according to their relative power, property, and prestige. (148)

2.   A form of social stratification in which some people own other people is SLAVERY. (149)

3.   A CASTE system is a form of social stratification in which individual status is determined by birth and is lifelong. (151)

4.   Caste societies use the practice of ENDOGAMY to make certain that boundaries between castes remain firm. (151)

5.   According to Marx, the tools, factories, land, and investment capital used to produce wealth is THE MEANS OF PRODUCTION. (153)

6.   According to Marx, the awareness of a common identity based on one's position in the means of production is CLASS CONSCIOUSNESS. (153)

7.   Karl Marx's term for the mistaken identification of workers with the interests of capitalists was FALSE CONSCIOUSNESS. (153)

8.   MELVIN TUMIN was the first sociologist to point out what he saw as major flaws in the functionalist position on stratification. (155)

9.   GAETANO MOSCA was the forerunner of the contemporary conflict view regarding social stratification. (155)

10.   The DIVINE RIGHT OF KINGS is the idea that the king's authority comes directly from God. (156)

11.   COLONIZATION is the process in which one nation takes over another nation, usually for the purpose of exploiting its labor and natural resources. (163)

12.   World system theory was developed by IMMANUEL WALLERSTEIN. (163)

13.   GLOBALIZATION is the extensive interconnections among world nations resulting from the expansion of capitalism. (163)

14.   CULTURE OF POVERTY is a culture that perpetuates poverty from one generation to the next. (165)

15.   Companies that operate across many national boundaries are MULTINATIONAL CORPORATIONS. (165)

ANSWERS TO MATCH THESE SOCIAL SCIENTISTS WITH THEIR CONTRIBUTIONS

1. d   Karl Marx: *false consciousness*
2. e   Kingsley Davis and Wilbert Moore: *the functionalist view on stratification*
3. f   Gaetano Mosca: *forerunner of the conflict view on stratification*
4. a   Immanuel Wallerstein: *world system theory*
5. g   Michael Harrington: *neocolonialism*
6. c   John Kenneth Galbraith: *stressed the culture of poverty*
7. h   Max Weber: *class based on property, prestige and power*
8. b   Melvin Tumin: *criticism of the functionalist view on stratification*

CHAPTER 8
SOCIAL CLASS IN THE UNITED STATES

☞ CHAPTER SUMMARY

- Most sociologists have adopted Weber's definition of social class as a large group of people who rank closely to one another in terms of wealth, power, and prestige. The three criteria for measuring social class are wealth, consisting of property and income, power, consisting of the ability to carry out one's will despite the resistance of others, and prestige, consisting of the regard or respect accorded an individual or social position.

- Most people are status consistent, meaning that they rank high or low on all three dimensions of social class. People who rank high on some dimensions and low on others are status inconsistent. The frustration of status inconsistency tends to produce political radicalism.

- Sociologists use two main models to portray the social class structure. Erik Wright developed a four class model based on the ideas of Karl Marx. Dennis Gilbert and Joseph Kahl developed a six class model based on the ideas of Max Weber.

- Social class leaves no aspect of life untouched. Class membership affects life chances, physical and mental health, family life, politics, religion, and education.

- Poverty is unequally distributed in the United States. Minorities, children, female-headed households, and the rural poor are more likely to be poor. Sociologists generally focus on structural factors, such as employment opportunities, in explaining poverty.

- In studying the mobility of individuals within society, sociologists look at intergenerational mobility, the individual changes in social class from one generation to the next; exchange mobility, the movement of large numbers of people from one class to another; and structural mobility, the social and economic changes that affect the social class position of large numbers of people. The Horatio Alger myth encourages people to strive to get ahead, and blames failures on individual shortcomings.

☞ LEARNING OBJECTIVES

As you read Chapter 8, use these learning objectives to organize your notes. After completing your reading, briefly state an answer to each of the objectives, and review the text pages in parentheses.

1. Define social class and compare the three components of social class. (172-178)
2. Define status inconsistency and discuss the consequences in terms of individual behavior. (178-179)
3. Explain Erik Wright's updated model of Marx's class theory. (179)
4. Discuss Gilbert and Kahl's updated model of Weber's perspective. (179-182)
5. Use Gilbert and Kahl's model to explain the reality of social classes in the automobile industry and among our nation's homeless. (182-183)
6. Examine the consequences of social class on family life, politics, religion, and illness and health care. (184-186)
7. Indicate how the poverty line is drawn. State the major characteristics of the poor in the United States. (186-190)
8. Contrast short and long-term poverty. (190)
9. Assess individual versus structural explanations of poverty. (190-191)

10.   Distinguish between the different types of social mobility, discuss the patterns of social mobility within the United States, and note some of the costs of such mobility. (191-192)
11.   Identify the social functions of the Horatio Alger myth. (193)

☞ **CHAPTER OUTLINE**

I.   **What Is Social Class?**
      A.   Social class can be defined as a large group of people who rank close to each other in wealth, power, and prestige.
      B.   Wealth consists of property (what we own) and income (money we receive). Wealth and income are not always the same--a person may own much property yet have little income, or vice versa. Usually, however, wealth and income go together.
            1.   Ownership of property (real estate, stocks and bonds, etc.) is not distributed evenly: 10 percent of the U.S. population owns 68 percent of the wealth, and the wealthiest 0.5 percent of U.S. residents own 27 percent of the nation's wealth.
            2.   Income is also distributed disproportionately: the top 20 percent of U.S. residents acquire 44 percent of the income; the bottom 20 percent receive less than 5 percent. Each fifth of the U.S. population receives approximately the same proportion of national income today as it did in 1945.
            3.   Apart from the very rich, the most affluent group in U.S. society is the executive officers of the largest corporations. Their median income (excluding stock options) is about $1 million a year.
      C.   Power is the ability to carry out your will in spite of resistance. Power is concentrated in the hands of a few--the "power elite"--who share the same ideologies and values, belong to the same clubs, and reinforce each other's world view. No major decision in U.S. government is made without their approval.
      D.   Prestige is the respect or regard people give to various occupations and accomplishments.
            1.   Occupations are the primary source of prestige. Occupations with the highest prestige pay more, require more education, entail more abstract thought, and offer greater autonomy. Occupational prestige rankings tend to be consistent across countries and over time.
            2.   For prestige to be valuable, people must acknowledge it. The elite traditionally has made rules to emphasize their higher status.
            3.   Status symbols, which vary according to social class, are ways of displaying prestige. In the United States, they include designer label clothing, expensive cars, prestigious addresses, and attending particular schools.
      E.   Status inconsistency is the term used to describe the situation of people who have a mixture of high and low rankings in the three components of social class (wealth, power, and prestige).
            1.   Most people are status consistent--they rank at the same level in all three components. People who are status inconsistent want others to act toward them on the basis of their highest status, but others tend to judge them on the basis of their lowest status.
            2.   Sociologist Gerhard Lenski determined that people suffering the frustrations of status inconsistency are more likely to be radical and approve political action aimed against higher status groups.

II.   **Sociological Models of Social Class**
   A.   How many classes exist in industrial society is a matter of debate, but there are two main models, one that builds on Marx and the other on Weber.
   B.   Sociologist Erik Wright realized that not everyone falls into Marx's two broad classes (capitalists and workers, which were based upon a person's relationship to the means of productions). For instance, although executives, managers, and supervisors would fall into Marx's category of workers, they act more like capitalists.
      1.   Wright resolved this problem by regarding some people as simultaneously members of more than one class, occupying what he called contradictory class locations.
      2.   Wright identified four classes: capitalists (owners of large enterprises); petty bourgeoisie (owners of small businesses); managers (employees who but have authority over others); and workers.
   C.   Using the framework originally developed by Weber, sociologists Dennis Gilbert and Joseph Kahl created a model to describe class structure in the U.S. and other capitalist countries.
      1.   The capitalist class (1 percent of the population) is composed of investors, heirs, and a few executives; it is divided into "old" money and "new" money. The children of "new" money move into the old money class by attending the right schools and marrying "old" money.
      2.   The upper-middle class (14 percent of the population) is composed of professionals and upper managers, almost all of whom have attended college or university and frequently have postgraduate degrees.
      3.   The lower-middle class (30 percent of the population) is composed of lower managers, craftspeople and foremen. They have at least a high school education.
      4.   The working class (30 percent of the population) is composed of factory workers and low-paid white collar workers. Most have high school educations.
      5.   The working poor (22 percent of the population) is composed of relatively unskilled blue-collar and white-collar workers, and those with temporary and seasonal jobs. If they graduated from high school, they probably did not do well in school.
      6.   The underclass (3 percent of the population) is concentrated in the inner cities and has little connection with the job market. Welfare is their main support.
   D.   The homeless are so far down the class structure that their position must be considered even lower than the underclass. They are the "fallout" of industrialization, especially the post-industrial developments that have contributed to a decline in the demand for unskilled labor.

III.   **Consequences of Social Class**
   A.   Social class plays a role in family life.
      1.   Children of the capitalist class are under great pressure to select the right mate in order to assure the continuity of the family line. Parents in this social class play a large role in mate selection.
      2.   Marriages are more likely to fail in the lower social classes; the children of the poor thus are more likely to live in single-parent households.
   B.   Political views and involvement are influenced by social class.
      1.   People in lower classes are more likely to vote Democrat, and those in higher classes to vote Republican; parties are seen as promoting different class interests.

2.   People in higher classes are more likely to be conservative on economic issues (lower taxes, etc..) and more liberal on social issues (individual rights, etc.).

3.   Political participation is not equal; the higher classes are more likely to vote and get involved in politics than those in lower social classes.

C.   All aspects of religious orientation follow class lines. Classes tend to cluster in different denominations; and patterns of worship also follow class lines.

D.   Social class affects our health, with lower classes having more sickness and higher death rates. This pattern is influenced by the unequal access to medical care.

1.   Mental health is also affected by social class. Studies show that the mental health of the lower classes is worse than that of the higher classes. These higher rates are due to the stresses of poverty.

2.   Social class is also a deciding factor in how the mentally ill are treated, with poorer individuals having less access to mental health facilities.

IV.   Poverty

A.   The U.S. government classifies the poverty line as being families whose incomes are less than three times a low-cost food budget. Any modification of this measure instantly adds or subtracts millions of people, and thus has significant consequences.

B.   Certain social groups are disproportionately represented among the poor population.

1.   Race is a major factor. Although 2 out of 3 poor people are white, racial minorities are much more likely to be poor: 11 percent of whites, 29 percent of Hispanics, and 33 percent of African-Americans live in poverty.

2.   Although the percentage of poor people over age 65 is practically the same as their overall percentage, elderly Hispanic Americans and African Americans are two to three times more likely to be poor than elderly white Americans.

3.   The sex of the person who heads a family is the greatest predictor or whether or not a family is poor. Most poor families are headed by women. They are several times more likely to be poor than families headed by two parents. The major causes of this phenomenon, called the feminization of poverty, are divorce, births to unwed mothers, and the lower wages paid to women.

C.   The poverty rate for the rural poor is higher than the national average. While they show the same racial/ethnic characteristics as the nation as a whole, they are less likely to be on welfare or to be single parents, less skilled and less educated, and the jobs available to them pay less.

D.   Children are more likely to live in poverty than are adults or the elderly. This holds true regardless of race, but poverty is much greater among minority children: two out of every five Hispanic-American children and almost one out of every two African-American children are poor.

E.   In the 1960s Michael Harrington and Oscar Lewis suggested that the poor get trapped in a "culture of poverty" as a result of having values and behaviors that make them "fundamentally different" from other U.S. residents.

1.   Economist Patricia Ruggles subsequently studied national statistics and determined that about half the poor are short-term poor, moving out of poverty within a few years, while the other half are long-term poor, living in poverty for at least 8 years.

2.   Contrary to popular belief, most poor children do not grow up to be poor. Only about 20 percent of those who were poor as children grow up to be poor as adults.

3.   Since the number of people who live in poverty remains fairly constant, this means that as many people move into poverty as move out of it.

4.   Those who remain in long-term poverty are more likely to be African American, unemployed, and live in female-headed households. About half are unmarried mothers with children.

F.   In trying to explain poverty, the choice is between focusing on individual explanations or on social structural explanations.

1.   Sociologists look to such factors as inequalities in education, access to learning job skills, racial, ethnic, age, and gender discrimination, and large-scale economic change to explain the patterns of poverty in society.

2.   Edward Banfield argued that people's orientation to time helps to explain poverty. The poor are "present oriented" and seek immediate gratification while the middle class are "future oriented" and defer gratification.

G.   The poor have little or no control over what happens to them in life, and it therefore is difficult for them to plan ahead. The desire for immediate gratification thus can be a consequence, not a cause, of poverty.

V.   **Social Mobility**

A.   There are three basic types of social mobility: intergenerational, structural, and exchange.

1.   Intergenerational mobility is the change that family members make in their social class from one generation to the next. As a result of individual effort, a person can rise from one level to another; in the event of individual failure, the reverse can be true.

2.   Sociologists are more interested in structural mobility--social changes that affect large numbers of people. By way of example, as the economy shifted from manual labor to factory machines to computers vast numbers of new jobs were created, with shifts from blue-collar jobs to white-collar positions.

3.   Exchange mobility is movement of people up and down the social class system, where, on balance, the system remains the same. The term refers to general, overall movement of large numbers of people that leaves the class system basically untouched.

B.   Studies of social mobility in the United States have focused on men, since large numbers of women in the work force is a relatively new phenomenon. Compared with their fathers one-half of all men have moved up in social class; one-third have stayed in the same place; and one-sixth have moved down.

1.   Structural changes in the U.S. economy have created opportunities for women to move up the social class ladder. One study indicated that women that did move up were encouraged by their parents to postpone marriage and get an education.

2.   Structural mobility can also work in the opposite direction; if the U.S. does not keep pace with global changes its economic position will decline. This would result in the next generation having slightly less status than their parents.

C.   The costs of social mobility include risking the loss of one's roots. One study of working class families, in which the adult children had achieved upward social mobility because parental sacrifices enabled them to get an education, found that the parent-adult child relationship was marked by estrangement, lack of communication, and bitterness.

D. Despite real-life examples of people from humble origins who climbed far up the social ladder, the widely-held belief of most U.S. residents (including minorities and the working poor) that they have a chance of getting ahead (the Horatio Alger myth) obviously is a statistical impossibility. Functionalists would stress that this belief is functional for society because it encourages people to compete for higher positions, while placing the blame for failure squarely on the individual.

☞ GLOSSARY OF DIFFICULT-TO-UNDERSTAND WORDS

abject poverty: greatest degree of most miserable poverty (172)

albeit: although (181)

assembly-line worker: someone employed in a factory, whose work involves doing the same task over and over again (179)

capital gains: gains from selling an asset held for investment (174)

coalesce: come together (175)

cockeyed: slightly crazy; ridiculous (172)

curtsies: bending the knees and slightly bowing in a gesture of respect (177)

debutante balls: formal dances at which young women from socially prominent families are "presented" to society (176)

disjunction: a separation (172)

estrangement: separation between people who formerly were friendly (192)

fallout: an chance result of product of something else happening (183)

flesh this out: make this discussion more complete (172)

generic sheepskin: degree from a college not having much prestige (178)

gleaned: collected (178)

hefty: very large or heavy (173)

indolence: laziness (191)

juxtaposing: placing things side by side (172)

malnourished: not fed enough food to be healthy (189)

mortgage payments: payments to a back or loan company on a home loan (173)

ne'er-do-wells: people who never do well or right (182)

on-site: activity that take place on the spot (192)

philanthropic: charitable (181)

piqued: to stir up an interest in something (175)

psyche: soul and intellect (193)

pyramid: a solid shape that is broad at the base and narrows to a point at the top (179)

share-cropping: a system of farming in which the farmer is provided with credit for seed, tools, living quarters, and food in exchange for working the land. When the crop is harvested, the farmer receives an agreed upon share of the value for the crop minus the credit charges (181)

sleight-of-hand: deceiving, as with magic tricks (187)

spontaneous: occurring naturally, instead of from ritual (184)

stock options: the opportunity to acquire shares in a company (174)

taint: a mark or influences that is contaminating (181)

vibrant: full of life or activity (175)

vulnerability: capable of being wounded (186)

☞ KEY TERMS TO DEFINE

After studying the chapter, define each of the following terms. Then check your work by referring to the answers beginning at page 133 of this Study Guide.

contradictory class location
culture of poverty
deferred gratification
downward social mobility
exchange mobility
feminization of poverty
Horatio Alger myth
income

intergenerational mobility
poverty line
power
power elite
prestige
property
social class
status

status consistent
status inconsistency
structural mobility
underclass
upward social mobility
wealth

☞ KEY PEOPLE

State the major theoretical contributions or findings of these people.

Edward Banfield
Jonathan Cobb
G. William Domhoff
Dennis Gilbert

Joseph Kahl
Michael Katz
Gerhard Lenski
Elliot Liebow

C. Wright Mills
Patricia Ruggles
W. Richard Sennett
Erik Wright

☞ SELF-TEST

After completing this self-test, check your answers against the Answer Key beginning on page 133 of this Study Guide and against the text on page(s) indicated in parentheses.

MULTIPLE CHOICE QUESTIONS

1.   According to your text, most sociologists agree that social class: (172)
    a.   has a clear-cut, accepted definition in sociology.
    b.   is best defined by the two classes as set out by Marx.
    c.   is best defined by Weber's dimensions of social class.
    d.   has no clear-cut, accepted definition and, thus, is used differently by all sociologists.

2.   It is safe to say that in the United States wealth is: (173)
    a.   fairly evenly distributed among the top one-third of the population.
    b.   concentrated within the largest segment of our population--the middle class.
    c.   somewhat concentrated at the top, with about half held by the top 20 percent of U.S. families.
    d.   highly concentrated, with more than one-quarter held by less than one percent of U.S. families.

3.   According to Paul Samuelson, if an income pyramid were made out of a child's blocks, most
     U.S. residents would be: (174)
     a.   near the top of the pyramid.
     b.   near the middle of the pyramid.
     c.   near the bottom of the pyramid.
     d.   None of the above.

4.   The term "power elite" was coined by: (175)
     a.   C. Wright Mills.
     b.   G. William Domhoff.
     c.   Gary Marx.
     d.   W. Lloyd Warner.

5.   Two of the major "power elite" theorists are: (175-176)
     a.   Mills and Domhoff.
     b.   Gilbert and Kahl.
     c.   Cobb and Sennett.
     d.   Marx and Wright.

6.   All of the following are true regarding jobs that have the most prestige, except: (176)
     a.   they pay more.
     b.   they require more education.
     c.   they require special talent or skills.
     d.   they offer greater autonomy.

7.   Capitalists, petty bourgeoisie, managers, and workers are the four classes in U.S. society,
     according to: (179)
     a.   Erik Wright.
     b.   C. Wright Mills.
     c.   Dennis Gilbert and Joseph Kahl.
     d.   Gary Marx.

8.   Capitalist, upper-middle, lower-middle, working class, working poor, and underclass are the six
     classes in the United States, according to: (179-181)
     a.   Erik Wright.
     b.   C. Wright Mills.
     c.   Dennis Gilbert and Joseph Kahl.
     d.   W. Lloyd Warner.

9.   According to Gilbert and Kahl, people who have made fortunes in entertainment or sports would
     be in the _____ category. (181)
     a.   old money
     b.   new money
     c.   upper-middle
     d.   None of the above.

10. All of the following are characteristics of the working class, <u>except</u>: (181)
   a.   most are employed in relatively unskilled blue-collar and white-collar jobs.
   b.   most have attended college for one or two years.
   c.   most hope to get ahead by achieving seniority on the job.
   d.   about thirty percent of the population belong to this class.

11. According to your text, the typical mechanic in a Ford dealership would be in the: (183)
   a.   upper-middle class.
   b.   lower-middle class.
   c.   working class.
   d.   underclass.

12. One area of life which is <u>not</u> affected by social class is: (184)
   a.   choice of mate.
   b.   politics.
   c.   sickness and health.
   d.   none of the above.

13. People in the _____ classes are more likely to be conservative on economic issues and more liberal on social issues. (184)
   a.   upper
   b.   middle
   c.   lower
   d.   None of the above.

14. Which social class experiences the most stress in daily life? (186)
   a.   upper class
   b.   middle class
   c.   lower class
   d.   All of the above experience about the same amount of stress, although the kind of stress and the source of stress may be different.

15. The official measure of poverty calculated to include those whose incomes equal less than three times a low-cost food budget is the: (186)
   a.   adjusted income level.
   b.   the welfare distribution scale.
   c.   the poverty line.
   d.   the welfare line.

16. According to your text, what is the greatest predictor of whether a U.S. family is poor? (187)
   a.   age
   b.   race
   c.   sex of the head of household
   d.   place of residence, (e.g. urban vs. rural)

17.   In the United States, the poor are most likely to be: (187-190)
        a.   the elderly and women.
        b.   racial minorities, children and women.
        c.   the elderly and children.
        d.   racial minorities and the elderly.

18.   According to U.S. Senator Daniel Moynihan, the increase in the rate of child poverty is due to: (189)
        a.   cutbacks in social welfare money.
        b.   the breakdown of the U.S. family.
        c.   the increase in illegal immigration across our borders.
        d.   a liberalization of the definition of poverty.

19.   According to a study by Patricia Ruggles, about _____ of the poor are considered short-term poor. (190)
        a.   one-quarter
        b.   one-third
        c.   one-half
        d.   two-thirds

20.   The assumption that the values and behaviors of the poor make them fundamentally different from other people and that these factors are largely responsible for their poverty is referred to as: (191)
        a.   deferred gratification.
        b.   immediate gratification.
        c.   feminization of poverty.
        d.   None of the above.

21.   A homeless person whose father was a physician has experienced: (191)
        a.   exchange mobility.
        b.   structural mobility.
        c.   upward mobility.
        d.   downward mobility.

22.   As computers were introduced into the workplace many new white-collar jobs opened up overnight. Taking advantage of these new opportunities, many workers switched from blue-collar to white-collar employment. This is an example of: (191)
        a.   exchange mobility.
        b.   structural mobility.
        c.   upward mobility.
        d.   job mobility.

23.   As compared with their fathers, most U.S. men: (191)
        a.   have a status higher than that of their fathers.
        b.   have the same status their fathers did.
        c.   have a status lower than that of their fathers.
        d.   It is impossible to compare the relative statuses of fathers and sons because of structural mobility.

24. Research by Higginbotham and Weber on women professionals, managers, and administrators from working class backgrounds indicates that: (192)
    a. intergenerational mobility was greater for sons than for daughters.
    b. upwardly mobile women achieved higher class positions despite their parents reservations.
    c. upwardly mobile women achieved higher class positions because of parental encouragement that began when they were just little girls.
    d. any upward mobility was due entirely to structural changes in the economy rather than individual effort or parental influences.

25. The Horatio Alger myth: (192)
    a. is beneficial for society, according to the functionalists.
    b. reduces pressures on the social system.
    c. motivates people to try harder to succeed because anything is possible.
    d. all of the above.

TRUE-FALSE QUESTIONS

T F 1. Most sociologists question Weber's views on social class. (172)
T F 2. Wealth and income are the same thing. (173)
T F 3. Sixty-eight percent of the total net worth of all U.S. families is owned by just ten percent of those families. (173)
T F 4. Apart from the very rich, the most affluent group in U.S. society consists of the chief executive officers of the nation's largest corporations. (174)
T F 5. Occupational prestige rankings vary widely across countries and over time. (176)
T F 6. Most U.S. residents are not very conscious of prestige. (178)
T F 7. College professors typically are an example of status inconsistency. (179)
T F 8. According to Gilbert and Kahl, the capitalist class has the ability to shape the consciousness of the nation. (180)
T F 9. The capitalist class is the one most shaped by education. (181)
T F 10. The underclass is concentrated in the inner city and has little or no connection with the job market. (182)
T F 11. The homeless are the "fallout" of industrialization, especially of post-industrial developments. (183)
T F 12. Social class affects a person's chances of living and dying. (184)
T F 13. People in the higher classes are more likely to be conservative on social issues. (184)
T F 14. In combination, about one-quarter of the U.S. population is part of the working poor or the underclass. (186)
T F 15. The greatest predictor of whether or not a U.S. family is poor is race. (187)
T F 16. The rural poor do not differ significantly from the urban poor. (188)
T F 17. Research has shown that most poverty is intergenerational, with most children of the poor growing up to be poor. (190)
T F 18. Sociological explanations of poverty tend to focus on structural features of society more than life orientations. (190)
T F 19. Structural mobility refers to social and economic changes that affect the status of large numbers of people. (191)
T F 20. Exchange mobility leaves the class system basically untouched. (192)

FILL-IN QUESTIONS

1.   According to Max Weber, the three dimensions of social class are: (1)_____;
        (2)_____; and (3)_____. (172)
2.   _____, which encompasses buildings, land, cars, stocks, and bank accounts, is a form
        of wealth. (172)
4.   Money received as wages, rents, interest, royalties, or proceeds from a business are
        _____. (173)
4.   According to C. Wright Mills, the _____ makes the big decisions in U.S. society.
        (175)
5.   A person is considered to be _____ if he or she ranks high on some dimensions of
        social class and low on others. (178)
6.   A position in the class structure that generates conflicting interests is _____. (179)
7.   According to Gilbert and Kahl, the capitalist class can be divided into two groups: (1)
        _____ and (2) _____. (180-181)
8.   The _____ consists of a small group of people for whom poverty persists year after
        year and across generations. (182)
9.   The official measure of poverty is referred to as _____. (186)
10.   _____ is a trend whereby most poor families in the U.S. are headed by women. (188)
11.   That the poor have values and beliefs that set them apart from the rest of society is the main
        argument of the _____ theory. (190)
12.   Foregoing something in the present in hope of achieving greater gains in the future is
        _____. (190)
13.   _____ is movement up the social class ladder. (191)
14.   Movement up or down the social class ladder that is attributed to changes in the structure of
        society, not to individual efforts, is _____. (191)
15.   The _____ is the belief that anyone can get ahead if only he or she tries hard enough.
        (193)

MATCH THESE SOCIAL SCIENTISTS WITH THEIR CONTRIBUTIONS

___1. Gerhard Lenski   a. *studied short and long term poverty*
___2. C. Wright Mills   b. *hidden injuries of class*
___3. Erik Wright   c. *power elite*
___4. Dennis Gilbert & Joseph Kahl   d. *status inconsistency*
___5. William Domhoff   e. *continued the tradition of C. Wright Mills*
___6. Edward Banfield   f. *updated Marx's model*
___7. Elliot Liebow   g. *street corner men in Washington, D.C.*
___8. W. Richard Sennett & Jonathan Cobb   h. *the immediate gratification of the poor*
___9. Patricia Ruggles   i. *criticized the way in which the poverty line is drawn*
___10. Michael Katz   j. *updated Weber's model*

"DOWN-TO-EARTH SOCIOLOGY"

1. Study Figure 8.3 on page 175. How could you explain the consistency of income distribution across the years to someone who is unfamiliar with U.S. society?
2. What are your occupational goals? Can you find your future occupation listed in Table 8.1 on page 177? If it is ranked high on this table, was prestige a consideration in your decision to work towards this occupation? If it is ranked lower on the scale, are there factors other than prestige that make it appealing to you? What are those factors?
3. After reading on page 182 about how domestic workers respond to the social stigma of doing low-paid, low-status, dead-end jobs, can you image how you would react if placed in similar circumstances? Most domestic workers are women; do you think this fact affects the kinds of strategies they follow in trying to maintain dignity? Would male workers similarly employed in low-paying, low-status, dead-end jobs respond the same way?
4. Do you think it was right to deny Terry Takewell medical treatment because he was too poor to pay his medical bills (p. 185)? Is it right to relegate the poor mentally ill to state hospitals (p. 186)? What do these strategies suggest about our society's values?
5. After reading "Children in Poverty" on page 189, think about the following questions: Is child poverty a concern only for the poor or is it a concern for everyone in society? What steps do you think should be taken to relieve the problem? Where would the money come from to implement your plans?
6. As a result of attending college, will you move into a higher social class than your parents? In terms of your relationship with them, have you experienced any changes similar to the ones described by Sennett and Cobb in the study of upwardly mobile Boston families (p. 192)?

☞ ANSWERS FOR CHAPTER 8

DEFINITIONS OF KEY TERMS

contradictory class location: Erik Wright's term for a position in the class structure that generates contradictory interests

culture of poverty: the values and behaviors of the poor that are assumed to make them fundamentally different from other people; these factors are assumed to be largely responsible for their poverty, and parents are assumed to perpetuate poverty across generations by passing these characteristics on to their children

deferred gratification: forgoing something in the present in the hope of achieving greater gains in the future

downward social mobility: movement down the social class ladder

exchange mobility: about the same numbers of people moving up and down the social class ladder, such that, on balance, the social class system shows little change

feminization of poverty: a trend in U.S. poverty whereby most poor families are headed by women

Horatio Alger myth: belief that anyone can get ahead if only he or she tries hard enough; encourages people to strive to get ahead and deflects blame for failure from society to the individual

income: money received as wages, rents, interest, royalties, or the proceeds from business

intergenerational mobility: the change that family members make in social class from one generation to the next

poverty line: the official measure of poverty; calculated as three times a low-cost food budget

power: the ability to get your way, even over the resistance of others

power elite: C. Wright Mills's term for the top leaders of corporations, military, and politics who make the nation's major decisions

prestige: respect or regard

property: a form of wealth, such as buildings, land, animals, machinery, cars, stocks, bonds, businesses, and band accounts

social class: a large number of people with similar amounts of income and education who work at jobs that are roughly comparable in prestige

status: the position that someone occupies in society or a social group; one's social ranking

status consistent: people who rank high or low on all three dimensions of social class

status inconsistency: a contradiction or mismatch between statuses; a condition in which a person ranks high on some dimensions of social class and low on others

structural mobility: movement up or down the social class ladder that is attributable to changes in the structure of society, not to individual efforts

underclass: a small group of people for whom poverty persists year after year and across generations

upward social mobility: movement up the social class ladder

wealth: property and income

ANSWERS FOR MULTIPLE CHOICE QUESTIONS

1. c   According to your text, most sociologists agree with Max Weber that social class is best defined by employing three dimensions of social class. (172)
2. d   It is safe to say that in the United States wealth is highly concentrated, with more than one-quarter held by less than one percent of U.S. families. (173)
3. c   According to economist Paul Samuelson, if an income pyramid were made out of a child's blocks, most U.S. residents would be near the bottom of the pyramid. (174)
4. a   The term "power elite" was coined by C. Wright Mills. (175)
5. a   Two of the major "power elite" theorists are Mills and Domhoff. (175-176)
6. c   All of the following are true regarding jobs that have the most prestige--they pay more, require more education, and offer greater autonomy. They do not necessarily require special talent or skills. (176)
7. a   Capitalists, petty bourgeoisie, managers, and workers are the four classes in U.S. society, according to Erik Wright. (179)
8. c   Capitalist, upper-middle, lower-middle, working class, working poor, and underclass are the six classes in the United States, according to Dennis Gilbert and Joseph Kahl. (179-181)
9. b   According to Gilbert and Kahl, people who have made fortunes in entertainment or sports would be in the new money category. (181)
10. b   All of the following are characteristics of the working class: most are employed in relatively unskilled blue-collar and white-collar jobs; most hope to get ahead by achieving seniority on the job; and about thirty percent of the population belong to this class. However, most have not attended college for one or two years. (181)

11. c According to your text, the typical mechanic in a Ford dealership would be in the working class. (183)
12. d The correct answer is "d." In most cases, choice of mate, politics, and even sickness and health are affected by one's social class. (184)
13. a People in the upper classes are more likely to be conservative on economic issues and more liberal on social issues. (184)
14. c Members of the lower class experience more stress in daily life than members of either the middle or upper classes. The poor have less job security, lower wages, more unpaid bills, more divorce, more alcoholism, greater vulnerability to crime, more physical illnesses, and are constantly threatened by the possibility of eviction. All of these are likely to increase the amount of stress in one's life. (186)
15. c The official measure of poverty calculated to include those whose incomes equal less than three times a low-cost food budget is the poverty line. (186)
16. c The greatest predictor of whether a U.S. family is poor is the sex of the head of household; most poor families are headed by women. (187)
17. b In the United States, the poor are most likely to be racial minorities, children and women. The elderly are less likely to be poor because of programs such as Social Security and Medicare. (187-190)
18. b According to U.S. Senator Daniel Moynihan, the increase in the rate of child poverty is due to the breakdown of the U.S. family. As the rate of divorce and the rate of childbirth outside of marriage have both increased, the result has been an increase in the number of female-headed households whose children are being raised in poverty. (189)
19. c According to a study by Patricia Ruggles, about one-half of the poor are considered short-term poor, moving out of poverty in less than eight years. (190)
20. d None of the above is correct. The correct answer would be the culture of poverty, a theory that assumes that the values and behaviors of the poor make them fundamentally different from other people and that these factors are largely responsible for their poverty. (191)
21. d A homeless person whose father was a physician has experienced downward mobility. (191)
22. b As computers have been integrated into the workplace, opportunities for white-collar employment have expanded. Many blue-collar workers switched into white-collar jobs as a result. This type of upward mobility is the result of changes in employment opportunities and is referred to as structural mobility. (191)
23. a As compared with their fathers, most U.S. men have a status higher than that of their fathers. (191)
24. c Higginbotham and Weber studied women professionals from working class backgrounds and found parental encouragement for postponing marriage and getting an education. (192)
25. d All of the above is correct. The Horatio Alger myth is beneficial to society, according to the functionalists, because it shifts the blame for failure away from the social system and onto the shoulders of the individual, thereby reducing pressures on the system. It also motivates people to try harder to succeed because "anything is possible." (192)

ANSWERS FOR TRUE-FALSE QUESTIONS

1. *False.* Most sociologists accept Weber's views on social class, using the components of wealth, power and prestige in studying social class. (172)
2. *False.* Wealth and income are not the same; wealth includes both property and income. (173)
3. *True.* (173)

4.   *True.* (174)
5.   *False.* Occupational prestige rankings are remarkably consistent across countries and over time. (176)
6.   *False.* Most U.S. residents are highly conscious of prestige. (178)
7.   *True.* (179)
8.   *True.* (180)
9.   *False.* The upper-middle class, not the capitalist class, is the one most shaped by education. (181)
10.   *True.* (182)
11.   *True.* (183)
12.   *True.* (184)
13.   *False.* People in the higher classes are more likely to be conservative on economic issues and more liberal on social issues. (184)
14.   *True.* (186)
15.   *False.* The greatest predictor of whether a U.S. family is poor is the sex of the person who heads the family. (187)
16.   *False.* The poverty rate among the rural poor is higher than the national average. This group is less likely than the non-rural poor to be on welfare and to live in single-parent households, are more likely than the non-rural poor to have low skills and less education. (188)
17.   *False.* Only about 20 percent of those who are poor as children grow up to be poor. (190)
18.   *True.* (190)
19.   *True.* (191)
20.   *True.* (192)

ANSWERS FOR FILL-IN QUESTIONS

1.   According to Max Weber, the three dimensions of social class are: (1) <u>WEALTH</u>; (2) <u>POWER</u>; and (3) <u>PRESTIGE</u>. (172)
2.   <u>PROPERTY</u>, which encompasses buildings, land, cars, stocks, and bank accounts, is a form of wealth. (172)
3.   Money received as wages, rents, interest, royalties, or proceeds from a business is <u>INCOME</u>. (173)
4.   According to C. Wright Mills, the <u>POWER ELITE</u> makes the big decisions in U.S. society. (175)
5.   A person is considered to be <u>STATUS INCONSISTENT</u> if he or she ranks high on some dimensions of social class and low on others. (178)
6.   A position in the class structure that generates conflicting interests is <u>CONTRADICTORY CLASS LOCATION</u>. (179)
7.   According to Gilbert and Kahl, the capitalist class can be divided into two groups: (1) <u>OLD MONEY</u> and (2) <u>NEW MONEY</u>. (180-181)
8.   The <u>UNDERCLASS</u> consists of a small group of people for whom poverty persists year after year and across generations. (182)
9.   The official measure of poverty is referred to as <u>THE POVERTY LINE</u>. (186)
10.   <u>THE FEMINIZATION OF POVERTY</u> is a trend whereby most poor families in the U.S. are headed by women. (188)
11.   That the poor have values and beliefs that set them apart from the rest of society is the main argument of the <u>CULTURE OF POVERTY</u> theory. (190)

12.   Foregoing something in the present in hope of achieving greater gains in the future is DEFERRED GRATIFICATION. (190)
13.   UPWARD MOBILITY is movement up the social class ladder. (191)
14.   Movement up or down the social class ladder that is attributed to changes in the structure of society, not to individual efforts, is STRUCTURAL MOBILITY. (191)
15.   The HORATIO ALGER MYTH is the belief that anyone can get ahead if only he or she tries hard enough. (193)

ANSWERS TO MATCH THESE SOCIAL SCIENTISTS WITH THEIR CONTRIBUTIONS

1. d   Gerhard Lenski: *status inconsistency*
2. c   C. Wright Mills: *power elite*
3. f   Erik Wright: *updated Marx's model*
4. j   Dennis Gilbert and Joseph Kahl: *updated Weber's model*
5. e   William Domhoff: *continued the tradition of C. Wright Mills*
6. h   Edward Banfield: *immediate gratification of the poor*
7. g   Elliot Liebow: *street corner men in Washington, D.C.*
8. b   W. Richard Sennett & Jonathan Cobb: *hidden injuries of class*
9. a   Patricia Ruggles: *studied short and long term poverty*
10. i   Michael Katz: *criticized the way in which the poverty line is drawn*

CHAPTER 9
INEQUALITIES OF RACE AND ETHNICITY

☞ CHAPTER SUMMARY

- Race is a complex and often misunderstood concept. Race is a reality in the sense that inherited physical characteristics distinguish one group from another. However, race is a myth in the sense of one race being superior to another and of there being pure races. The *idea* of race is powerful, shaping basic relationships between people. An ethnic group is a group of people who identify with one another on the basis of common ancestry and cultural heritage. A minority group is defined as one singled out for unequal treatment by members of the dominant group and that regards itself as the object of collective discrimination. Both race and ethnicity can be a basis for unequal treatment.
- Prejudice is an attitude and discrimination is unfair treatment.
- Psychological theories explain the origin of prejudice in terms of stress frustration that gets directed towards scapegoats and in terms of the development of authoritarian personalities. Sociologists emphasize how different social environments affect levels of prejudice. They look at the benefits and costs of discrimination, the exploitation of racial-ethnic divisions by those in power, and the self-fulfilling prophecies that are the outcome of labeling.
- Individual discrimination is the negative treatment of one person by another, while institutional discrimination is discrimination built into society's social institutions.
- Dominant groups typically practice one of five policies toward minority groups: genocide, population transfer, internal colonialism, segregation, assimilation, or pluralism.
- White Anglo-Saxon Protestants have dominated American society since colonial times. Among minority groups in the United States, African Americans are the largest group, Latino Americans are the second largest, Asian Americans are the fastest growing group, and Native Americans are the worst off.
- The issues of multiculturalism in the United States today pertain to maintaining separate racial and ethnic identities and to tolerating this differences.
- The extent of ethnic identification depends upon the relative size of the group, its power, broad physical characteristics, and the amount of discrimination.
- Four principles for improving ethnic relations are equal status, common goals, solidarity, and institutional support.

☞ LEARNING OBJECTIVES

As you read Chapter 9, use these learning objectives to organize your notes. After completing your reading, briefly state an answer to each of the objectives, and review the text pages in parentheses.

1. Explain how race is defined and how it can be both a reality and a myth. (198-199)
2. Define ethnicity and explain what an ethnic group is. (199)
3. Define the terms "minority group" and "dominant group." (200)
4. Identify the characteristics shared by minority groups worldwide and explain the factors that affect their emergence within a society. (200-201)
5. Differentiate between prejudice and discrimination and explain the extent of prejudice among racial and ethnic groups. (201-202)

6.   Discuss the rise of racism on college campuses. (202-203)
7.   Compare and contrast individual and institutional discrimination and give examples of each type of discrimination. (203-204)
8.   Compare psychological and sociological perspectives on prejudice. Indicate why sociologists believe psychological explanations are inadequate. (205-207)
9.   List and describe the six patterns of intergroup relations. (207-210)
10.   Discuss the status of White Anglo-Saxon Protestants (WASPs) as a dominant group and, given this, relate the assimilation experiences of white ethnics in the United States. (210-212)
11.   Outline the history of the African American experience in the United States, discussing both the gains and setbacks African Americans have made since the Civil Rights Movement. (212-214)
12.   Summarize the current debate over the importance of race and social class. (214-217)
13.   Compare and contrast the experiences of different segments of the Latino and Asian American communities, including divisions within each of these broad ethnic groups. (217-220)
14.   Describe the treatment of Native Americans and explain why they can be considered an invisible minority. (221-222)
15.   Identify some of the signs that U.S. society is becoming truly multicultural. (222-223)
16.   List some of the problems created by encouraging multiculturalism. (223-225)
17.   Identify the factors that are related to the development of a sense of ethnic identity. (225-226)
18.   State the major principles for improving racial/ethnic relations. (226-227)

☞ CHAPTER OUTLINE

I.   **Laying the Sociological Foundation**
       A.   Race is a reality in the sense that humans come in different colors and shapes; however, two myths regarding race are that one race is superior to another, and that a pure race exists. These myths make a difference for social life because people believe they are real.
       B.   Race and ethnicity are often confused due to the cultural differences people see and the way they define race. Ethnicity refers to cultural characteristics that distinguish a people.
       C.   Minority groups are people singled out for unequal treatment and who regard themselves as objects of collective discrimination.
              1.   Shared characteristics of minorities worldwide: the physical or cultural traits that distinguish them are held in low esteem by the dominant group; they are unequally treated by the dominant group; they tend to marry within their own group; and they tend to feel strong group solidarity.
              2.   They are not necessarily in the numerical minority. Sociologists refer to those who do the discriminating as the dominant group--they have greater power, more privileges, and higher social status. The dominant group attributes its privileged position to its superiority, not to discrimination.
              3.   A group becomes a minority through expansion of political boundaries by another group. Another way for group to become a minority is by migration into a territory, either voluntarily or involuntarily.
       D.   Examples of prejudice and discrimination exist throughout the world, in, for example, Northern Ireland, Israel, and Japan.
              1.   Discrimination is unfair treatment directed toward someone. When based on race, it is known as racism. It also can be based on features such as age, sex, sexual preference, religion, or politics.

2. Prejudice is prejudging of some sort, usually in a negative way.
3. Ethnocentrism is so common that each racial/ethnic group views other groups as inferior in at least some way. Studies confirm that there is less prejudice among the more educated and among younger people. People who are prejudiced against one group are likely to be prejudiced against others.

E. Sociologists distinguish between individual and institutional discrimination.
   1. Individual discrimination (negative treatment of one person by another) is too limited a perspective because it focuses only on one individual treating another badly.
   2. Institutional discrimination (negative treatment of a minority group that is built into a society's institutions) focuses on human behavior at the group level. Examples include certain medical procedures, mortgage lending, and overall life chances.

II. **Theories of Prejudice**
   A. Psychological Perspectives
      1. According to John Dollard, prejudice results from frustration: people unable to strike out at the real source of their frustration find scapegoats to unfairly blame.
      2. According to Theodor Adorno, highly prejudiced people are characterized by excess conformity, intolerance, insecurity, respect for authority, and submission to superiors; he called this complex of personality traits the authoritarian personality.
      3. Subsequent studies have generally concluded that people who are older, less educated, less intelligent and from a lower social class are more likely to be authoritarian.
   B. Sociological Perspectives
      1. To functionalists, the social environment can be deliberately arranged to generate either positive or negative feelings about people. Prejudice is functional in that it creates in-group solidarity and out-group antagonism. It is dysfunctional in that it destroys social relationships and intensifies conflict.
      2. To conflict theorists, the ruling class benefits because it systematically pits group against group by: (1) creating a split labor market, dividing workers along racial ethnic lines and weakening solidarity among the workers; and (2) maintaining higher unemployment rates for minorities, creating a reserve labor force from which owners can draw when they need to expand production temporarily. The reserve labor force is a constant threat to white workers, who modify their demands rather than lose their jobs to unemployment.
      3. To symbolic interactionists, the labels people learn color their perception, leading people to see certain things and be blind to others. Racial and ethnic labels are especially powerful because they are shorthand for emotionally laden stereotypes. These stereotypes that we learn not only justify prejudice and discrimination, but they also lead to a self-fulfilling prophecy, stereotypical behavior in those who are stereotyped.

III. **Patterns of Intergroup Relations**
   A. Genocide in the actual or attempted systematic annihilation of a race or ethnic group who has been labeled as less than fully human by the dominant group. The Holocaust and the U.S. government's treatment of Native Americans are examples.

B.   Population transfer is involuntary movement of a minority group. Indirect transfer involves making life so unbearable that members of a minority then leave; direct transfer involves forced expulsion. A combination of genocide and population transfer occurred in Bosnia, part of the former Yugoslavia, as Serbs engaged in ethnic cleansing, the wholesale slaughter of Muslims and Croats, with survivors forced to flee the area.

C.   Internal colonialism is a society's policy of exploiting a minority by using social institutions to deny it access to full benefits. Slavery is an extreme example.

D.   Segregation, the formal separation of groups, often accompanies internal colonialism.

E.   Assimilation is the process by which a minority is absorbed into the mainstream. Forced assimilation occurs when the dominant group prohibits the minority from using its own religion, language, customs. Permissive assimilation is when the minority adopts the dominant group's patterns in its own way/at its own speed.

F.   Multiculturalism (pluralism) permits or encourages ethnic variation. Switzerland provides an outstanding example of this.

IV.   **Race and Ethnic Relations in the United States**

A.   In the United States, the dominant group is made up of whites whose ancestors immigrated here from European countries.

     1.   White Anglo-Saxon Protestants (WASPs) established the basic social institutions in the U. S. when they settled the original colonies.

     2.   White ethnics are white immigrants to the United States whose culture differs from that of WASPs. They include the Irish, Germans, Poles, Jews, and Italians. They were initially discriminated against by WASPs who felt that something was wrong with people whose customs were different.

     3.   Subsequent immigrants were expected to speak English and adopt the Anglo-Saxon way of life.

     4.   With the larger number of immigrants from western Europe, the meaning of WASP expanded to include people of this descent. The institutional and cultural dominance of Western Europeans set the stage for current ethnic relations.

B.   African Americans face a legacy of racism.

     1.   In 1955, African Americans in Montgomery, Alabama, using nonviolent tactics advocated by Martin Luther King, Jr., protested laws believed to be unjust. This led to the civil rights movement that challenged existing patterns of racial segregation throughout the south.

     2.   The 1964 Civil Rights Act (banning discrimination in public facilities) and 1965 Voting Rights Act (banning literacy tests) heightened expectations. Frustration over the pace of change led to urban riots and passage of the 1968 Civil Rights Act.

     3.   Since then, African Americans have made political and economic progress. For example, African Americans have quadrupled their membership in the U.S. House of Representatives in just 15 years, and enrollment in colleges and graduate schools continues to increase. African Americans such as Jesse Jackson, Douglas Wilder, and Clarence Thomas have gained political prominence.

     4.   Despite these gains, however, African Americans continue to lag behind in politics, economics, and education. Only one U.S. senator is African American; African Americans average 57 percent of whites' incomes; only 12 percent of African Americans graduate from college.

5. According to William Wilson social class (not race) is the major determinant of quality of life. The African American community today is divided into two groups, the outcome of civil rights legislation that opened new opportunities. Middle-class African Americans seized them and advanced economically, moving out of the inner city; they have moved up the class ladder, live in good housing, have well-paid jobs, and send their children to good schools. However, as opportunities for unskilled labor declined, a large group of poorly educated and unskilled African Americans were left behind; they still live in poverty, face violent crime and dead-end jobs, attend terrible schools, and live in hopelessness and despair.

6. Charles Willie challenges this, arguing that discrimination on the basis of race persists, despite gains made by some African Americans.

7. It is likely that both discrimination and social class contribute to the African American experience.

C. Latino Americans are the second largest ethnic group in the United States, and include Chicanos, Puerto Ricans, Cuban Americans, and people from Central or South America. While most are legal residents, large numbers have entered the United States illegally and avoid contact with public officials. Concentrated in four states (California, Texas, New York, and Florida), they are causing major demographic shifts.

1. The Spanish language distinguishes them from other minorities: perhaps half are unable to speak English without difficulty. This is a major obstacle to getting well-paid jobs.

2. Divisions based on social class and country of national origin prevent political unity.

3. Compared with non-Hispanic whites and Asian Americans, Latinos are worse off on all indicators of well-being. The country of origin is significant, with Cuban Americans scoring much higher on indicators of well being and Puerto-Rican Americans scoring the lowest.

4. The large number of illegal immigrants has led to a growing resentment. Immigrants are perceived as taking away jobs from citizens and as an economic drag on taxpayers. Whether illegal immigrants pay more in taxes than they cost in benefits, or the other way around, has become a heated debate.

D. Asian Americans have long faced discrimination in the United States.

1. The history of Asian Americans is one of discrimination and prejudice. Chinese Americans frequently were victims of vigilante groups and anti-Chinese legislation. After the attack on Pearl Harbor in World War II, hostilities towards Japanese Americans increased, with many being imprisoned in "relocation camps."

2. Today Asian Americans are the fastest growing minority in the U.S. They are a diverse group divided by separate cultures. Although there are variations in income among Asian American groups, on the average Asian Americans have been extremely successful. This success can be traced to four factors: (1) a close family life; (2) a supportive community; (3) educational achievement; and (4) assimilation into the mainstream.

3. Recent immigration has been mainly from Vietnam. Despite initial problems of settlement, these immigrants have adjusted well.

E.   Due to the influence of old movie westerns, many Americans tend to hold stereotypes of Native Americans as uncivilized savages, as a single group of people subdivided into separate bands.

    1.   In reality, however, Native Americans represent a diverse group of people with a variety of cultures and languages. Although originally numbering 5 million, their numbers were reduced to a low of 500,000 at the beginning of the 20th Century, due to a lack of immunity to European diseases and warfare. Today there are about 2 million Native Americans.

    2.   At first, relations between European settlers and the Native Americans were peaceful. However, as the number of settlers increased, tension increased. Because they stood in the way of expansion, many were slaughtered. Government policy shifted to population transfer, with Native Americans confined to reservations.

    3.   Today, they are an invisible minority. Almost half live in rural areas, with one-third concentrated in Oklahoma, California, and Arizona; most other Americans are hardly aware of them. They have the highest rates of poverty, unemployment, suicide, and alcoholism of any U. S. minority . These negative conditions are the result of Anglo domination.

    4.   In the 1960's Native Americans won a series of legal victories that restored their control over the land and their right to determine economic policy. Many Native Americans have opened businesses on their land, ranging from industrial parks to casinos.

    5.   Today many Native Americans are interested in recovering and honoring their own traditions. Pan-Indianism is an emphasis on common elements that run through Native American cultures in an attempt to develop self-identification that goes beyond any particular tribe.

V.   Multiculturalism in the United States

A.   There are signs that the United States is becoming a multicultural society.

    1.   Ethnic restaurants and neighborhoods flourish; different religions co-exist.

    2.   Studies of population trends indicate significant changes in the U.S. racial/ethnic mix; by the middle of the 21st century, the "average" American will trace ancestry to almost any part of the world but Europe.

    3.   As U.S. society becomes more diverse, those who have enjoyed a privileged status (White Americans), are unlikely to welcome these changes. Some Anglos, called nativists, perceive the growing use of Spanish as a threat and have initiated an "English only" movement and have succeeded in getting states to consider making English their official language.

    4.   The proper role of affirmative action in a multicultural society is likely to remain an issue into the future.

    5.   Changing racial balances call for a rethinking of U.S. history and the motives and treatment of different ethnic/racial groups.

B.   Some people feel an intense sense of ethnic identity while others feel very little.

    1.   An individual's sense of ethnic identity is influenced by the relative size and power of the ethnic group, its appearance, and the level of discrimination aimed at the group. If a group is relatively small, has little power, has a distinctive appearance, and is an object of discrimination, its members will have a heightened sense of ethnic identity.

2.   Ethnic work refers to how ethnicity is constructed and includes enhancing and maintaining a group's distinctiveness or attempting to recover ethnic heritage.

VI.   **Principles for Improving Racial and Ethnic Relations**

A.   Since it is impossible to pass laws against prejudice, it is necessary to outlaw discrimination.

B.   Gordon Allport propose four guidelines to decrease prejudice: (1) groups should possess equal status; (2) groups should seek common goals; (3) groups should feel the need to pull together; and (4) authority, law and custom should support interaction between groups.

☞ GLOSSARY OF DIFFICULT-TO-UNDERSTAND WORDS

aloof: reserved or indifferent (203)

backlash: a strong negative reaction to a recent political or social development (219)

blackface skits: theatrical performance in which whites blacken their skin and mimic the actions and behavior of African Americans (203)

boycott: an organized decision not to dealings with someone, usually in order to express disapproval and to force acceptance of certain conditions (213)

car pools: an arrangement in which different drivers take turns driving (213)

cohesiveness: the quality of sticking together (220)

credit histories: a written record of an individual's loans from banks and credit companies (203)

czarist Russia: Russia during the time it was ruled by czars (monarchs) (208)

deflected: to turn aside or to turn off course (207)

deleterious: harmful (222)

discrepancy: a disagreement or difference (208)

disheveled: unkempt; to be in disarray (198)

endemic: native to a particular people or country (212)

flunkies: servants who obediently obey their superiors (206)

genetic mutations: changes in genes over time (198)

innate: existing from birth (200)

iron-fisted: acting in both a harsh and ruthless manner (208)

plummeting: rapidly falling (201)

rampant: spreading rapidly (201)

relentless: stubborn, persistent (221)

ruthlessly: to show no mercy (208)

sabotage: deliberately damage (219)

scowled: facial expression showing contempt or disgust (198)

swastikas: a symbol used by the Nazis (201)

tallied: counted (217)

unkempt: tangled, not combed (198)

utterances: statements (205)

vaudeville skit: short stage show intended to be funny (203)

☞ KEY TERMS TO DEFINE

After studying the chapter, define each of the following terms. Then check your work by referring to the answers beginning at page 152 of this Study Guide.

assimilation	individual discrimination	race
authoritarian personality	institutional discrimination	racism
Chicanos	internal colonialism	reserve labor force
compartmentalize	melting pot	rising expectations
discrimination	minority group	scapegoat
dominant group	multiculturalism	segregation
ethnic cleansing	Pan-Indianism	selective perception
ethnic work	pluralism	split labor market
ethnicity and ethnic	population transfer	WASP
genocide	prejudice	white ethnics

☞ KEY PEOPLE

State the major theoretical contributions or findings of these people.

Theodor Adorno	John Dollard	William Wilson
Gordon Allport	Muzafer & Carolyn Sherif	Louis Wirth
Ashley Doane	Charles Willie	

☞ SELF-TEST

After completing this self-test, check your answers against the Answer Key beginning on page 152 of this Study Guide and against the text on page(s) indicated in parentheses.

MULTIPLE CHOICE QUESTIONS

1. Race: (198)
    a. means having distinctive cultural characteristics.
    b. means having inherited physical characteristics that distinguish one group from another.
    c. means people who are singled out for unequal treatment.
    d. is relatively easy to determine.

2. People often confuse race and ethnicity because: (200)
    a. they dislike people who are different from themselves.
    b. of the cultural differences people see and the way they define race.
    c. they are unaware of the fact that race is cultural and ethnicity is biological.
    d. All of the above.

3. A minority group: (200)
    a. is discriminated against because of physical or cultural differences.
    b. is discriminated against because of personality factors.
    c. does not always experience discrimination.
    d. All of the above.

4. The dominant group in a society almost always considers its position to be due to: (200)
    a. its own innate superiority.
    b. its ability to oppress minority group members.
    c. its ability to control political power.
    d. All of the above.

5. Prejudice and discrimination: (202)
    a. are less prevalent in the United States than in other societies.
    b. are more prevalent in the United States than in other societies.
    c. appear to characterize every society.
    d. appear to characterize only large societies.

6. Prejudice: (202)
    a. is an attitude.
    b. may be positive or negative.
    c. often is the basis for discrimination.
    d. All of the above.

7. Racism on college campuses: (202)
    a. is limited to members of fraternities and sororities.
    b. is directed only against African Americans.
    c. has become a major social issue.
    d. all of the above.

8. The negative treatment of one person by another on the basis of personal characteristics is: (203)
    a. individual discrimination.
    b. individual prejudice.
    c. institutional discrimination.
    d. institutional prejudice.

9. As compared with a white baby, an African American baby: (204)
    a. has a better chance of surviving infancy.
    b. has the same chance of surviving infancy.
    c. has a slightly higher chance of dying in infancy.
    d. has twice the chance of dying in infancy.

10. The idea that prejudice is the result of frustration was suggested by: (205)
    a. John Dollard.
    b. Theodor Adorno.
    c. Muzafer and Carolyn Sherif.
    d. George Simpson and Milton Yinger.

11. According to conflict theorists, prejudice: (206-207)
    a. benefits capitalists by splitting workers along racial or ethnic lines.
    b. contributes to the exploitation of workers by producing a split-labor market.
    c. keeps workers from demanding higher wages and better working conditions.
    d. All of the above.

12.   _____ refers to the unemployed whose employment depends upon market forces. (207)
    a.   reserve labor force.
    b.   secondary labor force.
    c.   split-labor market.
    d.   the underclass.

13.   Symbolic interactionists stress that prejudiced people: (207)
    a.   are born that way.
    b.   have certain types of personalities.
    c.   learn their prejudices in interaction with others.
    d.   None of the above.

14.   Genocide: (207-208)
    a.   occurred when Hitler attempted to destroy all Jews.
    b.   is the systematic annihilation of a race or ethnic group.
    c.   often requires the cooperation of ordinary citizens.
    d.   All of the above.

15.   When a minority is expelled from a country or from a particular area of a country, the process is called: (208)
    a.   population redistribution.
    b.   direct population transfer.
    c.   indirect population transfer.
    d.   expelled population transfer.

16.   A society's policy of exploiting a minority group, using social institutions to deny the minority access to the society's full benefits is referred to as: (209)
    a.   segregation.
    b.   pluralism.
    c.   internal colonialism.
    d.   genocide.

17.   The process of being absorbed into the mainstream culture is: (209)
    a.   pluralism.
    b.   assimilation.
    c.   cultural submersion.
    d.   internal colonialism.

18.   The U.S. Congress passed the Voting Rights Act in: (213)
    a.   1945.
    b.   1955.
    c.   1965.
    d.   1975.

19. According to _____, social class--not race--is the major determinant of the quality of life for African Americans in the United States today. (214)
    a. Gordon Allport
    b. William Wilson
    c. John Dollard
    d. Robert Merton

20. According to your text, Latinos are distinguished from other ethnic minorities in the United States by: (217)
    a. the Spanish language.
    b. the fact that virtually all Latinos entered the United States illegally.
    c. the length of time Latinos have been in the United States.
    d. All of the above.

21. Today, the fastest-growing minority in the U.S. is: (219)
    a. African Americans.
    b. Asian Americans.
    c. Latinos.
    d. Native Americans.

22. Of all American minorities, the worst off are: (222)
    a. African Americans.
    b. Asian Americans.
    c. Latinos.
    d. Native Americans.

23. Which of the following is <u>not</u> only of the factors that influences the sense of ethnic identity? (225-226)
    a. size of the ethnic group
    b. power of the ethnic group
    c. experiences with discrimination
    d. education

24. Activities that range from trying to trace one's family line to preserving the food, language and holidays are considered: (226)
    a. the melting pot.
    b. ethnic work.
    c. forced assimilation.
    d. one's heritage.

25. According to Gordon Allport, the key to decreasing prejudice is: (227)
    a. support by dominant groups.
    b. having groups seek common goals.
    c. customs that encourage diversity.
    d. all of the above.

TRUE-FALSE QUESTIONS

T F   1.   In some societies a "pure" race exists. (199)

T F   2.   Sociologists often use the terms race and ethnicity interchangeably. (199)

T F   3.   Physical or cultural differences can be a basis of unequal treatment in societies. (200)

T F   4.   A group must represent a numerical minority to be considered a minority group. (200)

T F   5.   Certain characteristics are shared by minorities worldwide. (200)

T F   6.   Minorities often have a shared sense of identity and of common destiny. (200)

T F   7.   After the United States defeated Mexico in war and annexed the Southwest, the Mexicans living there were transformed into the dominant group, because they were the majority ethnic group. (201)

T F   8.   Sociologists believe that individual discrimination is an adequate explanation for discrimination in the U.S. (203)

T F   9.   Research shows that African Americans and Latinos are 60 percent more likely than whites to be rejected for mortgages, all other factors being similar. (203)

T F   10.   People with prejudice against one racial or ethnic group are likely to be prejudiced against other groups. (205)

T F   11.   Persons with an authoritarian personality are characterized by prejudice and high rankings on scales of conformity, intolerance, insecurity, and excessive respect for authority. (205-206)

T F   12.   The Sherif study demonstrates that the social environment can be deliberately arranged to generate either positive or negative feelings about people. (206)

T F   13.   Functionalists focus on the role of the capitalist class in exploiting racism and ethnic inequalities. (206-207)

T F   14.   Symbolic interactionists stress that prejudiced people learn their prejudices in interaction with others. (207)

T F   15.   Genocide often relies on labeling and compartmentalization. (208)

T F   16.   Segregation allows the dominant group to exploit the labor of the minority while maintaining social distance. (209)

T F   17.   Most white ethnics are not assimilated into the mainstream American culture. (210)

T F   18.   Social class and national origin are major obstacles to Latino political unity. (217-218)

T F   19.   Most Native Americans were not granted United States citizenship until 1924. (219)

T F   20.   It is accurate to describe the experiences of Native Americans as ranging from genocide to containment. (221)

FILL-IN QUESTIONS

1.   _____ is inherited physical characteristics that distinguish one group from another. (198)

2.   The term minority group was defined by sociologist _____. (200)

3.   _____ is discrimination on the basis of race. (202)

4.   _____ discrimination is the negative treatment of a minority group that is built into a society's institutions. (203)

5.   Theodor Adorno's term for people who are prejudiced and rank high on scales of conformity, intolerance, insecurity, respect for authority, and submissiveness to superiors is _____. (205)

6.   _____ theorists believe that prejudice can be both functional and dysfunctional. (206)

7. Split-labor market is used by _____ theorists to explain how the racial and ethnic strife can be used to pit workers against one another. (206)
8. The term used to describe the unemployed who can be put to work during times of high production and then discarded when no longer needed is _____. (207)
9. _____ is the ability to see certain points but remain blind to others. (207)
10. The systematic annihilation or attempted annihilation of a race or ethnic group is _____. (208)
11. The types of population transfer are: (1) _____ and (2) _____. (208)
12. The policy of forced expulsion and genocide is referred to as _____. (209)
13. _____ is the process of being absorbed into the mainstream culture. (209)
14. In the period immediately following passage of the Civil Rights Act, many African Americans experienced _____, a belief that better conditions were in sight. (213)
15. Activities designed to discover, enhance, or maintain ethnic and racial identity are called _____. (225)

MATCH THESE CONCEPTS WITH THEIR DEFINITIONS

___1. race
___2. assimilation
___3. scapegoat
___4. prejudice
___5. population transfer
___6. genocide
___7. ethnicity
___8. dominant group
___9. discrimination
___10. ethnic cleansing

a. *having distinctive cultural characteristics*
b. *the group with the most power, privileges, and social status*
c. *a political policy that includes expulsion and genocide*
d. *inherited physical characteristics that distinguish one group from another*
e. *an act of unfair treatment directed against an individual or group*
f. *the process of being absorbed into the mainstream culture*
g. *an individual or group unfairly blamed for someone else's troubles*
h. *systematic annihilation or attempted annihilation of a race or ethnic group*
i. *involuntary movement of a minority group*
j. *prejudging, usually in a negative way*

"DOWN-TO-EARTH SOCIOLOGY"

1. According to "Clashing Cultures" (p. 201) what produces backlash against immigrants with a country? What could be done to improve intergroup relations among people?
2. Read "Racism on College Campuses" (p. 203). Have there been similar incidents on your own campus? Are the situations described in your text racist? Why or why not? Why do some consider an act racist, while others would not? Is there a difference when racism is expressed by a minority rather than a dominant group? Do college and university administrators have a responsibility to deal with racism on campus?
3. After reading about the Haitian experience with assimilation (p.212), why do you think the immigrant experience is more difficult for black immigrants than non-black immigrants? Do you think blacks coming from African nations have the same problems as Haitians? Why or why not? Would the social class background of the immigrant make a difference?
4. Think back over history textbooks you read in school. Were balanced in presenting the accomplishments of the many racial/ethnic groups and both genders? Why or why not? How was the history of U.S. race/ethnic relations presented in this chapter new to you?

☞ ANSWERS FOR CHAPTER 9

DEFINITIONS OF KEY TERMS

assimilation: the process of being absorbed into the mainstream culture

authoritarian personality: Theodor Adorno's term for people who are prejudiced and rank high on scales of conformity, intolerance, insecurity, respect for authority, and submissiveness to superiors

Chicanos: Latinos whose country of origin is Mexico

compartmentalize: to separate acts from feelings or attitudes

discrimination: an act of unfair treatment directed against an individual or a group

dominant group: the group with the most power, greatest privileges, and highest social status

ethnic cleansing: a policy of population elimination, including forcible expulsion and genocide

ethnic work: activities designed to discover, enhance, or maintain ethnic/racial identification.

ethnicity (and ethnic): having distinctive cultural characteristics

genocide: the systematic annihilation or attempted annihilation of a race or ethnic group

individual discrimination: the negative treatment of one person by another on the basis of that person's perceived characteristics

institutional discrimination: negative treatment of a minority group that is built into a society's institutions

internal colonialism: the systematic economic exploitation of a minority group

melting pot: the idea that Americans of various backgrounds would melt into a sort of ethnic stew

minority group: people who are singled out for unequal treatment on the basis of their physical and cultural characteristics, and who regard themselves as objects of collective discrimination

multiculturalism (also called pluralism): a policy that permits or encourages groups to express their individual, unique racial and ethnic identities

pan-Indianism: the emphasis on the common elements in Native American culture in order to develop a mutual self-identity and to work toward the welfare of all Native Americans

pluralism: see *multiculturalism*

population transfer: involuntary movement of a minority group

prejudice: an attitude or prejudging, usually in a negative way

race: inherited physical characteristics that distinguish one group from another

racism: prejudice and discrimination on the basis of race

reserve labor force: the term used by conflict theorists for the unemployed, who can be put to work during times of high production and then discarded when no longer needed

rising expectations: the sense that better conditions are soon to follow, which, if unfulfilled, creates mounting frustration

scapegoat: an individual or group unfairly blamed for someone else's troubles

segregation: the policy of keeping racial or ethnic groups apart

selective perception: seeing certain features of an object or situation but remaining blind to others

split-labor market: a term used by conflict theorists for the practice of weakening the bargaining power of workers by splitting them along racial, ethnic, sex, age, or any other lines

WASP: a white Anglo-Saxon Protestant; narrowly, an American of English descent; broadly, an American of western European ancestry

white ethnics: white immigrants to the United States whose culture differs from that of WASPs.

ANSWERS FOR MULTIPLE CHOICE QUESTIONS

1. b   Race is inherited physical characteristics that distinguish one group from another. (198)
2. b   People often confuse race and ethnicity because of the cultural differences people see and the way they define race. (200)
3. a   A minority group is discriminated against because of physical or cultural differences. (200)
4. a   The dominant group in a society almost always considers its position to be due to its own innate superiority. (200)
5. c   Prejudice and discrimination appear to characterize every society. (202)
6. d   All of the above is correct. Prejudice is an attitude, it may be positive or negative, and it often is the basis for discrimination. (202)
7. c   Racism on college campuses is not only limited to members of fraternities and sororities, nor is it directed only against African Americans. Many feel that it has become a major social issue. (202)
8. a   The negative treatment of one person by another on the basis of that person's characteristics is referred to as individual discrimination. (203)
9. d   As compared with a white baby, an African American baby has twice the chance of dying in infancy. (204)
10. a   The idea that prejudice is the result of frustration was suggested by John Dollard. (205)
11. d   All of the above is correct. According to conflict theorists, prejudice benefits capitalists by splitting workers along racial or ethnic lines; contributes to the exploitation of workers by producing a split-labor market; and is a factor in keeping workers from demanding higher wages and better working conditions. (206-207)
12. a   The term used by conflict theorists for the unemployed who can be put to work during times of high production and then discarded when no longer needed is reserve labor force. (207)
13. c   Symbolic interactionists stress that prejudiced people learn their prejudices in interaction with others. (207)
14. d   All of the above is correct. Genocide occurred when Hitler attempted to destroy all Jews. Genocide is the systematic annihilation of a race or ethnic group, and it often requires the cooperation of ordinary citizens. (207-208)
15. b   When a minority is expelled from a country or from a particular area of a country, the process is called direct population transfer. (208)
16. c   A society's policy of exploiting a minority group, using social institutions to deny the minority access to the society's full benefits, is referred to as internal colonialism. (209)
17. b   The process of being absorbed into the mainstream culture is assimilation. (209)
18. c   The U.S. Congress passed the Voting Rights Act in 1965. (213)
19. b   According to William Wilson, social class--not race--is the major determinant of the quality of life for African Americans in the United States today. (214)
20. a   According to your text, Latinos are distinguished from other ethnic minorities in the United States by the Spanish language. (217)
21. b   Today, the fastest-growing minority in the U.S. is Asian Americans, whose numbers have doubled in just the past ten years. (219)
22. d   Of all American minorities, the worst off are Native Americans. (222)
23. d   Size of the ethnic group, power of the ethnic group, experiences with discrimination, as well as appearance are all factors that influences the sense of ethnic identity. The factor that is not related to the sense of ethnic identity is education. (225-226)

24. b   Activities that range from trying to trace one's family line to preserving the food, language and holidays are considered ethnic work. (226)
25. b   Gordon Allport suggested that prejudice could be decreased under social conditions in which all groups sought common goals, where all groups had equal status, where they felt the need to work together to achieve those goals, and where authority, laws and customs supported interaction between groups. (227)

ANSWERS FOR TRUE-FALSE QUESTIONS

1.   *False.* The notion of a "pure" race exists is a myth. Thus, no societies have a "pure race." (199)
2.   *False.* Race is physical characteristics; ethnicity is cultural. (199)
3.   *True.* (200)
4.   *False.* Sociologically speaking, size is not an important defining characteristics of minority group status. Being singled out for unequal treatment and objects of collective discrimination are. (200)
5.   *True.* (200)
6.   *True.* (200)
7.   *False.* After the United States defeated Mexico in war and annexed the Southwest, the Mexicans living there were transformed from the dominant group into a minority group. (201)
8.   *False.* In order to understand discrimination in the United States it is necessary to explain the patterns of institutional discrimination. (203)
9.   *True.* (203)
10.   *True.* (205)
11.   *True.* (205-206)
12.   *True.* (206)
13.   *False.* Conflict theorists, not functionalists, focus on the role of the capitalist class in exploiting racism and ethnic inequalities. (206-207)
14.   *True.* (207)
15.   *True.* (208)
16.   *True.* (209)
17.   *False.* Most white ethnics are assimilated into the mainstream U.S. culture. Some assimilated so successfully that many of their descendants are today only vaguely aware of their ethnic origins. However, in recent decades, many of the white ethnics have rediscovered their roots. (210)
18.   *True.* (217-218)
19.   *True.* (219)
20.   *True.* (221)

ANSWERS FOR FILL-IN QUESTIONS

1.   RACE is inherited physical characteristics that distinguish one group from another. (198)
2.   The term minority group was defined by sociologist LOUIS WIRTH. (200)
3.   RACISM is discrimination on the basis of race. (202)
4.   INSTITUTIONAL discrimination is the negative treatment of a minority group that is built into a society's institutions. (203)
5.   Theodor Adorno's term for people who are prejudiced and rank high on scales of conformity, intolerance, insecurity, respect for authority, and submissiveness to superiors is THE AUTHORITARIAN PERSONALITY. (205)
6.   FUNCTIONAL theorists believe that prejudice can be both functional and dysfunctional. (206)

7. Split-labor market is used by <u>CONFLICT</u> theorists to explain how the racial and ethnic strife can be used to pit workers against one another. (206)
8. The term used to describe the unemployed who can be put to work during times of high production and then discarded when no longer needed is <u>THE RESERVE LABOR FORCE</u>. (207)
9. <u>SELECTIVE PERCEPTION</u> is the ability to see certain points but remain blind to others. (207)
10. The systematic annihilation or attempted annihilation of a race or ethnic group is <u>GENOCIDE</u>. (208)
11. The types of population transfer are: (1) <u>DIRECT</u> and (2) <u>INDIRECT</u>. (208)
12. The policy of forced expulsion and genocide is referred to as <u>ETHNIC CLEANSING</u>. (209)
13. <u>ASSIMILATION</u> is the process of being absorbed into the mainstream culture. (209)
14. In the period immediately following passage of the Civil Rights Act, many African Americans experienced <u>RISING EXPECTATIONS</u>, a belief that better conditions were in sight. (213)
15. Activities designed to discover, enhance, or maintain ethnic and racial identity are called <u>ETHNIC WORK</u>. (225)

ANSWERS TO MATCH THESE CONCEPTS WITH THEIR DEFINITIONS

1. d   race: *inherited physical characteristics that distinguish one group from another*
2. f   assimilation: *the process of being absorbed into the mainstream culture*
3. g   scapegoat: *an individual or group unfairly blamed for someone else's troubles*
4. j   prejudice: *prejudging, usually in a negative way*
5. i   population transfer: *involuntary movement of a minority group*
6. h   genocide: *systematic annihilation or attempted annihilation of a race or ethnic group*
7. a   ethnicity: *having distinctive cultural characteristics*
8. b   dominant group: *the group with the most power, greatest privileges, and highest social status*
9. e   discrimination: *an act of unfair treatment directed against an individual or group*
10. c   ethnic cleansing: *a political policy that includes expulsion and genocide*

CHAPTER 10
INEQUALITIES OF GENDER AND AGE

☞ CHAPTER SUMMARY

- Each society establishes a structure that, on the basis of sex and gender, permits or limits access to power, property, and prestige; this structure is referred to as gender stratification. Sex refers to biological distinctions between males and females; gender refers to what a society considers to be proper behaviors and attitudes for its males and females. In the "nature versus nurture" debate, almost all sociologists take the side of nurture.

- Male dominance, or patriarchy, appears to be universal. Different theories about how women became a minority group focus on the physical limitations imposed by childbirth, the relative size and strength of men and women, and the rise of private property.

- Although feminist movements in the United States have battled to eliminate some of the most blatant forms of gender discrimination, there are still many areas of inequality. More females than males now attend college, but both generally end up in gender-biased academic fields. There are signs of change, especially in the field of dentistry. There is evidence of unintended sexual discrimination in the area of medical care. In the workplace women face discrimination in hiring, pay and sexual harassment.

- Traditional gender patterns still exist in regard to violent behavior, especially murder patterns.

- Women in the U.S. have the numerical capacity to take over politics and transform society, but continue to encounter obstacles to their full participation as elected officials. As females come to play a larger role in decision-making processes of U.S. social institutions, stereotypes will be broken.

- Cultural attitudes and beliefs about aging affect people's outlook and behaviors in any society. The graying of America refers to the rising proportion of older people in the U.S. population.

- The symbolic interaction perspective stresses that age has no meaning in and of itself, but is given a meaning by society. Ageism is based on stereotypes which are influenced by the mass media.

- The functional perspective analyzes the withdrawal of the elderly from positions of responsibility. Disengagement and activity theories are two functional theories arising from research in this area.

- Conflict theorists study the competition for scarce resources by rival interest groups (e.g., how different age cohorts may be on a collision course regarding Social Security, Medicare, and Medicaid).

☞ LEARNING OBJECTIVES

As you read Chapter 10, use these learning objectives to organize your notes. After completing your reading, briefly state an answer to each of the objectives, and review the text pages in parentheses.

1. Define gender stratification and differentiate between sex and gender. (232-233)
2. Discuss the continuing controversy regarding biological and cultural factors which come into play in creating gender differences in societies. (233-234)
3. Explain why women are considered to be a minority group and summarize the theories of how male dominance occurred. (234-235)
4. Describe the major factors which led to the rise of feminism in the United States and note how successful this movement has been up to this point in time. (235-236)

157

5.   Discuss ways in which educational systems may perpetuate gender inequality. (236-238)
6.   Explain gender relations in the workplace, including changes in the labor force participation rate, differences in expectations, the pay gap, the "glass ceiling" and the "old boy network," and sexual harassment. (238-244)
7.   Explain what the author means why he says gender violence a "one-way street." (244-245)
8.   Explain why women historically have not taken over politics and transformed American life. (246-248)
9.   Describe what the future looks like in terms of gender relations in the United States. (248)
10.   Analyze the social factors in aging, using the Abkhasians' culture as an example. (248-250)
11.   Discuss the factors involved in the "graying" of industrialized nations. (250-252)
12.   Discuss the major conclusions drawn by symbolic interactionists regarding aging. (252-254)
13.   Summarize the functional perspective on aging and explain disengagement theory and activity theory. (254-256)
14.   Explain why conflict theorists see social life as a struggle between groups for scarce resources and note how this impacts different age cohorts. (256-258)

☞ CHAPTER OUTLINE

INEQUALITIES OF GENDER
I.   **Issues of Sex and Gender**
   A.   Gender stratification refers to men's and women's unequal access to power, prestige, and property.
   B.   Sex and gender reflect different bases.
      1.   Sex is biological characteristics distinguishing males and females--primary sex organs (organs related to reproduction) and secondary sex organs (physical distinctions not related to reproduction).
      2.   Gender is a social characteristic which varies from one society to another and refers to what the group considers proper for its males and females. The sociological significance of gender is that it serves as a primary sorting device by which society controls its members and thus is a structural feature of society.
   C.   There is disagreement as to what produces gender differences in behavior.
      1.   Some researchers argue that biological factors (two X chromosomes in females, one X and one Y in males) result in differences in the behavior of males (more aggressive and domineering) and females (more comforting and nurturing) conduct.
      2.   The dominant sociological position is that gender differences result from sex being used to mark people for special treatment. Symbolic interactionists stress that society interprets the physical differences; males and females then take the relative positions that society assigns to them.
   D.   Alice Rossi suggested that women are better prepared biologically for "mothering" than are men; nature provides biological predispositions which are overlaid with culture.
II.   **Global Considerations: How Females became a Minority Group**
   A.   Around the world, gender is *the* primary division between people. Because society sets up barriers to deny women equal access, they are referred to as a minority even though they outnumber men.

B. Although the origin of patriarchy (male dominance) is unknown, one theory points to the social consequences of human reproduction.

    1. As a result of pregnancy and breast-feeding, women were limited for much of their lives; they assumed tasks associated with the home and child care.

    2. Men took over tasks requiring greater speed and longer absences, such as hunting animals. This enabled men to make contact with other tribes and to wage war; male prestige was the result of their accumulation of possessions through trade and war with other groups. Little prestige was given to women's routine tasks.

    3. Eventually men took over society, using their weapons, their possessions, and their knowledge to guarantee that they held more social power than women.

C. There is no way to test this theory because answers lie buried in history. There may be many different causes, other than the biology of human reproduction.

    1. Marvin Harris argued that in prehistoric times, each group was threatened with annihilation by other groups, and each had to recruit members to fight enemies in dangerous, hand-to-hand combat. Men (bigger and stronger) were coaxed into this bravery by promises of rewards--sexual access to females.

    2. Frederick Engels suggested that male dominance developed in society with the emergence of private property.

    3. Today, male dominance is a continuation of millennia-old patterns.

III. Gender Inequality in the United States

A. U.S. women did not have the right to vote, hold property, or serve on a jury until this century.

    1. Males did not willingly surrender their privileges; but used social institutions to maintain their position.

    2. Women's rights resulted from a prolonged and bitter struggle. Feminism, the view that gender stratification is wrong, met with strong opposition.

    3. While women enjoy more rights today, gender inequality still exists.

B. Despite evidence of educational gains made by women--more females than males are enrolled in U.S. colleges and universities and females earn 54 percent of all bachelor's degrees--some traditional male-female distinctions persist.

    1. At college males and females are channeled into different fields; 89 percent of home economics degrees are awarded to females; 86 percent of engineering degrees are awarded to males.

    2. The proportion of females decreases in post-graduate work.

    3. There is gender stratification in both the rank and pay within higher educational institutions. Women are less likely to be in the higher ranks of academia, and at all levels are paid less than their male counterparts.

    4. Changes are taking place; the proportion of professional degrees earned by women has increased in recent years.

C. Researchers have found sex discrimination in the area of medicine and health care.

    1. Physicians sometimes dismiss the complaints of female patients as not serious. This neglect could be a matter of life and death; one example is in the area of heart disease.

    2. Physicians regard women's reproductive organs as "potentially disease producing," unnecessary after childbearing years. They recommend removal.

D. There have been significant changes in the workforce, as the number of working women has increased. However, discrimination against women is still very visible.

1. In 1900, one in five workers was female; today it is almost one in two.
2. Factors influencing a woman's decision to work include race or ethnicity, marital status, and age of children.
3. Sociologists refer to the continuing increase in the proportion of women in the workforce as a "quiet revolution." It has had profound effects on consumer patters, relations at work, self-concepts, and relationships with significant others.
4. Women in the work force average only 73 percent of men's wages. Despite the level of educational achievement women earn less than men; this is true even when they have more qualifications that male counterparts. Half this pay gap results from women entering lower-paying jobs. One study found that five years after graduation from college, the pay gap was even wider than it was upon entering the job market.
5. "Glass ceiling" describes an invisible barrier that women face in the work force. Even in companies where over half the professional employees are women, only 6 percent of senior management is female. In upper ranks, the gap is preserved through an "old boys"' network (acquaintances who bring access to jobs, promotions, opportunities). To combat this, some female professionals develop alternative networks to help their own careers.

E. Until the 1970s, women did not draw a connection between unwanted sexual advances on the job and their subordinate positions at work.
1. As women began to discuss the problem, they named it and came to see unwanted sexual advances by men in powerful positions as a structural problem. The change resulted from reinterpreting women's experiences--giving them a name.
2. Sexual harassment may be a single encounter or a series of incidents; it may be a condition to being hired, retained, or promoted. The Equal Employment Opportunity Commission defines it as all unwelcome sexual attention that affects an employee's job conditions or creates a hostile work environment.
3. As more women move into positions of authority over men, the problem of sexual harassment is no longer exclusively a female problem.

IV. **Gender and Violence**
A. Every year in the U.S. 83 out of every 100,000 females are raped. Of increased concern today is the widespread incidence of date rape. Studies show that this occurs most commonly between couples who have known each other about one year.
B. Males are more likely to commit murder than females; males commit 91 percent of the murders involving women victims and 86 percent of the murders involving males victims.
C. Feminists use symbolic interactionism to understand violence against women. They stress that U.S. culture promotes violence by males. It teaches men to associate power, dominance, strength, virility and superiority with masculinity. Men use violence to try and maintain a higher status.
D. To solve violence we must first break the link between violence and masculinity.

V. **The Changing Face of Politics**
A. Despite the gains U.S. women have made in recent elections, they continue to be underrepresented in political office, especially in higher office. There are different factors that contribute to this pattern.
1. Women are still underrepresented in law and business, the careers from which most politicians are drawn.

    2.   Women do not see themselves as a voting bloc who need political action to overcome discrimination.

    3.   Women still find the roles of mother and politician incompatible.

    4.   Males seldom incorporate women into the centers of decision making or present them as viable candidates.

  B.   Trends in the 1990s indicate that women will participate in political life in far greater numbers than in the past.

  C.   As women play a fuller role in the decision-making processes, and as gender stereotypes are abandoned, further structural obstacles to women's participation in society will give way.

INEQUALITIES OF AGING

VI.   The Global Context of Aging

  A.   In Abkhasia (a remote agricultural region in the former Soviet Union) the people commonly live to be 100, or even older. Possible reasons for their longevity include sexual abstinence (other than through marriage); work (from childhood to the end of life); diet and eating customs (overeating is considered dangerous); and social integration (active, valued, contributing members of the society, never isolated from family and community).

  B.   In the United States, as in other industrialized nations, life expectancy is increasing; to an extent, this is because of a safer water supply and the control of certain diseases.

    1.   The graying of America refers to the proportion of older persons in the U.S. population. Almost 13 percent of the population has achieved age 65.

    2.   Because the proportion of non-whites in the U.S. is growing, the number of minority elderly is also increasing, and therefore differences in cultural attitudes about aging, types of family relationships, work histories, and health practices will be important areas of sociological investigation in the coming years.

  C.   All industrialized nations are encountering this graying trend, which places a greater burden on the young to pay the benefits that the elderly need.

VII.   The Symbolic Interactionist Perspective

  A.   Robert Butler coined the term ageism to refer to prejudice, discrimination, and hostility directed at people because of their age. Ageism is not limited to industrialized nations, but can also be found in more traditional societies.

  B.   While in U.S. society today the general image of old age is negative, researchers have found that at one time, old age had more positive meanings.

    1.   Few made it to old age, so those who did were listened to concerning how to live a long life.

    2.   Old age was associated with virtue.

    3.   In the days before Social Security provided for retirement, the elderly worked and were seen as wise and knowledgeable about work skills.

  C.   Industrialization eroded traditional bases of respect.

    1.   With improved sanitation and health care, living to an old age was no longer unique.

    2.   The morality of the elderly was seen as out-dated, as new lifestyles and relationships supplanted traditional ones.

    3.   Mass education stripped away the mystique that surrounded the elderly's possession of superior knowledge that was to be "handed down" to the next generation.

VIII. **The Functionalist Perspective**

A. Functionalists examine age from the standpoint of how those persons who are retiring and those who will replace them in the work force make mutual adjustments.

B. Elaine Cumming and William Henry developed disengagement theory to explain how society prevents disruption to society when the elderly retire. The elderly are rewarded in some way (pensions) for giving up positions rather than wait until they become incompetent or die; this allows for a smooth transition of positions. It is criticized because it assumes that the elderly disengage and then sink into oblivion.

C. Activity theory examines people's reactions to exchanging one set of roles for another. Older people who maintain a high level of activity tend to be more satisfied with life than those who do not. Level of activity is connected to key factors such as social class, health, and individual orientation.

IX. **The Conflict Perspective**

A. Conflict theorists examine social life as a struggle between groups for scarce resources. Social Security legislation is an example of that struggle.

   1. In the 1920s-30s, two-thirds of all citizens over 65 had no savings and could not support themselves. Francis Townsend enrolled one-third of all Americans over 65 in clubs that sought a national sales tax to finance a monthly pension for all Americans over age 65. To avoid the plan without appearing to be opposed to old-age pensions, Social Security was enacted by Congress.

   2. Conflict theorists state that Social Security was not a result of generosity, but rather of competition among interest groups.

B. Since equilibrium is only a temporary balancing of social forces, some form of continuing conflict between the younger and the older appears inevitable.

   1. The huge costs of Social Security have become a national concern. The dependency ratio (number of workers compared with number of recipients) is currently five working-age Americans paying to support each person over 65; by the year 2035 it will be two to one. Meanwhile, other groups are organizing to fight the elderly for these resources.

   2. Some argue that the elderly and children are on a collision course. Data indicate that as the number of elderly poor decreased, children in poverty increased. It has been argued that the comparison is misleading because the money that went to the elderly did not come from money intended for the children. Framing the issue in this way is an attempt to divide the working class, and to force a choice between suffering children and suffering elderly.

☞ GLOSSARY OF DIFFICULT-TO-UNDERSTAND WORDS

astride: on top of (232)

carjacking: forcing the driver of a car out of the car while it is in motion and then stealing it away from him or her (244)

collision course: a situation in which two forces are set to run headlong into one another (258)

demure: modest, shy (232)

disequilibrium: things not being in balance (256)

encumbered: to be burdened by something, or weighed down by something (235)

entice: lure or tempt (235)

erogenous zone: body areas that are sexually stimulating (249)

gunslinging heroes: cowboys in the Wild West who wore guns in holsters and engaged in gun fights (245)

home economics: a course of study in which activities associated with maintaining a home and family are stressed (236)

hovered: stayed more or less in one place; very slight movement (239)

idyllic: careful or romantic; rustic or pastoral (255)

incontinent: having to control over one's bladder (255)

internships: supervised work experiences while still a student in preparation for a particular career (242)

lethal barrage: a prolonged, deadly burst of gunfire (232)

longevity: long lifetime (249)

mystique: a combination of mystical ideas and attitudes that develop around something or someone (254)

"old boys'" network: a term used to refer to the informal social ties that exist among men, growing out of associations formed in college and carried through into the business world (243)

picket line: a line formed by protesters, usually marching in front of some building (236)

prerogatives: special privileges based on status (236)

ramifications: consequences (242)

steered away: discouraged from following a particular course of action (243)

sweatshop: a workplace where people work long hours for low pay (242)

tenacious: persistence (236)

vegetate: engage in no activities (250)

veil of foliage: an area with a mass of plants and trees that may conceal things (232)

virility: a characteristic in which masculinity is associated with being able to impregnate a woman (245)

wheezing: breathing with difficulty; the breathing is often accompanied by a whistling sound (255)

widowhood: being single as a result of spouse's death (256)

☞ KEY TERMS TO DEFINE

After studying the chapter, define each of the following terms. Then check your work by referring to the answers beginning at page 169 of this Study Guide.

activity theory	feminism	life span
age cohort	gender	patriarchy
ageism	gender stratification	quiet revolution
dependency ratio	graying of America	sex
disengagement theory	life expectancy	sexual harassment

☞ KEY PEOPLE

State the major theoretical contributions or findings of these people.

Sula Benet	Rex Fuller	Alice Rossi
Robert Butler	Marvin Harris	Richard Schoenberger
Elaine Cumming	William Henry	Felice Schwartz
Frederick Engels	Meredith Minkler	Francis Townsend
Sue Fisher	Ann Robertson	

☞ SELF-TEST

After completing this self-test, check your answers against the Answer Key beginning on page 169 of this Study Guide and against the text on page(s) indicated in parentheses.

MULTIPLE CHOICE QUESTIONS

1. Gender stratification: (232)
    a. cuts across all aspects of social life.
    b. represents a primary division between people.
    c. refers to men's and women's unequal access to power, prestige, and property on the basis of their sex.
    d. All of the above.

2. The term "sex" refers to: (232)
    a. the social characteristics that a society considers proper for its males and females.
    b. the biological characteristics that distinguish females and males.
    c. masculinity and femininity.
    d. All of the above.

3. According to sociologists, if biology were the principal factor in human behavior, around the world we would find: (233)
    a. things to be just like they are.
    b. men and women to be much more like each other than they currently are.
    c. women to be one sort of person and men another.
    d. None of the above.

4. In regard to the prestige of work: (235)
    a. greater prestige is given to activities which are considered to be of great importance to a society, regardless of whether they are performed by females or males.
    b. greater prestige is given to female activities that males cannot perform, such as pregnancy and lactation.
    c. greater prestige is given to male activities.
    d. None of the above.

5. Patriarchy: (235)
    a. is a society in which men dominate women.
    b. has existed throughout most of history.
    c. is universal.
    d. All of the above.

6. Feminism is the view that: (236)
    a. female traits are superior to male traits.
    b. gender stratification is wrong and should by resisted.
    c. females should have dominance over males.
    d. All of the above

7. Gender inequality in education: (236)
   a. has virtually disappeared today.
   b. is allowed by law.
   c. is perpetuated by the use of sex to sort students into different academic disciplines.
   d. None of the above.

8. The continuing increase in the proportion of women in the workforce since the 1960s is referred to as the "quiet revolution" because: (236-239)
   a. women are generally quieter than men.
   b. the changes have been gradual, while the implications are profound.
   c. most people aren't even aware of it, because their lives are not affected by it.
   d. women have been employed in "quiet" occupations like clerical or nursing.

9. The pay gap between men and women: (239-243)
   a. is found primarily in low-skilled jobs.
   b. is found primary in the professions.
   c. is found in both low-skilled jobs and in the professions.
   d. largely has disappeared in both low-skilled jobs and in the professions.

10. According to Felice Schwartz, what is it that keeps women from breaking through the glass ceiling? (243)
    a. a lack of self-confidence on the part of the women themselves
    b. being "detoured" away from core positions from which executives are recruited
    c. a lack of educational credentials
    d. the burden of childcare responsibilities

11. The use of one's position to force unwanted sexual demands on someone is referred to as: (243)
    a. sexual harassment.
    b. sexual provocation.
    c. sexual maladjustment.
    d. sexual conquest.

12. Sexual harassment: (243-244)
    a. is still exclusively a female problem.
    b. has a clear legal definition based on Supreme Court rulings.
    c. involves a person in authority using the position to force unwanted sex on subordinates.
    d. All of the above.

13. The pattern of date rape shows: (244)
    a. that it is not an isolated event.
    b. that it is more likely to happen with couples who have dated for a period of time.
    c. that most date rapes go unreported.
    d. All of the above.

14. Women continue to be underrepresented in politics because: (247-248)
    a.   they are not really interested in pursuing political careers.
    b.   they are not viewed as serious candidates by the voters.
    c.   their roles as mothers and wives are incompatible with political roles.
    d.   they lack the proper educational backgrounds.

15. According to the author, which of the following is most likely to result in breaking the stereotypes that lock both males and females into traditional gender activities? (248)
    a.   stricter laws
    b.   equal pay
    c.   increased female participation in the decision-making processes of social institutions
    d.   increased male participation in nurturing activities

16. The Abkhasians are an interesting example regarding age because they: (249)
    a.   live such short lives.
    b.   live such long lives.
    c.   have so many words in their language for "old people."
    d.   quit working when they were quite young.

17. Social factors which are likely to shorten life include: (249-250)
    a.   isolation from family and community.
    b.   participating in too many activities.
    c.   too many goals to fulfill and not enough time.
    d.   All of the above.

18. The increase in life expectancy in industrialized nations is due to: (250)
    a.   improvements in sanitation.
    b.   developments in medicine.
    c.   the control of deadly childhood diseases.
    d.   All of the above.

19. The process by which older persons make up an increasing proportion of the United States population is referred to as: (250-251)
    a.   the aging process.
    b.   the graying of America.
    c.   the gentrification process.
    d.   None of the above.

20. Prior to industrialization, old people in U.S. society: (254)
    a.   were considered a burden.
    b.   were generally neglected by their families.
    c.   were viewed in a positive light, seen as wise and virtuous.
    d.   were not as productive as they are today.

21. Some researchers believe that the process of disengagement begins: (256)
    a. when a person first starts a job.
    b. during middle age.
    c. at retirement.
    d. about one year after retirement.

22. _____ suggests that satisfaction in old age depends on one's level/quality of activity. (256)
    a. activity theory.
    b. recreational theory.
    c. satisfaction theory.
    d. None of the above.

23. Conflict theorists believe that retirement benefits are the result of: (256)
    a. generous hearts in Congress.
    b. a struggle between competing interest groups.
    c. many years of hard work by elderly Americans.
    d. None of the above.

24. The dependency ratio refers to: (257)
    a. the number of dependents in a household relative to the number of working people.
    b. the number of workers it takes to pay one person's Social Security.
    c. the number of welfare recipients relative to employed workers.
    d. the number of working women relative to non-working women.

25. Trends in poverty over the past 30 years indicate that: (258-259)
    a. the percentage of elderly who are poor has increased.
    b. the percentage of elderly who are poor has decreased.
    c. both childhood and elderly poverty has decreased.
    d. elderly poverty has increased and childhood poverty has decreased.

TRUE-FALSE QUESTIONS

T F 1. The terms sex and gender basically mean the same thing to sociologists. (232-233)
T F 2. The emergence of female warriors in Tamil society was due to changes in their biology. (233)
T F 3. Sociologist Alice Rossi has argued that nature provides biological predispositions which are overlaid with culture. (234)
T F 4. Women are considered to be a minority group because there are fewer women than men in the United States. (234)
T F 5. Patriarchy is a society in which men dominate women. (235)
T F 6. According to anthropologist Marvin Harris, females became the reward to encourage males to become a society's defenders and attackers. (235)
T F 7. In the U.S. women's rights were gained by a prolonged and bitter struggle. (236)
T F 8. While women outnumber men on college campuses today, they earn less than one-half of all bachelor's degrees. (236)
T F 9. Research indicates that the highest prestige universities are least likely to discriminate against women in terms of academic hiring and promotion. (236)

T F 10. Today women and men have equal levels of achievement in higher education. (236-238)

T F 11. In the legal profession, women are only half as likely as men to receive partnerships in their legal firms. (243)

T F 12. Once sexual harassment was defined as a problem, women saw some of their experiences in a different light. (243)

T F 13. Both males and females are victims of male violence. (245)

T F 14. Around the world, males kill at about the same rate as that of females. (245)

T F 15. Women in the United States are still vastly underrepresented in political decision making. (245-247)

T F 16. The Abkhasians believe that one of the reasons why they live longer is because they conserve their sexual energy. (249)

T F 17. One reason why the Abkhasians live so long is because they retire while they are still young enough to enjoy life. (250)

T F 18. Not all industrialized nations have the increase in life expectancy experienced in the United States. (250)

T F 19. That racial and ethnic groups have different proportions of elderly within their populations is due to biological factors. (251)

T F 20. Problems of ageism are largely limited to industrialized societies. (253)

T F 21. Disengagement theory is used to explain how society prevents disruption by having the elderly vacate their positions of responsibility. (256)

T F 22. Activity theorists believe that older people who maintain a high level of activity tend to be more satisfied with life than those who do not. (256)

T F 23. According to conflict theorists, the passage of social security legislation is an example of the struggle between the young and old in society. (257)

T F 24. The dependency ratio is the number of workers required to support one person on Social Security. (257)

T F 25. According to conflict theorists Meredith Minkler and Ann Robertson, the increase in child poverty has paralleled the decrease in elderly poverty is the result of shifting funds away from children and towards old people. (258)

FILL-IN QUESTIONS

1. _____ refers to biological characteristics that distinguish females and males, consisting of primary and secondary sex characteristics. (232)

2. Around the world, _____ is the primary division between people. (234)

3. Patriarchy was attributed to warfare and physical strength by anthropologist _____. (235)

4. _____ is the philosophy that gender stratification is wrong and should be resisted. (236)

5. The _____ prevents women from advancing to top executive positions. (243)

6. _____ is a particular form of violence directed exclusively against women. (246)

7. The process by which older persons make up an increasing proportion of the United States population is called _____. (250)

8. _____ is the discrimination against people because of their age. (253)

9. The belief that society prevents disruption by having the elderly vacate their positions of responsibility is _____. (256)

10. _____ theory asserts that satisfaction during old age is related to a person's level and quality of activity. (257)

MATCH THESE CONCEPTS WITH THEIR DEFINITIONS

___1. gender   a. *biological traits that separate male from female*
___2. gender stratification   b. *unequal access to power, prestige, and property on the basis of sex*
___3. patriarchy   c. *a society in which men dominate women*
___4. sex   d. *using one's position to make unwanted sexual demands on another*
___5. sexual harassment   e. *the characteristics that society considers proper for its males and females*
___6. ageism   f. *satisfaction in old age is related to a one's level and quality of activity*
___7. dependency ratio   g. *people born at the same time and go through the life course together*
___8. activity theory   h. *the number of workers required to support one person on Social Security*
___9. life span   i. *the maximum length of life of a species*
___10. age cohort   j. *prejudice, discrimination, and hostility because of one's age*

"DOWN-TO-EARTH SOCIOLOGY"

1. What factors do you think were responsible for the break-up of Altagracia Ortiz's marriage (p. 242)? Could the couple have done anything differently in order to hold their marriage together? Where does the blame for the failure lie?

2. What do you think would occur in the United States if the public relations department of a corporation put a cover girl on the company magazine and showed the woman taking off one more piece of clothing each month? What happened when this occurred in Japan? (See "Sexual Harassment in Japan," p. 244.)

3. What was your reaction to the piece on female circumcision (pp. 246-247)? How is the purpose of this procedure fundamentally different from male circumcision? Do you think that international pressure should be applied to end this procedure? Why or why not?

4. After reading about how some other cultures deal with the care of their elderly ("Trouble in Paradise," p. 255), think again about our own society. How do you think we should care for the elderly? What kind of treatment do you expect when you are old?

☞ ANSWERS FOR CHAPTER 10

DEFINITIONS OF KEY TERMS

activity theory: the view that satisfaction during old age is related to a person's level and quality of activity

age cohort: people born at roughly the same time who pass through the life course together

ageism: prejudice, discrimination, and hostility directed against people because of their age; can be directed against any age group, including youth

dependency ratio: the number of workers required to support one person on Social Security

disengagement theory: the view that society prevents disruption by having the elderly vacate their positions of responsibility so that the younger generation can step into their shoes

feminism: the philosophy that men and women should be politically, economically, and socially equal, and organized activity on behalf of this principle

gender: the social characteristics that a society considers proper for its males and females; masculinity and femininity

gender stratification: men's and women's unequal access to power, prestige, and property on the basis of sex

graying of America: the process by which older people make up an increasing proportion of the U.S. population

life expectancy: the age to which people can expect to live

life span: the maximum length of life

patriarchy: a society in which authority is vested in males; male control of a society or group

quiet revolution: the fundamental changes in society that follow when vast numbers of women enter to work force

sex: biological characteristics that distinguish females and males, consisting of primary and secondary sex characteristics

sexual harassment: usually defined as the use of one's occupational position to force unwanted sexual demands on someone

ANSWERS FOR MULTIPLE CHOICE QUESTIONS

1. d   All of the above is correct. Gender stratification cuts across all aspects of social life and represents a primary division between people. The term refers to men's and women's unequal access to power, prestige, and property on the basis of their sex. (232)
2. b   The term "sex" refers to the biological characteristics that distinguish females and males. (232)
3. c   According to sociologists, if biology were the principal factor in human behavior, around the world we would find women to be one sort of person and men another. (233)
4. c   In regard to the prestige of work, greater prestige is given to male activities. (235)
5. d   All of the above is correct. Patriarchy is a society in which men dominate women. Patriarchy has existed throughout most of history, and it is universal. (235)
6. b   Feminism is the view that gender stratification is wrong and should by resisted by both men and women. (236)
7. c   Gender inequality in education is perpetuated by the use of sex to sort students into different academic disciplines. (236)
8. b   The continuing increase in the proportion of women in the workforce since the 1960s is referred to as the "quiet revolution" because the changes have been gradual, while the implications, in terms of consumer patterns, relations at work, self-concepts, and relationships with significant others, are profound. (236-239)
9. c   The pay gap between men and women is found in both low-skilled jobs and in the professions. (239-243)
10. b   According to Felice Schwartz, what keeps women from breaking through the glass ceiling is not a lack of self-confidence, educational credentials, or the burden of childcare responsibilities. Rather, women are often "detoured" away from the core positions which serve as springboards

to executive positions. Seen as more suited for jobs that provide "support," such as public relations and human services, women do not get the corporate experience required for top management. (243)

11. a   The use of a person's position to force unwanted sexual demands on someone is referred to as sexual harassment. (243)

12. c   Sexual harassment involves a person in authority, usually a male, who uses that position to force unwanted sexual actions on a subordinate, usually a female. (243-244)

13. d   Date rape is not an isolated event; it is more likely to happen after a couple has dated for a period of time rather than on the first few dates; and most date rapes go unreported. (244)

14. c   Women are reluctant to get involved in politics because the demands of political life are in conflict with the demands of their roles as wives and mothers. (247-248)

15. c   Increased female participation in decision-making processes of social institutions is most likely going to result in breaking down the stereotypes that lock both males and females into traditional gender activities. (248)

16. b   The Abkhasians are an interesting example regarding age because they live such long lives. (249)

17. a   Social factors which are likely to shorten life include isolation from family and community. (249-250)

18. d   The increase in life expectancy in industrialized nations is due to improvements in sanitation, developments in medicine, and the control of deadly childhood diseases. (250)

19. b   The process by which older persons make up an increasing proportion of the United States population is referred to as the "graying of America." (250-251)

20. c   Prior to industrialization, old people in U.S. society were viewed in a positive light, seen as wise and virtuous. In a time when many died before reaching old age, those who survived were listened to for advise about how to live a long life; they provided guidance on how to live a good life; and they were seen as knowledgeable about work skills. (254)

21. b   Some researchers believe that the process of disengagement begins during middle age. (256)

22. a   The belief that satisfaction during old age is related to a person's level and quality of activity is called activity theory. (256)

23. b   Conflict theorists believe that retirement benefits reflect competition among interest groups. (256)

24. b   The dependency ratio refers to the number of workers it takes to pay one person's Social Security. (257)

25. b   Trends in poverty over the past 30 years indicate that the percentage of elderly who are poor has decreased. At the same time, the percentage of children living in poverty has increased. Some argue that the young have suffered at the expense of the old, a view that is challenged by conflict theorists such as Meredith Minkler and Ann Robertson. (258-259)

ANSWERS FOR TRUE-FALSE QUESTIONS

1.   *False.* Sex refers to biological characteristics that distinguish females and males. Gender refers to social characteristics that a society considers proper for its males and females. (232-233)

2.   *False.* The emergence of female warriors in Tamil society was not due to changes in their biology but, instead, was due to changes in their social conditions. (233)

3.   *True.* (234)

4.   *False.* Women are considered to be a minority group, but not because there are fewer women than men in the United States. They are considered to be a minority group because they are discriminated against--economically, in education, in politics, and in everyday life--on the basis of physical characteristics. (234)

5.   *True.* (235)
6.   *True.* (235)
7.   *True.* (236)
8.   *False.* While it is true that women outnumber men on college campuses today, it is not true that they earn less than one-half of all bachelor's degrees. Rather, they earn 54 percent of all bachelor's degrees. (236)
9.   *False.* The highest prestige universities are most likely to discriminate against women in the area of academic rank and salaries. (236)
10.   *False.* While women have made gains in terms of the proportion of degrees earned, and exceed men in earning bachelor's of arts degrees, they still lag behind in post-graduate and professional degrees. (236-238)
11.   *True.* (243)
12.   *True.* (243)
13.   *True.* (245)
14.   *False.* Around the world, males kill at a rate several times that of females. (245)
15.   *True.* (245-247)
16.   *True.* (249)
17.   *False.* Among the Abkhasian retirement is unknown and unthinkable; even the very old continue to work, averaging about 4 hours daily. (250)
18.   *False.* The United States is not alone in the "graying" trend. All industrialized nations are graying because industrialization brings health measures that allow a larger proportion of a population to reach an advanced age. (250)
19.   *False.* The fact that different racial and ethnic groups differ in terms of the proportion of elderly within their populations is due not to biological factors, but social class factors; groups with a disproportionate number of poor will have a smaller percentage of elderly than those that do not. (251)
20.   *False.* Contrary to our expectations, ageism is just a likely to exist in traditional societies as it is in modern industrialized societies. (253)
21.   *True.* (256)
22.   *True.* (256)
23.   *True.* (257)
24.   *True.* (257)
25.   *False.* Conflict theorists Minkler and Robertson caution against this interpretation of the trends. They argue that increasing expenditures for one group does not automatically result in a reduction in resources to another group; rather, the pattern of spending is a reflection of government decision-making. Framing the issue in terms of gains and losses simply leads to divisions among groups. (258)

ANSWERS FOR FILL-IN QUESTIONS

1.   <u>SEX</u> refers to biological characteristics that distinguish females and males, consisting of primary and secondary sex characteristics. (232)
2.   Around the world, <u>GENDER</u> is the primary division between people. (234)
3.   Patriarchy was attributed to warfare and physical strength by anthropologist <u>MARVIN HARRIS</u>. (235)
4.   <u>FEMINISM</u> is the philosophy that gender stratification is wrong and should be resisted. (236)
5.   The <u>GLASS CEILING</u> prevents women from advancing to top executive positions. (243)

6.   <u>FEMALE CIRCUMCISION</u> is a particular form of violence directed exclusively against women. (246)
7.   The process by which older persons make up an increasing proportion of the United States population is called <u>THE GRAYING OF AMERICA</u>. (250)
8.   <u>AGEISM</u> is the discrimination against people because of their age. (253)
9.   The belief that society prevents disruption by having the elderly vacate their positions of responsibility is <u>DISENGAGEMENT THEORY</u>. (256)
10.   <u>ACTIVITY</u> theory asserts that satisfaction during old age is related to a person's level and quality of activity. (257)

ANSWERS TO MATCH THESE CONCEPTS WITH THEIR DEFINITIONS

1. e   Gender: *characteristics that a society considers proper for its males and females*
2. b   Gender stratification: *unequal access to power, prestige, and property on the basis of sex*
3. c   Patriarchy: *a society in which men dominate women*
4. a   Sex: *biological characteristics that distinguish females and males*
5. d   Sexual harassment: *using one's position to make unwanted sexual demands on another*
6. j   ageism: *prejudice, discrimination, and hostility because of one's age*
7. h   dependency ratio: *the number of workers required to support one person on Social Security*
8. f   activity theory: *satisfaction during old age is related to a one's level and quality of activity*
9. i   life span: *the maximum length of life of a species*
10. g   age cohort: *people born at about the same time and go through the life course together*

CHAPTER 11
POLITICS AND THE ECONOMY:
LEADERSHIP AND WORK IN THE GLOBAL VILLAGE

☞ CHAPTER SUMMARY

- Authority refers to the legitimate use of power, while coercion is its illegitimate use. The state is a political entity that claims a monopoly on violence over a particular territory. Three types of authority--traditional, rational-legal, and charismatic--were identified by Max Weber. The orderly transfer of authority at the death, resignation, or incapacitation of a leader is critical for social stability.

- Three forms of government are monarchies (power is based on hereditary rule), democracies (power is given by the citizens), and dictatorships and oligarchies (power is seized by an individual or a small group). Although democracies are fairly new in world history, the concept of democracy and citizenship is now transforming global politics.

- In the United States, with its winner-takes-all electoral system, the two main political parties must appeal to the center, and minority parties make little headway. The more people feel they have a stake in the political system, the more likely they are to vote. Special interest groups, with their lobbyists and PACs, play a significant role in U.S. politics.

- Functionalists and conflict theorists have very different views on who rules the United States. According to the functionalists, no one group holds power; the outcome is that the competing interest groups balance one another (pluralism). According to conflict theorists, the United States is governed by a ruling class made up of members drawn from the elite (power elite).

- The earliest hunting and gathering societies were characterized by subsistence economies; economic systems became more complex as people discovered how to cultivate (horticultural and pastoral societies), farm (agricultural societies) and manufacture (industrial societies). Trade followed the emergence of a surplus; one outcome of trade was the creation of social inequality, as some people began to accumulate more than others.

- The two major economic systems are capitalism, in which the means of production are privately owned, and socialism, in which the means of production are state owned. In recent years, each of these systems has adopted features of the other.

- The term corporate capitalism is used to describe the economic dominance by giant corporations today. At the top is an inner circle, intent on making sure that corporate capitalism is protected. The rise of the multinational corporations means that the interests of this inner circle lies beyond national boundaries.

- There are indications that a new world order is developing, as communications, transportation, and trade expand globally. The consequences of this transformation for human welfare are still unclear; predictions range from excellent to calamitous.

☞ LEARNING OBJECTIVES

As you read Chapter 11, use these learning objectives to organize your notes. After completing your reading, briefly state an answer to each of the objectives, and review the text pages in parentheses.

1. Distinguish between power and authority, and discuss the role of the state in the exercise of legitimate violence. (264-265)

2.   Describe the sources of authority identified by Weber, and explain how the orderly transfer of authority is achieved under each type of authority. (265-267)
3.   Differentiate between monarchies, democracies, and dictatorships and oligarchies. (267-267)
4.   Explain the nature of the two-party system in the United States and consider why third parties do poorly within this system. (269-270)
5.   Describe American voting patterns, identify those most and least likely to vote in elections, and explain the social factors behind these patterns. (270-271)
6.   Analyze the ways in which special-interest groups influence the political process. (271-274)
7.   Distinguish between the functionalist and conflict perspectives on how the U.S. political process operates, and compare the power elite perspective of C. Wright Mills with William Domhoff's ruling class theory. (274-276)
8.   Trace the transformation of the economic systems through each of the historical stages and state the degree to which social inequality existed in each of the economies. (276-279)
9.   Discuss some of the ominous contemporary trends within the U.S. economy, including downsizing, the "Great U-Turn," and the U.S.'s status as the world's largest debtor. Analyze the possibilities for improvement in the U.S. economy. (279-281)
10.   State the essential features of capitalism and socialism and explain why neither exists in its "pure" form. (281-283)
11.   Identify the ideologies of capitalism and socialism. (283)
12.   State criticisms of capitalism and socialism, describe the recent changes in socialist economies, and explain why some theorists believe the two systems are converging. (283-284)
13.   Define corporations, interlocking directorates, and multinational corporations and discuss the role each plays in the global economy. (284-285)
14.   Explain why some theorists believe that there is a possibility that global political and economic unity could come about. (285-286)

☞ CHAPTER OUTLINE

POLITICS: ESTABLISHING LEADERSHIP
I.   **Power and Authority**
        A.   Max Weber noted that power--the ability to get your way, even over the resistance of others--can be either legitimate or illegitimate.
                1.   Authority is legitimate power that people accept as right, while coercion is power that people do not accept as just.
                2.   The state is the source of legitimate force or violence in society; violence is the ultimate foundation of political order. The ultimate proof of the state's authority is that the state can kill someone because he or she has done something which is considered absolutely horrible; an individual can't, without facing consequences.
        B.   Three sources of authority were identified by Max Weber.
                1.   Traditional authority (based on custom) is prevalent in preliterate groups, where custom sets relationships. When society changes, traditional authority is undermined, but does not die, even in postindustrial societies. For example, parental authority is a traditional authority.
                2.   Rational-legal authority (based on written rules, also called bureaucratic authority) derives from the position an individual holds, not from the person. Everyone (no matter how high the office) is subject to the rules.

3.   Charismatic authority (based on an individual's personal following) may pose a threat. Because charismatic leaders work outside the established political system and may threaten it, the authorities are often quick to oppose this type of leader.

C.   Orderly transfer of authority upon death, resignation, or incapacity of a leader is critical for stability. Succession is more of a problem with charismatic authority than with traditional or rational-legal authority. Routinization of charisma refers to the transfer of authority from a charismatic leader to either traditional or rational-legal authority.

II.   Types of Government

A.   As cities developed, each city-state (an independent city whose power radiated outward, bringing adjacent areas under its rule) had its own monarchy, a type of government headed by a king or queen.

1.   As city-states warred with one another, the victors would extend their rule, eventually over an entire region.

2.   As the size of these regions grew, people developed an identification with the region; over time this gave rise to the state.

B.   A democracy is a government whose authority derives from the people.

1.   Direct democracy (voters meet together to discuss issues and make decisions) emerged about 2,000 years ago in Athens.

2.   Representative democracy (voters elect representatives to govern and make decisions on their behalf) emerged as the United States became more populous, making direct democracy impossible.

3.   Today, citizenship (citizens have basic rights) is taken for granted in the U. S. Universal citizenship (everyone having the same basic rights) came into practice very slowly and only through fierce struggle.

C.   Dictatorship is government where power is seized and held by an individual; oligarchy results when a small group of individual seizes power. Dictators and oligarchies can be totalitarian; this is when the government exercises almost total control of a people.

III.   The U.S. Political System

A.   The Democratic and Republican parties emerged by the time of the Civil War.

1.   The Democrats are often associated with the poor and the working class and the Republicans with people who are financially better off.

2.   Since each appeals to a broad membership, it is difficult to distinguish conservative Democrats from liberal Republicans; however, it is easy to discern the extremes. Those elected to Congress may cross party lines, because although office holders support their party's philosophy, they do not necessarily support all of its specific proposals.

3.   Despite their differences, however, both parties support fundamentals of U.S. society such as freedom of religion, free public education, and capitalism.

4.   Third parties do play a role in U.S. politics, although generally they receive little public support. Ross Perot's "United We Stand" party is one exception.

B.   Voting Patterns

1.   U.S. voting patterns are consistent: the percentage of people who vote increases with age; whites are more likely to vote than African Americans or Asian Americans, while Latinos are considerably less likely to vote than either; those with higher levels of education are more likely to vote, as are people with higher levels of income; about the same proportion of males and females vote in presidential elections.

2.   The more that people feel they have a stake in the system, the more likely they are to vote. Those who have been rewarded by the system feel more socially integrated and perceive that elections directly affect their lives and the society in which they live.

3.   People who gain less from the system in terms of education, income, and jobs are more likely to be alienated.

4.   Voter apathy is indifference/inaction to the political process. As a result of apathy, two out of five eligible American voters do not vote for president; less than half of the nation's eligible voters vote for members of Congress.

C.   Special-interest groups are people who think alike on a particular issue and can be mobilized for political action.

1.   Lobbyists are people who try to influence legislation on behalf of their clients; they have become a major force in politics. In an effort to curb the influence of lobbyists, Congress passed legislation in the 1970s that set limits on the amount of money that special-interest groups can donate to political candidates.

2.   Political action committees (PACs) solicit and spend funds to influence legislation and bypass laws intended to limit the amount any individual, corporation, or group can give a candidate. PACs have become a powerful influence, bankrolling lobbyists and legislators, and PACs with the most clout gain the ear of Congress.

D.   The major criticism against lobbyists and PACs is that their money buys votes. Rather than representing the people who elected them, legislators support the special interests of groups able to help them stay in power.

IV.   **Who Rules the United States?**

A.   The functionalists say that pluralism, the diffusion of power among interest groups, prevents any one from gaining control of the government. Functionalists believe it helps keep the government from turning against its citizens.

1.   To balance the interests of competing groups, the founders of the U.S. system of government created a system of checks and balances in which separation of powers among the three branches of government ensures that each is able to nullify the actions of the other two, thus preventing the domination of any single branch.

2.   According to this perspective, each group within society pursues its own interests and is balanced by other groups pursuing theirs. As groups negotiate with one another and reach compromises, conflict is minimized.

B.   According to the conflict perspective, lobbyists and even Congress are not at the center of decision making; rather, the power elite makes the decisions that direct the country and shake the world.

1.   As stated by C. Wright Mills, the power elite (heads of leading corporations, powerful generals and admirals in the armed forces, and certain elite politicians) rule the United States. The power elite views capitalism as essential to the welfare of the country; thus, business interests come first.

2.   According to William Domhoff, the ruling class (the wealthiest and most powerful individuals in the country) run the United States. Its members control the U.S.'s top corporations and foundations; presidential cabinet members and top ambassadors to the most powerful countries are chosen from this group, which promotes the view that positions come through merit and that everyone has a chance of becoming rich.

3.   The ruling class does not act in complete unity; at times the interests of one segment may conflict with those of another. At the same time the members generally see eye to eye; they have a mutual interest in solving the problems of business.

C.   While the functionalist and conflict views of power in U.S. society cannot be reconciled. it is possible to employ both. The middle level of C. Wright Mills's model best reflects the functionalist view of competing interests holding each other at bay. At the top is an elite that follows its special interests, as conflict theorists suggest.

THE ECONOMY: WORK IN THE GLOBAL VILLAGE

V.   **The Transformation of Economic Systems**

A.   The transformation of preindustrial societies, from hunting-and-gathering to agricultural, was accompanied by growing inequality.

1.   Earliest hunting and gathering societies had subsistence economies, characterized by little trade with other groups, and a high degree of social equality.

2.   In pastoral and horticultural economies, people created more dependable food supplies. The creation of a surplus allowed groups to grow in size, to settle in a single place, to develop a specialized division of labor, and to trade with other groups, all of which fostered social inequality.

3.   Agricultural economies brought even greater surpluses, magnifying prior trends in social, political and economic inequality. More people were freed from food production, a more specialized division of labor developed, and trade expanded.

B.   The surplus (and greater inequality) grew in industrial societies. As the surplus increased emphasis changed from production of goods to consumption (Thorstein Veblen coined the term conspicuous consumption).

C.   Postindustrial societies are characterized by three types of work: primary (extraction of natural resources from the environment), secondary (processing of raw materials into finished products), and tertiary (provision of services).

1.   According to Daniel Bell, postindustrial economies have six traits: (1) a service sector so large that it employs the majority of workers; (2) a large surplus of goods; (3) even more extensive trade among nations; (4) a wide variety and amount of goods available to the average person; (5) an information explosion; and (6) a "global village" with instantaneous, worldwide communications.

2.   The key to the postindustrial society is the "information explosion" with large numbers of people managing information and designing and servicing products.

3.   The consequence of this explosion is that the transformation of the world is uneven; some will live comfortably while others will continue the struggle just to survive.

D.   In recent years some ominous economic trends have emerged within the United States.

1.   The average work week has increased. U.S. firms are trying to remain competitive in the global marketplace by demanding that employees work longer hours; the cost of overtime is lower than having to pay the unemployment, medical and retirement benefits of additional workers.

2.   Income inequalities continue to plague our society. The distribution of income reassembles an inverted pyramid.

3.   Many Americans find their standard of living stagnating or even declining. There has been a net decline in wages and the standard of living (the great American U-Turn) since the early 1970s.

4.   The United States has gone from being the world's largest creditor to the world's largest debtor in the space of a few short years. The national debt is so large that the interest alone is greater that the combined expenditures for health, science, space, agriculture, housing, protecting the environment, and the entire justice system.

5.   If these trends continue, the United States will become a "two-thirds society." At the top would be the one-third of the population that is well-educated and securely employed. In the middle third would be the working class, insecure in their jobs, earning a more-or-less adequate income. At the bottom would be the unemployed and the underemployed.

VI.   **World Economic Systems**

A.   Capitalism has three essential features: (1) the private ownership of the means of production; (2) the pursuit of profit; and (3) market competition.

    1.   Pure (laissez faire) capitalism exists only when market forces are able to operate without interference from the government.

    2.   The United States today has welfare (or state) capitalism. Private citizens own the means of production and pursue profits, but do so within a vast system of laws designed to protect the public welfare (market restraints).

B.   Socialism also has three essential features: (1) the public ownership of the means of production; (2) central planning; and (3) the distribution of goods without a profit motive.

    1.   Under socialism, the government owns the means of production, and a central committee determines what the country needs instead of allowing supply and demand to control production and prices.

    2.   Socialism is designed to eliminate competition, to produce goods for the general welfare, and to distribute them according to people's needs, not their ability to pay.

    3.   Socialism does not exist in pure form. Although the ideology of socialism calls for resources to be distributed according to need rather than position, socialist nations found it necessary to offer higher salaries for some jobs in order to entice people to take greater responsibilities.

    4.   Some nations (e.g., Sweden and Denmark) have adopted democratic or welfare socialism: both the state and individuals engage in production and distribution, although the state owns certain industries (steel, mining, forestry, telephones, television stations, and airlines) while retail stores, farms, and most service industries remain in private hands.

C.   Capitalism and socialism represent distinct ideologies.

    1.   Capitalists believe that market forces should determine both products and prices, and that it is good for people to strive for profits. Capitalists see that socialists violate basic human rights of freedom of decision and opportunity.

    2.   Socialists believe that profit is immoral and represents excess value extracted from workers. Socialists see that capitalists violate basic human rights of freedom from poverty.

D.   The primary criticism of capitalism is that it leads to social inequality (a top layer of wealthy, powerful people, and a bottom layer of people who are unemployed or underemployed). Socialism has been criticized for not respecting individual rights, and for not being capable of producing much wealth (thus the greater equality of socialism actually amounts to almost everyone having an equal chance of being poor).

E.   As societies industrialize they display comparable divisions of labor, a similar emphasis on higher education, and a trend towards extensive urbanization. According to convergence theory, as both capitalist and socialist systems adopt features of the other, the result may be the emergence of a hybrid or mixed economy in the future.

VII.   **Capitalism in a Global Economy**

A.   The corporation (joint ownership of a business enterprise, whose liabilities are separate from those of its owners) has changed the face of capitalism.

1.   Corporate capitalism refers to the domination of the economic system by giant corporations. One of the most significant aspects of large corporations is the separation of ownership and management, producing ownership of wealth without appreciable control, and control of wealth without appreciable ownership.

2.   Because of the dispersion of ownership, a power vacuum is created. Often, stockholders will simply rubber-stamp management's recommendations at annual stockholders' meetings. However, a stockholders' revolt (stockholders of a corporation refuse to rubber stamp decisions made by the management) is likely to occur if the profits do not meet expectations.

B.   Interlocking directorates occur when individuals serve as directors of several companies, concentrating power and minimizing competition.

C.   As corporations have outgrown national boundaries, the result is the creation of multinational corporations.

1.   The sociological significance of multinational companies is that they have loyalty to profit and market share rather than to a regional or cultural value system.

2.   On the negative side, the world's market dominated by a handful of corporate leaders. On the positive side, global interconnections, which transcend national loyalties, may promote global peace.

VIII.   **A New World Order?**

A.   The historical trend has been for states to grow larger and larger. Today the worldwide flow of information, capital and goods has made national boundaries less meaningful. At the same time national boundaries and national patriotism are deeply entrenched continuing the divisions among the world's population.

B.   Some speculate as to what kind of global political and economic unity will result. If the trend towards greater rights of citizens and greater political participation continues, the potential for human welfare is enhanced. If totalitarianism occurs, then the world's resources and people could come under the control of a dictatorship or oligarchy.

☞ GLOSSARY OF DIFFICULT-TO-UNDERSTAND WORDS

Black Maria: police wagon (265)
distill: reduce (281)
dyed-in-the-wool: holding inflexible opinions (270)
engenders: produces or generates (286)
faze: disturb (264)
flock: a large number of people attracted to a leader (266)
gain the ear of: get access to; are heard by (272)
hallmark: a distinguishing characteristic, trait, or feature (265)
heretic: nonbeliever (264)

Holsteins: a breed of cattle (271)
incapacitation: to make ineligible or incapable of performance (267)
innumerable: too many in number to be counted (265)
levy: to impose a fee (265)
martyr: person who suffers greatly for a cause (266)
palladium: a silver-white metallic element of the platinum group used as a catalyst (286)
preliterate: existing prior to the emergence of written language (265)
remittance: payment (282)
rubber-stamp: approve almost without thinking about it (288)
ruthless: without mercy, cruel (269)
sojourners: temporary residents; transients (272)
sovereign: being of the most supreme kind (285)
subvert: to overturn or overthrow from the foundation (272)
synonymous: alike in meaning or significance (265)
vested: to give someone power or authority to do something (268)

☞ KEY TERMS TO DEFINE

After studying the chapter, define each of the following terms. Then check your work by referring to the answers beginning at page 188 of this Study Guide.

anarchy	direct democracy	rational-legal authority
authority	economy	representative democracy
bureaucratic authority	interlocking directorates	routinization of charisma
capitalism	laissez-faire capitalism	ruling class
charismatic authority	lobbyists	socialism
checks and balances	market forces	special-interest group
citizenship	market restraints	state
city-state	mechanical solidarity	stockholders' revolt
coercion	monarchy	subsistence economy
conspicuous consumption	multinational corporations	totalitarianism
convergence theory	oligarchy	traditional authority
corporate capitalism	organic solidarity	universal citizenship
corporation	pluralism	voter apathy
democracy	political action committee (PAC)	welfare (or state) capitalism
democratic socialism	power	
dictatorship	power elite	

☞ KEY PEOPLE

State the major theoretical contributions or findings of these people.

Daniel Bell	William Form	C. Wright Mills
Barry Bluestone	Bennett Harrison	Thorstein Veblen
William Domhoff	Clark Kerr	Max Weber

☞ SELF-TEST

After completing this self-test, check your answers against the Answer Key beginning on page 188 of this Study Guide and against the text on page(s) indicated in parentheses.

MULTIPLE CHOICE QUESTIONS

1. Power: (264)
    a. was defined by Max Weber.
    b. is the ability to carry out one's will in spite of resistance from others.
    c. is an inevitable part of everyday life.
    d. All of the above.

2. Traditional authority: (265)
    a. is the hallmark of preliterate groups.
    b. is based on custom.
    c. was identified by Max Weber.
    d. All of the above.

3. The least stable type of authority is the: (267)
    a. traditional.
    b. rational-legal.
    c. charismatic.
    d. monarchy.

4. Democracy: (268)
    a. first occurred in the United States.
    b. is a system of government in which authority derives from elected officials.
    c. is basically a modern idea.
    d. None of the above.

5. An individual who seizes power and imposes his will onto the people is known as a: (269)
    a. charismatic leader.
    b. dictator.
    c. totalitarian leader.
    d. monarch.

6. A form of government that exerts almost total control over the people is a(n): (269)
    a. monarchy.
    b. dictatorship.
    c. totalitarian regime.
    d. oligarchy.

7. Studies of voting patterns in the United States: (271)
    a. are inconsistent.
    b. show that voting varies by age, race/ethnicity, education, employment, and income.
    c. show that younger people are more likely to vote than older individuals.
    d. All of the above.

8. Today in the United States, approximately _____ out of every five eligible voters do not vote for the President of the United States. (271)
    a. one
    b. two
    c. three
    d. four

9. Lobbyists: (271-272)
    a. are people paid to influence legislation on behalf of their clients.
    b. are employed by special-interest groups.
    c. are a major force in American politics.
    d. All of the above.

10. Functionalists believe that any one group is prevented from gaining control of the government because of: (274-275)
    a. the existence of pluralism.
    b. the use of checks and balances.
    c. the presence of many interest groups to which politicians must pay attention.
    d. All of the above.

11. According to conflict theorists, the ruling class is: (276)
    a. a group that meets together and agrees on specific matters.
    b. a group which tends to have complete unity on issues.
    c. made up of people whose backgrounds and orientations to life are so similar that they automatically share the same goals.
    d. a myth.

12. Hunting and gathering societies are characterized by a: (277)
    a. market economy.
    b. surplus economy.
    c. subsistence economy.
    d. maintenance economy.

13. Industrial economies: (277)
    a. are based on machines powered by fuels.
    b. created a surplus unlike anything the world had seen.
    c. emerged following the invention of the steam engine.
    d. All of the above.

14.   Workers who package fish, process copper into wire, and turn trees into lumber are in the: (277)
 a.   primary sector.
 b.   secondary sector.
 c.   tertiary sector.
 d.   None of the above.

15.   Postindustrial economies are characterized by: (278)
 a.   a large surplus of goods.
 b.   extensive trade among nations.
 c.   a "global village."
 d.   All of the above.

16.   A primary reason why the average work week of U.S. workers has increased recent is: (279)
 a.   that Republican members of the U.S. Congress have passed legislation mandating a longer work week.
 b.   that U.S. firms are struggling to remain competitive in the global marketplace and find it cheaper to pay overtime than to hire more workers.
 c.   that unions have negotiated salary increases in exchange for longer work days.
 d.   that people just have more to do today than in the past.

17.   Private ownership of the means of production is an essential feature of: (281)
 a.   communism.
 b.   socialism.
 c.   democracy.
 d.   capitalism.

18.   The term "welfare capitalism" refers to a system in which: (281)
 a.   the government gives financial breaks to businessmen.
 b.   former socialist economies are replaced by a "kinder and gentler" form of capitalism.
 c.   a kind of underground economy in which the entrepreneurs are not only receiving welfare but are also engaged in economic activities that generate a profit.
 d.   private individuals own the businesses and pursue profits, but they do so within a system of laws designed to protect the welfare of the population.

19.   An economic system characterized by the public ownership of the means of production, central planning, and the distribution of goods without a profit motive is: (282)
 a.   democratic socialism.
 b.   socialism.
 c.   capitalism.
 d.   communism.

20.   Unemployment compensation, housing subsidies, minimum wage, and Social Security are examples of: (283)
 a.   government handouts.
 b.   outdated Democratic party programs.
 c.   socialist practices.
 d.   inflated government budget expenditures.

21. The joint ownership of a business enterprise, whose liabilities and obligations are separate from those of its owners is a(n): (284)
   a. oligopoly.
   b. monopoly.
   c. corporation.
   d. interlocking directorate.

22. The elite who sit on the boards of directors of not just one but several companies are referred to as: (285)
   a. vertical integrators.
   b. interlocking trustees.
   c. interlocking directorates.
   d. oligopolies.

23. The sociological significance of multinational corporations is that: (285)
   a. more and more U.S. workers are employed by multinationals.
   b. increasingly they have become detached from the interests and values of their country of origin.
   c. they help to control the problem of interlocking directorates because they recruit an international elite to serve on their boards.
   d. the are less likely to exploit labor and natural resources because they operate in a world economy rather than a national economy.

24. Today, national boundaries are becoming less meaningful as: (285)
   a. more and more nations embrace capitalism.
   b. information, capital and goods flow worldwide.
   c. large economic and political units like the European Union are formed.
   d. all of the above.

25. As societies industrialize, they become based on: (286)
   a. mechanical solidarity.
   b. organic solidarity.
   c. social solidarity.
   d. None of the above.

TRUE-FALSE QUESTIONS

T F   1.   In every group, large or small, some individuals have power over others. (264)
T F   2.   Coercion refers to legitimate power. (264)
T F   3.   Even with industrialization some forms of traditional authority go unchallenged. (265)
T F   4.   Rational-legal authority is based on written rules. (265)
T F   5.   Routinization of charisma involves the transfer of authority from a charismatic leader to either traditional or rational-legal authority. (267)
T F   6.   Direct democracy was impossible in the U.S.as population grew and spread out. (268)
T F   7.   The concept of representative democracy based on citizenship may be the greatest gift the United States has given to the world. (268)
T F   8.   The idea of universal citizenship caught on quickly in the United States. (268-269)

T F   9.   Employment and income do not affect the probability that people will vote. (271)

T F   10.   Most political action committees represent broad social interests such as environmental protection. (272)

T F   11.   Functionalists believe that pluralism prevents any one group from gaining control of the government and using it to oppress the people. (274)

T F   12.   Conflict theorists believe that the ruling class is a group that meets together and agrees on specific matters. (276)

T F   13.   Hunting and gathering societies were the first economies to have a surplus. (277)

T F   14.   In pastoral and horticultural economies, some individuals were able for the first time in human history to develop their energies to tasks other than food production. (277)

T F   15.   Industrial economies are based on information processing and providing services. (277-278)

T F   16.   The richest fifth of Americans earn about 44 percent of all the income in the United States. (279)

T F   17.   In welfare capitalism, private citizens own the means of production and pursue profits, but do so within a vast system of laws. (281)

T F   18.   Socialists believe that profit is immoral. (283)

T F   19.   According to convergence theory, as nations industrialize they are likely to adopt more and more of the characteristics of capitalism rather than socialism. (283)

T F   20.   The term "corporate capitalism" is used to describe the dominance of the economic system by giant corporations. (284)

FILL-IN QUESTIONS

1.   _____, synonymous with government, is the source of legitimate violence in society. (265)

2.   _____ is based on custom. (265)

3.   Bureaucratic authority also is called _____. (265)

4.   An independent city whose power radiates outward, bringing the adjacent area under its rule is a _____. (267)

5.   _____ is a form of democracy in which the eligible voters meet together to discuss issues and make their decisions. (268)

6.   The concept that birth and residence in a country impart basic rights is known as _____. (268)

7.   A form of government that exerts almost total control over the people is _____. (269)

8.   _____ refers to indifference and inaction on the part of individuals or groups with respect to the political process. (271)

9.   _____ refers to the top people in leading corporations, the most powerful generals and admirals of the armed forces, and certain elite politicians. (275)

10.   _____ is the term for a system of distribution of goods and services. (276)

11.   Barry Bluestone and Bennett Harrison use the expression " _____ " to refer to the net decline in the wages and standard of living of U.S. workers. (280)

12.   Under _____ both the state and individuals engage in the production and distribution of goods and services. (283)

13.   The view that as capitalist and socialist economic systems each adopt features of the other, a hybrid (or mixed) economic system may emerge is _____. (283)

14.   The refusal of a corporation's stockholders to rubber-stamp decisions made by its managers is referred to as _____. (285)

15.   Durkheim's term for the unity that comes from being involved in similar occupations or activities is _____. (286)

MATCH THESE CONCEPTS WITH THEIR DEFINITIONS

___1. charismatic authority   a. *the laws of supply and demand*
___2. market restraints   b. *the ability to carry out one's will, even over others' resistance*
___3. totalitarianism   c. *authority based on individual traits*
___4. power   d. *laws/regulations limiting capacity to manufacture or distribute goods*
___5. economy   e. *government that exerts almost complete control over the people*
___6. market forces   f. *a system for distributing goods and services*

"DOWN-TO-EARTH SOCIOLOGY"

1.   After reading "Ethnicity and Class in the Path of Political Participation," (p. 272), do you think that recent immigrants will follow the same political route to overcoming discrimination that earlier immigrants took? In what ways might this be more difficult today than in the past? In what ways might it be easier?
2.   Were you surprised at the profile of the American voter that is contained in Table 11.2 on page 273? How would you characterize you own attachment to the political process? Do you vote? Do your friends vote? Why or why not?
3.   After reading about "The Economic Adaptation of the New Chinese Immigrants" on page 280, why do you think these immigrants' economic experiences are so different from those of native-born U.S. citizens or other immigrant groups? What lessons can the Chinese teach us about economic success?

☞ ANSWERS FOR CHAPTER 11

DEFINITIONS OF KEY TERMS

anarchy: a condition of lawlessness or political disorder caused by the absence or collapse of governmental authority
authority: power that people accept as rightly exercised over them
bureaucratic authority: see *rational-legal authority*
capitalism: an economic system characterized by the private ownership of the means of production, the pursuit of profit, and market competition
charismatic authority: authority based on an individual's outstanding traits, which attract followers
checks and balances: the separation of powers among the three branches of U.S. government-- legislative, executive and judicial--so that each is able to nullify the actions of the other two, thus preventing the domination any single branch
citizenship: the concept that birth (and residence) in a country impart basic rights

city-state: an independent city whose power radiates outward, bringing the adjacent areas under its rule

coercion: illegitimate power that people do not accept as just

conspicuous consumption: Thorstein Veblen's term for a change from the Protestant ethic to an eagerness to show off wealth by the elaborate consumption of goods

convergence theory: the view that as capitalist and socialist economic systems each adopt features of the other, a hybrid (or mixed) economic system may emerge

corporate capitalism: the domination of the economic system by giant corporations

corporation: the joint ownership of a business enterprise, whose liabilities and obligations are separate from those of the owners

democracy: a system of government in which authority derives from the people

democratic socialism: a hybrid economic system in which capitalism is mixed with state ownership

dictatorship: a form of government in which power is seized by an individual

direct democracy: a form of democracy in which the eligible voters meet together to discuss issues and make their decisions

economy: a system of distribution of goods and services

interlocking directorates: the phenomenon of one person serving on the board of directors in several companies

laissez-faire capitalism: unrestrained manufacture and trade (literally, "hands off" capitalism)

lobbyists: people who try to influence legislation on behalf of their clients

market forces: the law of supply and demand

market restraints: laws and regulations that limit the capacity to manufacture and sell products

mechanical solidarity: Durkheim's term for the unity or shared consciousness that comes from being involved in similar occupations or activities

monarchy: a form of government headed by a king or queen

multinational corporation: companies that operate across national boundaries

oligarchy: a form of government in which power is held by a small group of individuals; the rule of the many by the few

organic solidarity: Durkheim's term for the interdependence that results from people's needing others to fulfill their jobs; solidarity based on the division of labor

pluralism: the diffusion of power among many interest groups, preventing any single group from gaining control of the government

political action committee (PAC): an organization formed by one or more special-interest groups to solicit and spend funds for the purpose of influencing legislation

power: the ability to get your way, even over the resistance of others

power elite: C. Wright Mills's term for the top leaders of U.S. corporations, military, and politics who make the nation's major decisions

rational-legal authority: authority based on law or written rules and regulations; also called *bureaucratic authority*

representative democracy: a form of democracy in which voters elect representatives to govern and make decisions on their behalf

routinization of charisma: the transfer of authority from a charismatic figure to either a traditional or a rational-legal form of authority

ruling class: term used by William Domhoff to refer to the power elite

socialism: an economic system characterized by the public ownership of the means of production, central planning, and the distribution of goods without a profit motive

special-interest group: people who have a particular issue in common and can be mobilized for political action

state: the political entity that claims a monopoly on the use of violence within a territory

stockholders' revolt: the refusal of a corporation's stockholders to rubber-stamp decisions made by its managers

subsistence economy: the type of economy in which human groups live off the land with little or no surplus

totalitarianism: a form of government that exerts almost total control over the people

traditional authority: authority based on custom

universal citizenship: the idea that everyone has the same basic rights by virtue of being born in a country (or by immigrating and becoming a naturalized citizen)

voter apathy: indifference and inaction on the part of individuals or groups with respect to the political process

welfare (or state) capitalism: an economic system in which individuals own the means of production but the state regulates many economic activities for the welfare of the population

ANSWERS FOR MULTIPLE CHOICE QUESTIONS

1. d   All of the above is correct. Power was defined by Max Weber; is the ability to carry out one's will in spite of resistance from others; and it is an inevitable part of everyday life. (264)
2. d   All of the above is correct. Traditional authority is the hallmark of preliterate groups; it is based on custom; and it was identified by Max Weber. (265)
3. c   The least stable type of authority is the charismatic. (267)
4. d   None of the above is correct. Democracy first occurred in Athens, not the United States. Democracy is a system of government in which authority derives from the people, not from elected officials. Democracy was practiced in Athens two thousand years ago, so it is not a modern idea. (268)
5. b   An individual who seizes power and imposes his will onto the people is a dictator. (269)
6. c   A form of government that exerts almost total control is a totalitarian regime. (269)
7. b   Studies of voting patterns in the United States show that voting varies by age, race/ethnicity, education, employment, and income. (271)
8. b   Today in the United States, approximately two out of every five eligible voters do not vote for the President of the United States; this low voter turnout reflects both alienation (the feeling that voting will not affect your life one way or another) and apathy (the feeling that your vote won't make a difference anyway). (271)
9. d   All of the above is correct. Lobbyists are people paid to influence legislation on behalf of their clients; are employed by special-interest groups; and are a major force in American politics. (271)
10. d   All of the above is correct. Functionalists believe that any one group is prevented from gaining control of the government because of the existence of pluralism, the use of checks and balances, and the presence of many interest groups to which politicians must pay attention. (274-275)
11. c   According to conflict theorists, the ruling class is made up of people whose backgrounds and orientations to life are so similar that they automatically share the same goals. (276)
12. c   Hunting and gathering societies are characterized by a subsistence economy. (277)
13. d   All of the above is correct. Industrial economies are based on fuel-powered machines, created a tremendous, and emerged following the invention of the steam engine. (277)
14. b   Workers who package fish, process copper into electrical wire, and turn trees into lumber and paper are in the secondary sector. (277)
15. d   All of the above is correct. Postindustrial economies are characterized by a large surplus of goods; extensive trade among nations; and a "global village." (278)

16. b A primary reason why the average work week of U.S. workers has increased in recent years is because, as U.S. firms struggle to remain competitive in the global marketplace, they find it cheaper to pay overtime than to hire more workers; additional workers means additional payments for unemployment, medical, and retirement benefits. (279)

17. d Private ownership of the means of production is an essential feature of capitalism. (281)

18. d The term "welfare capitalism" refers to a system in which private individuals own the businesses and pursue profits, but they do so within a system of laws designed to protect the welfare of the population. This is the kind of capitalism that now exists in the United States. (281)

19. b An economic system characterized by the public ownership of the means of production, central planning, and the distribution of goods without a profit motive is socialism. (282)

20. c Unemployment compensation, subsidized housing, welfare, minimum wage, and Social Security are all examples of socialist practices that are now part of U.S. society. (283)

21. c The joint ownership of a business enterprise, whose liabilities and obligations are separate from those of its owners, is a corporation. (284)

22. c The elite who sit on the boards of directors of not just one but several companies are referred to as interlocking directorates. (285)

23. b The sociological significance of multinational corporations is that increasingly they have become detached from the interests and values of their country of origin. They owe allegiance not to any nation but only to profits and market shares. (285)

24. d "All of the above" is correct. Today, national boundaries are becoming less meaningful because of the embrace of capitalism by more and more nations, the worldwide flow of information, capital and goods, and the formation of large economic and political units like the European Union. (285)

25. b As societies industrialize, they become based on organic solidarity. (286)

ANSWERS FOR TRUE-FALSE QUESTIONS

1. *True.* (264)
2. *False.* Authority, not coercion, refers to legitimate power. (264)
3. *True.* As societies industrialize, traditional authority is undermined; however, it never totally dies out. Parental authority provides an excellent example. (265)
4. *True.* (265)
5. *True.* (267)
6. *True.* (268)
7. *True.* (268)
8. *False.* The idea of universal citizenship caught on very slowly in the United States. (268-269)
9. *False.* Employment and income do affect the probability that people will vote. (271)
10. *False.* Most political action committees do not represent broad social interests but rather, stand for narrow financial concerns, such as the dairy, oil, banking, and construction industries. (272)
11. *True.* (274)
12. *False.* Conflict theorists do not believe that the ruling class is a group that meets together and agrees on specific matters. Rather, it consists of people whose backgrounds and orientations to life are so similar that they automatically share the same goals. (276)
13. *False.* Pastoral and horticultural societies, not hunting and gathering societies, were the first economies to have a surplus. (277)
14. *True.* (277)
15. *False.* Postindustrial economy is based on information processing and providing services. (277)

16.   *True.* (279)
17.   *True.* (281)
18.   *True.* (283)
19.   *False.* According to convergence theory, as nations industrialize they will become more similar to one another. However, rather than adopting the traits of one type of economic system or another, they will reflect a hybrid or mixed economy, combining elements of both. (283)
20.   *True.* (284)

ANSWERS FOR FILL-IN QUESTIONS

1.   STATE, synonymous with government, is the source of legitimate violence in society. (265)
2.   TRADITIONAL AUTHORITY is based on custom. (265)
3.   Bureaucratic authority also is called RATIONAL-LEGAL AUTHORITY. (265)
4.   An independent city whose power radiates outward, bringing the adjacent area under its rule is a CITY-STATE. (267)
5.   DIRECT DEMOCRACY is a form of democracy in which the eligible voters meet together to discuss issues and make their decisions. (268)
6.   The concept that birth and residence in a country impart basic rights is known as CITIZENSHIP. (268)
7.   A form of government that exerts almost total control over the people is TOTALITARIANISM. (269)
8.   VOTER APATHY refers to indifference and inaction on the part of individuals or groups with respect to the political process. (271)
9.   POWER ELITE refers to the top people in leading corporations, the most powerful generals and admirals of the armed forces, and certain elite politicians. (275)
10.   ECONOMY is the term for a system of distribution of goods and services. (276)
11.   Barry Bluestone and Bennett Harrison use the expression "THE GREAT AMERICAN U-TURN" to refer to the net decline in the wages and standard of living of U.S. workers. (280)
12.   Under DEMOCRATIC SOCIALISM both the state and individuals engage in the production and distribution of goods and services. (283)
13.   The view that as capitalist and socialist economic systems each adopt features of the other, a hybrid (or mixed) economic system may emerge is CONVERGENCE THEORY. (283)
14.   The refusal of a corporation's stockholders to rubber-stamp decisions made by its managers is referred to as STOCKHOLDERS' REVOLT. (285)
15.   Durkheim's term for the unity that comes from being involved in similar occupations or activities is MECHANICAL SOLIDARITY. (286)

ANSWERS TO MATCH THESE CONCEPTS WITH THEIR DEFINITIONS

1. c   charismatic authority: *authority based on individual traits*
2. d   market restraints: *laws/regulations limiting the capacity to manufacture or distribute goods*
3. e   totalitarianism: *government that exerts almost complete control over the people*
4. b   power: *the ability to carry out one's will, even over others' resistance*
5. f   economy: *a system for distributing goods and services*
6. a   market forces: *the laws of supply and demand*

CHAPTER 12
MARRIAGE AND FAMILY

☞ CHAPTER SUMMARY

- Because there are so many cultural variations on family structure, it is hard to define. Nevertheless, family is defined broadly as two or more people who consider themselves related by blood, marriage or adoption. Marriage and family patterns vary remarkably across cultures, but four universal themes in marriage are mate selection, descent, inheritance, and authority.

- According to the functionalist perspective, the family carries out important social functions. Conversely, conflict theorists focus on how families help perpetuate inequality, especially gender relations. Symbolic interactionists focus on the meanings that people give their marital relationships, particularly in regard to communication between the partners.

- The family life cycle is analyzed in terms of love and courtship, marriage, childbirth, child rearing, and the family in later life. Within the United States, patterns of marriage, childbearing, and childrearing vary by social class, age, religion, and race.

- Family diversity in U.S. culture includes social class as well as racial and ethnic differences. One-parent families, childless families, blended families, and gay families represent some of the different types of families today.

- Trends in U.S. families include postponement of marriage, cohabitation, grandparenting, the emergence of the "sandwich generation" who are caught between caring for their own children and caring for their elderly parents, and commuter marriages.

- Studies on divorce have focused on problems in measuring divorce, the impact of divorce on children and ex-spouses, and remarriage. While time seems to heal most children's wounds over the divorce of their parents, research suggests that a minority carry the scars of divorce into adulthood. Men and women experience divorce differently; for men, this event often results in a weakening of their relationships with children, for women it means a decline in their standard of living.

- Violence and abuse--including battering, marital rape, and incest --are the "dark side" of family life. Researchers have identified variables that help marriages last and be happy.

- The trends for the future include a continued increased in cohabitation, births to unmarried mothers, and postponement of marriage. The continuing growth in the numbers of working wives will impact on marital balance of power.

☞ LEARNING OBJECTIVES

As you read Chapter 12, use these learning objectives to organize your notes. After completing your reading, briefly state an answer to each of the objectives, and review the text pages in parentheses.

1. Explain why it is difficult to define the term "family." (292-293)
2. Identify the common cultural themes that run through marriage and the family. (293-294)
3. Discuss the functionalists, conflict, and symbolic interaction perspectives regarding marriage and family. (294-299)
4. Outline the major developments in each stage of the family life cycle. (299-304)
5. State the unique problems experienced by African-American, Latino, and Asian-American families. (304-307)

6. Identify the major concerns of one-parent families, families without children, blended families, and gay families. (307-309)
7. Describe the current trends affecting marriage and family life in the United States. (309-312)
8. State why it is difficult to measure divorce accurately. (312)
9. Note some of the adjustment problems of children and ex-spouses following divorce. (313-314)
10. Explain the "dark side" of family life. (314-316)
11. List some of the characteristics which tend to be present in marriages that work. Explain how happy couples approach problems. (316)
12. Summarize conclusions regarding the future of marriage and family in the United States. (316-317)

☞ CHAPTER OUTLINE

I. **Marriage and Family in Global Perspective**
   A. The term family is difficult to define as there are many types.
      1. In some societies men have more than one wife (polygyny) or women have more than one husband (polyandry).
      2. A broad definition of family is a group of two or more people who considers itself related by blood, marriage, or adoption, and lives together (or has lived together). A household, in contrast to a family, consists of all people who occupy the same housing unit.
      3. A family is classified as a nuclear family (husband, wife, and children) or an extended family (a nuclear family plus other relatives who live together).
      4. The family of orientation is the family in which a person grows up, while the family of procreation is the family formed when a couple's first child is born. A person who is married but has not had a child is part of a couple, not a family.
      5. Marriage is a group's approved mating arrangements, usually marked by a ritual.
   B. Common Cultural Themes
      1. Each group establishes norms to govern who can and cannot marry. Endogamy is the practice of marrying within one's own group, while exogamy is the practice of marrying outside of one's own group. Some norms of mate selection are written into law, others are informal.
      2. Three major patterns of descent (tracing kinship over generations) are: (a) bilateral (descent traced on both the mother's and the father's side); (b) patrilineal (descent traced only on the father's side); and (c) matrilineal (descent traced only on the mother's side).
      3. Mate selection and descent are regulated in all societies in order to provide an orderly way of passing property, etc., to the next generation. In a bilateral system, property passes to males and females; in a patrilineal system, property passes only to males; in a matrilineal system, property passes only to females.
      4. Patriarchy is a social system in which men dominate women; this type of organization characterizes all societies. No historical records exist of a true matriarchy (a system in which women as a group dominate men). In an egalitarian social system authority is more or less equally divided between men and women.
II. **Marriage and Family in Theoretical Perspective**

A.   The Functionalist Perspective
   1.   The family is universal because it serves functions essential to the well-being of society: economic production, socialization of children, care of the sick and aged, recreation, sexual control, and reproduction.
   2.   The incest taboo (rules specifying which people are too closely related to have sex or marry) helps the family avoid role confusion and forces people to look outside the family for marriage partners, creating a network of support.
   3.   The nuclear family has few people it can depend on for material and emotional support; thus, the members of a nuclear family are vulnerable to "emotional overload." The relative isolation of the nuclear family makes it easier for the "dark side" of families (incest and other types of abuse) to emerge.

B.   The Conflict Perspective
   1.   One of the consequences of married women working for pay is a reshuffling of power within the home. Disputes develop over how to change the traditional division of labor in order to accommodate women's outside labor.
   2.   Arlie Hochschild found that after an 8-hour day at work, women typically work a "second shift" at home; this means that wives work an extra month of 24-hour days each year. The result is that working wives feel deep discontent.

C.   The Symbolic Interactionist Perspective
   1.   Symbolic interactionists focus on meanings people give their marital relationships.
   2.   New couples merge their worlds (the feminine and the masculine) by conversation in which they share ideas and feelings and, over time, see things from increasingly closer perspectives. Talk is also an essential part of emotional labor, the building of intimacy by sharing deeply personal thoughts and feelings. Women typically do most of the couple's emotional labor.

III.   **The Family Life Cycle**
   A.   Romantic love provides the ideological context in which people in the U.S. seek mates and form families. Romantic love has two components: (1) emotional, a feeling of sexual attraction; and (2) cognitive, the feeling we describe as being "in love."
   B.   The social channels of love and marriage in the United States include age, education, social class, race, and religion.
      1.   Homogamy is the tendency of people with similar characteristics to marry one another, usually resulting from propinquity (spatial nearness). People living near one another tend to marry.
      2.   Interracial marriage is an exception to these social patterns. In the U.S., about 5 percent of the population marries someone from a different race. At the same time, interracial marriages are becoming more acceptable.
   C.   Marital satisfaction usually decreases with the birth of a child, according to Martin Whyte. Lillian Rubin found that social class influences how couples adjust to children. Working-class couples are more likely to have a baby nine months after marriage and have major interpersonal and financial problems; middle-class parents are more prepared because of more resources, postponement of the birth of the first child, and more time to adjust to one another.
   D.   Traditionally childrearing automatically fell on the mother. As more mothers become employed outside the home, this has changed.

1. In comparing the overall child care arrangements of married couples and single mothers, the arrangements appear to be quite similar. The main difference is the role played by the child's father while the mother is at work. For married couples, almost one of four children is cared for by the father, while for single mothers this arrangement occurs for about only one of fourteen children. Grandparents often help to fill the child care gap left by absent fathers in single mother homes.

2. Birth order is significant in child rearing: first-borns tend to be disciplined more than children who follow but also receive more attention; when the next child arrives, the first born competes to maintain attention.

3. Social class is also important in child rearing. According to Melvin Kohn, parents socialize children into the norms of their respective work worlds. Working-class parents want their children to behave in conformity with social expectations. Middle-class parents are more concerned that their children develop curiosity, self-expression, and self-control.

E. The empty nest is a married couple's domestic situation after the last child has left home.

1. The empty-nest is thought to signal a difficult adjustment for women; however Lillian Rubin argues that this syndrome is largely a myth because women's satisfaction generally increases when the last child leaves home. Many couples report a renewed sense of companionship at this time.

2. With prolonged education and a growing cost of establishing households, U.S. children are leaving home much later, or after initially leaving home they are returning.

3. Women are more likely than men to face the problem of adjusting to widowhood, for not only does the average woman live longer than a man but she has also married a man older than herself.

IV. **Diversity in U.S. Families**

A. As with other groups, the family life of African Americans differs with social class.

1. The upper class is concerned with maintaining family lineage and preserving their privilege and wealth; the middle-class focuses on achievement and respectability; poor African-American families face the problems that poverty brings.

2. Marriage squeeze (fewer unmarried males than unmarried females) exists among African Americans; women thus are more likely to marry men with less education, or who are unemployed or divorced, or to remain single.

B. The effects of social class on families also apply to Latinos. In addition, families differ by country of origin.

1. Latino families are distinguishable by the Spanish language, Roman Catholic religion, and strong family ties with a disapproval of divorce.

2. Machismo, the emphasis on male strength and dominance, also seems to be a characteristic of Latino families. As a result, the husband-father plays a stronger role than in white or African-American families, and the wife-mother deals with family and child-related decisions.

C. Bob Suzuki points out that while Chinese-American and Japanese-American families have adopted the nuclear family pattern of the United States, they have retained Confucian values that provide a distinct framework to family life: humanism, collectivity, self-discipline, hierarchy, respect for the elderly, moderation, and obligation.

D. There has been an increase in one-parent families.

1.   This increase is due to the high divorce rate and the sharp increase in unwed motherhood.

2.   Most of these families are poor; the reason for the poverty is that most are headed by women who earn less than men.

3.   Children from one-parent families are more likely to drop out of school, become delinquent, be poor as adults, divorce, and have children outside of marriage.

E.   There are a growing number of families who are voluntarily childless. There are different reasons why a couple chooses not to have a child: a weak relationship, financial constraints, or a demanding career are among the reasons researchers have identified.

1.   The highest rate of voluntary childlessness is among Asian Americans and whites, the lowest among Latinos.

2.   More education, careers for women, effective contraception, abortion, the costs of rearing children, as well as changing attitudes toward children and goals in life, all contribute the increase in childless and childfree marriages.

F.   A blended family is one whose members were once part of other families (two divorced persons marry, bringing children into a new family unit). Blended families are increasing in number and often experience complicated family relationships.

G.   Although marriage between homosexuals is illegal in the United States, many homosexual couples live in monogamous relationships that they refer to as marriage. They have the usual problems of heterosexual marriages: housework, money, careers, problems with relatives, and sexual adjustment.

V.   Trends in U.S. Families

A.   The average age of U.S. brides is the oldest it has been since records first were kept. Many young people postpone marriage, but not cohabitation; if cohabitation were counted as marriage, rates of family formation and age at first marriage would show little change.

B.   Cohabitation, living together as an unmarried couple, has increased about seven times in two decades. About half the couples who marry have cohabited; this rate is lower in the United States than in Canada and most European countries. Commitment is the essential difference between cohabitation and marriage: marriage assumes permanence; cohabiting assumes remaining together "as long as it works out."

C.   As previously discussed, there has been an increase in the number of births to unmarried mothers.

1.   In the ten industrialized nations for which data are available, all except Japan have experienced sharp increases in births to unmarried mothers--the U.S. rate falls in the middle third of these nations.

2.   Industrialization alone is too simple an explanation for this increase. To more fully understand this trend, future research must focus on customs and values embedded within particular cultures.

D.   With longer life expectancy, more people are living to see their grandchildren and great-grandchildren. Three main styles of grandparenting have been identified: "recreational specialists" who are involved in activities and outings with their grandchildren; "ritualists" who carry on a symbolic relationship with their grandchildren through letters and gifts; and "everyday actives" who participate in the routine care of their grandchildren.

E.   The "sandwich generation" refers to people who find themselves sandwiched between two generations, responsible for the care of their children and for their own aging parents.

F.   Commuter marriages, in which the partners live and/or work in different cities, states, or countries, are also on the increase. The primary benefits for couples in commuter marriages are career development, personal satisfaction, economic gains, independence, and self-sufficiency. However, commuter marriages are more fragile than those in which the husband and wife live together, and there are often feelings of loneliness and isolation.

VI.   Divorce and Remarriage

A.   The United States has the highest divorce rate in the industrialized world; estimates suggest that as many as two-third of all couples getting married today may eventually divorce.

      1.   Although the divorce rate is reported at 50 percent, this statistic is misleading because with rare exceptions those who divorce do not come from the group who married that year.

      2.   An alternative is to compare the number of divorces in a given year to the entire group of married couples; this amount to 2.1 percent of all married couples getting a divorce.

      3.   A third way is to calculate the number of divorce persons for every thousand married people; this measure shows that divorce has tripled in the last two decades, although it leveled off in about 1981.

B.   Each year over one million children are in families affected by divorce. Divorce threatens a child's world.

      1.   Research has found that the grown children of divorce feel more distant from parents than children from intact families, perhaps because they feel their parents backed out of an implicit contract to provide a stable home for their children.

      2.   Several factors help children adjust to divorce: both parents show understanding and affection; the parent with whom the child lives is making a good adjustment; family routines are consistent; the family has adequate money for its needs; and, according to preliminary studies, the child lives with the parent of the same sex.

      3.   Children adjust better when a second adult can be counted on for support.

C.   A new fathering pattern known as serial fatherhood is beginning to emerge.

      1.   Divorced fathers tend to live with, support, and play an active fathering role with children of the woman to whom they are currently married or with whom they are currently living.

      2.   Over time, contact with their children from a previous marriage diminishes; one study found that in a typical month, two-thirds of children of divorce have no contact with their biological father.

D.   Women are more likely than men to feel divorce gives them a new chance at life. Divorce likely spells economic hardship for women, especially mothers of small children; in the first post-divorce year, the standard of living for women with dependent children declines significantly.

E.   About 80 percent of divorced persons remarry, with an average lapse between divorce and remarriage of about two years.

      1.   Men are more likely than women to remarry, perhaps because they have a larger pool of potential mates from which to select.

      2.   The divorce rate for remarried people without children is the same as that of first marriages. Those who bring children into their new marriage, however, are more likely to divorce again; this suggests that remarriages with children are

more difficult because as a society we have not developed norms to govern these relationships.

VII. Two Sides of Family Life
A. Abuse: Battering, Marital Rape, and Incest
1. Although wives are about as likely to attack their husbands as husbands are to attack their wives, it is generally the husband who lands the last and most damaging blow. Family violence follows certain "social channels" making some individuals more likely to be abusers or victims than others.
2. Marital rape most commonly occurs during a marital separation or breakup. Non-battering rape is where a husband forces his wife to have sex, with no intent to hurt her physically. Battering rape adds the element of intentionally inflicting physical pain to retaliate for some supposed wrongdoing on the wife's part. Husbands who commit perverted rape seem to be sexually aroused by the violent elements of rape and force their wives to submit to unusual sexual acts.
3. Incest is sexual relations between relatives, such as brothers and sisters or parents and children. It is most likely to occur in families that are socially isolated, and is more common than it previously was thought to be.
B. There are a number of factors that make marriages work. Variables that produce happy marriages include: spending time together, appreciating one another, having a commitment to the marriage, using good communications, confronting and working through problems together, and putting more into the marriage than you take out.

VIII. The Future of Marriage and Family
A. Martin Whyte concluded that there is reason for optimism about the state of marriage in the United States. The vast proportion of Americans will continue to marry; many of those who divorce will remarry and "try again."
B. It is likely that cohabitation will increase, as will the age at first marriage, and the number of women joining the work force, with a resulting shift in marital power toward a more egalitarian norm.

☞ GLOSSARY OF DIFFICULT-TO-UNDERSTAND WORDS

bickering: arguing over trivial matters (302)
bolster: to re-enforce; to give a boost to (296)
driving a wedge: doing something that would result in a separation (305)
e-mail: electronic mail; communicating by using telephone lines to connect to computers (312)
enmeshed: tangled up in (295)
extols: praises highly (300)
facilitates: makes something possible (295)
fax: a method of communicating by sending messages between machines that are connected to telephone lines (312)
flagging: drooping (298)
nagged: complained (298)
rickety: not well built, thus dangerous (299)
subservient: subordinate (295)
willy-nilly: randomly (301)
wrenching away: painfully removing (304)

☞ KEY TERMS TO DEFINE

After studying the chapter, define each of the following terms. Then check your work by referring to the answers beginning at page 205 of this Study Guide.

bilateral system	family of orientation	matrilineal system
blended family	family of procreation	nuclear family
cohabitation	homogamy	patriarchy
emotional love	household	patrilineal system
empty nest	incest	polyandry
endogamy	incest taboo	polygyny
exogamy	machismo	romantic love
extended family	marriage	serial fatherhood
family	matriarchy	system of descent

☞ KEY PEOPLE

State the major theoretical contributions or findings of these people.

Peter Berger	Kathleen Gerson	Pepper Schwartz
Philip Blumstein	Christine Grella	Susan Steinmetz
Urie Bronfenbrenner	Arlie Hochschild	Nicholas Stinnett
Andrew Cherlin	William Jankowiak	Murray Straus
David Finkelhor	Hansfried Kellner	Bob Suzuki
Edward Fischer	Melvin Kohn	Lenore Weitzman
Frank Furstenberg	Lillian Rubin	Martin Whyte
Richard Gelles	Diana Russell	Kersti Yllo

☞ SELF-TEST

After completing this self-test, check your answers against the Answer Key beginning on page 205 of this Study Guide and against the text on page(s) indicated in parentheses.

MULTIPLE CHOICE QUESTIONS

1.   Polyandry is: (292)
        a.   a marriage in which a woman has more than one husband.
        b.   a marriage in which a man has more than one wife.
        c.   male control of a society or group.
        d.   female control of a society or group.

2.   The family of orientation: (293)
        a.   is the family formed when a couple's first child is born.
        b.   is the same thing as an extended family.
        c.   is the same as the family of procreation.
        d.   None of the above.

3.   Endogamy: (293)
      a.   is the practice or marrying outside one's group.
      b.   is the practice of marrying within one's own group.
      c.   is the practice of marrying someone within one's own family.
      d.   None of the above.

4.   In a matrilineal system: (293)
      a.   descent is figured only on the mother's side.
      b.   children are not considered related to their mother's relatives.
      c.   descent is traced on both the mother's and the father's side.
      d.   descent is figured only on the father's side.

5.   According to functionalists, the family: (294)
      a.   serves very different functions from society to society.
      b.   serves certain essential functions in all societies.
      c.   has very few functions left.
      d.   is no longer universal.

6.   The incest taboo: (295)
      a.   is rules specifying the degrees of kinship that prohibit sex or marriage.
      b.   helps families avoid role confusion.
      c.   facilitates the socialization of children.
      d.   All of the above.

7.   Marital communication is an important research topic for: (298)
      a.   functionalists.
      b.   conflict theorists.
      c.   symbolic interactionists.
      d.   None of the above.

8.   Among most people in the U.S., romantic love: (299)
      a.   is considered to be a relic of the past.
      b.   is considered to be the single most important factor in marriage.
      c.   is considered to be somewhat less important than the financial potential of the spouse.
      d.   None of the above.

9.   The tendency of people with similar characteristics to marry one another is: (301)
      a.   propinquity.
      b.   erotic selection.
      c.   homogamy.
      d.   heterogamy.

10.   A national survey found fathers are the caregivers for almost _____ percent of children. (303)
      a.   25
      b.   30
      c.   35
      d.   40

11.   The empty nest syndrome: (304)
        a.   is not a reality for most parents.
        b.   causes couples to feel a lack of companionship.
        c.   is easier for women who have not worked outside the home.
        d.   None of the above.

12.   According to your text, a major concern of upper class African-American families is: (305)
        a.   achievement and respectability.
        b.   problems of poverty.
        c.   maintaining family lineage.
        d.   All of the above.

13.   Machismo: (306)
        a.   distinguishes Latino families from other groups.
        b.   is an emphasis on male strength and dominance.
        c.   exists where the Chicano husband-father plays a strong role in his family.
        d.   All of the above.

14.   The primary source of strain for one-parent families is: (307)
        a.   divorce.
        b.   poverty.
        c.   delinquency.
        d.   All of the above.

15.   Children from single-parent families are more likely to: (307-308)
        a.   drop out of school.
        b.   become delinquent.
        c.   be poor as adults.
        d.   All of the above.

16.   A family whose members were once part of other families is known as a: (308)
        a.   reconstituted family.
        b.   mixed family.
        c.   blended family.
        d.   multiple nuclei family.

17.   Cohabitation: (310)
        a.   is the condition of living together as an unmarried couple.
        b.   has increased about seven times in just two decades.
        c.   has occurred before about half of all couples marry.
        d.   All of the above.

18.   The "sandwich generation" refers to: (311)
        a.   grandparents who are primary caregivers for latchkey grandchildren.
        b.   children who survive on peanut butter sandwiches.
        c.   people who find themselves responsible for the care of children and aging parents.
        d.   people caught between families due to divorce.

19.   The percentage of all divorced persons who remarry is: (314)
       a.   less than 50 percent.
       b.   about 50 percent.
       c.   about 80 percent.
       d.   unknown.

20.   The highest rates of marital violence are found among: (315)
       a.   families with high incomes.
       b.   families living in large urban areas.
       c.   people over thirty.
       d.   white-collar workers.

TRUE-FALSE QUESTIONS

T F   1.   Families are people who live together in the same housing unit. (293)
T F   2.   The best example of endogamy is the incest taboo, which prohibits sex and marriage among certain relatives. (293)
T F   3.   Functionalists believe that the incest taboo helps the family to avoid role confusion. (295)
T F   4.   Conflict theorists believe that one of the consequences of married women working for pay is a reshuffling of power in the home. (296)
T F   5.   The phrase "second shift" refers to the time a person spends on household chores following a full day's work. (297)
T F   6.   According to Arlie Hochschild, it is very important for a husband to express appreciation to his wife for her being so organized that she can handle both work for wages and the second shift at home. (298)
T F   7.   Men and women are equally involved in doing emotional labor. (299)
T F   8.   Love and marriage channels include age, education, social class, race, and religion. (301)
T F   9.   Social class does not affect the ways couples adjust to the arrival of children. (302)
T F   10.   Firstborns tend to be disciplined more than children who follow. (302)
T F   11.   Regardless of the type of household, less than one in five preschoolers of working parents is cared for in organized child care facilities. (303)
T F   12.   Researchers have found that most husbands and wives experience the empty nest when their last child leaves home. (304)
T F   13.   Women are about as likely as men to face the problem of adjusting to widowhood. (304)
T F   14.   Marriage between homosexuals is legal in several states, including California. (308)
T F   15.   Americans have become more tolerant of cohabitation. (310)
T F   16.   Among industrialized nations, the United States ranks at the top in terms of the rate of births to unmarried women. (310)
T F   17.   A "commuter marriage" involves a husband who commutes into the city to work and a wife who remains at home in the suburbs all day, caring for their children. (312)
T F   18.   The usually pattern of father-child contact following a divorce is for the contact to be fairly high for several years while the child is young, but then to drop off significantly as the child moves through adolescence. (313)
T F   19.   Different studies of marital rape suggest that this form of domestic violence occurs in approximately 10-15 percent of all marriages. (315)
T F   20.   In the future, between 90 and 95 percent of all Americans will continue to marry. (317)

FILL-IN QUESTIONS

1.   A marriage in which a man has more than one wife is _____. (292)
2.   A _____ consists of all people who occupy the same housing unit. (293)
3.   A(n) _____ is a family consisting of a husband, wife, and child(ren). (293)
4.   The family you grow up in is called your _____. (293)
5.   A social group's approval arrangement for mating, usually marked by a ritual ceremony of some sort, is _____. (293)
6.   Those societies in which descent is only counted on the father's side are _____. (293)
7.   _____ is the practice of marrying outside one's group. (293)
8.   Female control of a society or group is a(n) _____. (294)
9.   In general, women do more of the _____ in a relationship, because they are more attentive to another's emotional needs and share deep, personal thoughts, feelings and aspirations. (298)
10. Feelings of erotic attraction, accompanied by an idealization of the other, is the definition of _____. (299)
11. _____ is the tendency of people with similar characteristics to get married. (301)
12. A married couple's domestic situation after the last child has left home is sometimes referred to as the _____. (304)
13. An emphasis on male strength and dominance is _____. (306)
14. The term sociologists use to describe adults who are living together in a sexual relationship without being married is _____. (310)
15. The pattern of divorced fathers living with, supporting, and playing an active fathering role with the children of the woman with whom they are currently involved is known as _____. (313)

MATCH THESE CONCEPTS WITH THEIR DEFINITIONS

___1. bilateral
___2. romantic love
___3. household
___4. incest taboo
___5. homogamy
___6. blended family
___7. empty nest
___8. machismo
___9. marriage
__10. polyandry
__11. polygyny
__12. serial fatherhood
__13. emotional labor
__14. endogamy
__15. exogamy

a. *a system of descent that counts both parents' sides*
b. *practice of marrying outside one's group*
c. *marriage in which a woman has more than one husband*
d. *rules specifying the degree of kinship that prohibits sex or marriage*
e. *a couple's domestic situation after the last child leaves home*
f. *the approved mating arrangements, usually marked by a ritual*
g. *tendency of people with similar characteristics to marry one another*
h. *marriage in which man has more than one wife*
i. *feelings of erotic attention*
j. *practice of marrying within one's own group*
k. *efforts aimed at maintaining intimacy*
l. *all the persons occupying the same housing unit*
m. *an emphasis on male strength and dominance*
n. *a family whose members were once part of other families*
o. *when a man parents children of the woman with whom he is living*

"DOWN-TO-EARTH SOCIOLOGY"

1.   What was your reaction to the description family life in Sweden (p. 296)? Should similar benefits be available to new families in the U.S.? What consequences would this have for family life? What are some of the obstacles to having such a program in this country?

2.   Do you think the second shift (pp. 297-298), is a temporary problem or a long-range problem in many families? How will you resolve problems such as this in your family?

3.   Would you like to have your marriage arranged for you by your parents? Consider this as you read "East is East and West is West" (p. 300). What would you gain and lose by this?

4.   After reading about the experiences of Russian Jews in the United States (p. 305), in what ways can you say that the Russian family is both a help and a hinderance to assimilation? In general, what is it about the society and culture of each country that makes the Russian family functional in Russia and dysfunctional in the United States?

☞ ANSWERS FOR CHAPTER 16

DEFINITIONS OF KEY TERMS

bilateral system: a system of reckoning descent that counts both the mother's and the father's side

blended family: a family whose members were once part of other families

cohabitation: unmarried people living together in a sexual relationship

emotional labor: efforts to maintain intimacy, such as listening, being attentive to another's emotional needs, and sharing deep personal thoughts, feeling and aspirations

empty nest: a married couple's domestic situation after the last child has left home

endogamy: the practice of marrying within one's own group

exogamy: the practice of marrying outside one's group

extended family: a nuclear family plus other relatives, such as grandparents, uncles and aunts, who live together

family: two or more people who consider themselves related by blood, marriage, or adoption

family of orientation: the family in which a person grows up

family of procreation: the family formed when a couple's first child is born

homogamy: the tendency of people with similar characteristics to marry one another

household: all persons who occupy the same housing unit

incest: sexual relations between specified relatives, such as brothers and sisters or parents and children

incest taboo: rules specifying the degrees of kinship that prohibit sex or marriage

machismo: an emphasis on male strength and dominance

marriage: a group's approved mating arrangements, usually marked by a ritual of some sort

matriarchy: authority vested in females; female control of a society or group

matrilineal system: a system of reckoning descent that counts only the mother's side

nuclear family: a family consisting of a husband, wife, and child(ren)

patriarchy: a society in which authority is vested in males; male control of a society or group

patrilineal system: a system of reckoning descent that counts only the father's side

polyandry: a marriage in which a woman has more than one husband

polygyny: a marriage in which a man has more than one wife

romantic love: feelings of erotic attraction accompanied by an idealization of the other

serial fatherhood: a pattern of parenting in which a father, after divorce, reduces contact with his own children, serves as a father to the children of the woman he marries or lives with, then ignores them after moving in with or marrying another woman; this pattern repeats

system of descent: how kinship is traced over the generations

ANSWERS FOR MULTIPLE CHOICE QUESTIONS

1. a   Polyandry is a marriage in which a woman has more than one husband. (292)
2. d   None of the above is correct; family of orientation is the one in which a person grows up. (293)
3. b   Endogamy is the practice of marrying within one's own group. (293)
4. a   In a matrilineal system descent is figured only on the mother's side. (293)
5. b   According to functionalists, the family serves certain essential functions in all societies. (294)
6. d   All of the above is correct. The incest taboo is rules specifying the degrees of kinship that prohibit sex or marriage; helps families avoid role confusion; and facilitates the socialization of children. (295)
7. c   Marital communication is an important research topic for symbolic interactionists. (298)
8. b   Most people in the U.S. consider romantic love to be the single most important factor in marriage. (299)
9. c   The tendency of people with similar characteristics to marry one another is homogamy. (301)
10. a   A recent national survey found that 23 percent of children in two-parent households were being cared for by their fathers. (303)
11. a   The empty nest syndrome is not a reality for most parents. (304)
12. c   According to your text, a major concern of upper class African-American families is how to maintain family lineage. (305)
13. d   All of the above is correct. Machismo, an emphasis on male strength and dominance, distinguishes Latino families from other groups; and is seen in some Chicano families where the husband-father plays a strong role in his family. (306)
14. b   The primary source of stress for one-parent families is poverty. (307)
15. d   All of the above is correct. Children from single-parent families are more likely to drop out of school, become delinquent, and be poor as adults. (307-308)
16. c   A family whose members were once part of other families is known as a blended family. (308)
17. d   All of the above is correct. Cohabitation, the condition of living together as an unmarried couple, has increased about seven times in just two decades; it has occurred before about half of all couples marry. (310)
18. c   The "sandwich generation" refers to people who find themselves responsible for the care of their own children and their aging parents simultaneously. (311)
19. c   The percentage of all divorced persons who remarry is about 80 percent. (314)
20. b   The highest rates of marital violence are found among families living in large urban areas. (315)

ANSWERS FOR TRUE-FALSE QUESTIONS

1.   *False.* Households are people who live together in the same housing unit; families consist of two or more people who consider themselves related by blood, marriage or adoption. (293)
2.   *False.* The incest taboo, which prohibits sex and marriage among certain relatives, is an example of exogamy, not endogamy. (293)

3.   *True.* (295)
4.   *True.* (296)
5.   *True.* (297)
6.   *False.* According to Arlie Hochschild, one of the strategies used by some husbands to resist doing housework is "substitute offerings"--expressing appreciation to the wife for her being so organized that she can handle both work for wages and the second shift at home--when, instead, it would be better if he actually shared the work with her. (298)
7.   *False.* Sociologists have found that women, not men, do most of the emotional labor. (299)
8.   *True.* (301)
9.   *False.* Social class does significantly influence the way in which couples adjust to the arrival of children. (302)
10.   *True.* (302)
11.   *True.* (303)
12.   False. Researchers have found that most husbands and wives do not experience the empty nest when their last child leaves home. Often just the opposite occurs because the couple now has more time and money to use at their own discretion. (304)
13.   *False.* Women are more likely than men to face the problem of widowhood, not only because they live longer, but also because they are likely to have married older men. (304)
14.   *False.* Marriage between homosexuals is not legal in any state; however, some gay churches conduct marriage ceremonies which are not recognized in the eyes of the law. (308)
15.   *True.* (310)
16.   *False.* Among industrialized nations, the United States ranks in the middle one-third in terms of the rate of births to unmarried women. (310)
17.   *False.* A "commuter marriage" involves a husband and wife who live in separate cities, travelling on week-ends, to spend time together. (312)
18.   *False.* The pattern is for contact to be high during the first 1-2 years following the divorce and then decline rapidly. (313)
19.   *True.* (315)
20.   *True.* (317)

ANSWERS FOR FILL-IN QUESTIONS

1.   A marriage in which a man has more than one wife is POLYGYNY. (292)
2.   A HOUSEHOLD consists of all people who occupy the same housing unit. (293)
3.   A(n) NUCLEAR FAMILY is a family consisting of a husband, wife, and child(ren). (293)
4.   The family you grow up in is called your FAMILY OF ORIENTATION. (293)
5.   A social group's approval arrangement for mating, usually marked by a ritual ceremony of some sort, is MARRIAGE. (293)
6.   Those societies in which descent is only counted on the father's side are PATRILINEAL. (293)
7.   EXOGAMY is the practice of marrying outside one's group. (293)
8.   Female control of a society or group is a(n) MATRIARCHY. (294)
9.   In general, women do more of the EMOTIONAL LABOR in a relationship, because they are more attentive to another's emotional needs and share deep, personal thoughts, feelings and aspirations. (298)
10.   Feelings of erotic attraction, accompanied by an idealization of the other, is the definition of ROMANTIC LOVE. (299)
11.   HOMOGAMY is the tendency of people with similar characteristics to get married. (301)

12.   A married couple's domestic situation after the last child has left home is sometimes referred to as the <u>EMPTY NEST</u>. (304)
13.   An emphasis on male strength and dominance is <u>MACHISMO</u>. (306)
14.   The term sociologists use to describe adults who are living together in a sexual relationship without being married is <u>COHABITATION</u>. (310)
15.   The pattern of divorced fathers living with, supporting, and playing an active fathering role with the children of the woman with whom they are currently involved is known as <u>SERIAL FATHERHOOD</u>. (313)

ANSWERS TO MATCH THESE CONCEPTS WITH THEIR DEFINITIONS

1. a   bilateral: *a system of descent that counts both parents' sides*
2. i   romantic love: *feelings of erotic attention*
3. l   household: *all the persons occupying the same housing unit*
4. d   incest taboo: *rules specifying the degree of kinship that prohibits sex or marriage*
5. g   homogamy: *tendency of people with similar characteristics to marry one another*
6. n   blended family: *a family whose members were once part of other families*
7. e   empty nest: *a couple's domestic situation after the last child leaves home*
8. m   machismo: *an emphasis on male strength and dominance*
9. f   marriage: *the approved mating arrangements, usually marked by a ritual*
10. c   polyandry: *marriage in which a woman has more than one husband*
11. h   polygyny: *marriage in which man has more than one wife*
12. o   serial fatherhood: *when a man parents children of the woman with whom he is living*
13. k   emotional labor: *efforts aimed at maintaining intimacy*
14. j   endogamy: *practice of marrying within one's own group*
15. b   exogamy: *practice of marrying outside one's group*

CHAPTER 13
EDUCATION AND RELIGION

☞ CHAPTER SUMMARY

- Industrialized societies are credential societies; employers use diplomas and degrees to determine who is eligible for jobs. Educational certification provides evidence of a person's ability in societies that are large and anonymous and people lack personal knowledge of one another.

- In general, formal education is more extensive in the First World, undergoing extensive change in the Second World, and very spotty in the Third World.

- Functionalists emphasize the functions of education, including teaching knowledge and skills, transmitting cultural values, social integration, gatekeeping, and mainstreaming.

- Conflict theorists view education as a mechanism for maintaining social inequality and reproducing the social class system. Accordingly, they stress how mechanisms such as unequal funding of schools, culturally biased IQ tests, tracking, and the hidden curriculum reinforce basic social inequality.

- Symbolic interactionists examine classroom interaction. They study how teacher expectations cause a self-fulfilling prophecy, producing the very behavior the teacher is expecting.

- Problems facing the current U.S. educational system include falling SAT scores, grade inflation, social promotion, functional illiteracy, and violence in schools. Suggestions for reform include implementing and maintaining a secure and safe learning environment, increasing academic standards and expectations for both students and teachers.

- Durkheim identified the essential elements of religion: beliefs that separate the profane from the sacred, rituals, and a moral community.

- According to the functionalist perspective, religion meets basic human needs such as answering questions about ultimate meaning, providing emotional comfort, guidelines for everyday life, social control, support for the government, and social change. Functionalists also believe religion has two main dysfunctions: war and religious persecution.

- Symbolic interactionists focus on how religious symbols communicate meaning and how ritual and beliefs unite people into a community.

- Conflict theorists see religion as a conservative force that serves the needs of the ruling class by reflecting and reinforcing social inequality.

- Unlike Marx, Weber saw religion as a powerful force for social change. He analyzed how Protestantism gave rise to an ethic that stimulated "the spirit of capitalism." The result was capitalism, which transformed society.

- Sociologists have identified cults, sects, churches, and ecclesia as distinct types of religious organizations. All religions began as cults; although most ultimately fail, those that survive become sects. As a sect grows it may change into a church. Ecclesiae, or state religions, are rare. Religion in the United States is characterized by diversity, pluralism and freedom, competition, a fundamentalist revival, and the electronic church.

- Secularization, a shift from spiritual concerns to those of "this world," is the force behind the dynamics of religious organization. As a cult or sect evolves into a church, its teachings are adapted to reflect changes in the social status of its members. Dissatisfied members break away to form new cults or sects.

- Even in countries where a concerted effort was made to eliminate it, religion has continued to thrive. Religion apparently will continue to exist as long as humanity does.

📖 LEARNING OBJECTIVES

As you read Chapter 13, use these learning objectives to organize your notes. After completing your reading, briefly state an answer to each of the objectives, and review the text pages in parentheses.

1. Explain why the United States has become a credential society. (322-323)
2. Outline the major differences in the educational systems of Japan, the former Soviet Union, and Egypt. (323-325)
3. List and briefly explain the functions of education. (325-326)
4. Explain how education maintains social inequality, according to conflict theorists. (326-327)
5. Summarize symbolic interaction research regarding teacher expectations and the self-fulfilling prophecy. (328-330)
6. Identify the major problems with the U.S. educational system and discuss solutions. (330-333)
7. Define religion and explain Durkheim's essential elements of religion. (333-334)
8. Describe the functions and the dysfunctions of religion. (334-335)
9. Explain what aspects of religion are focused on by symbolic interactionists. (336-337)
10. Identify the conflict perspective on religion and note Marx's influence. (337-338)
11. Describe the relationship between religion and capitalism, as seen by Weber. (338-339)
12. Define cult, sect, church, and ecclesia, and describe the process by which some groups have moved from one category to another. (339-342)
13. State the major characteristics of religion in the U.S. (342-344)
14. Explain what is meant by secularization of religion. (342-344)
15. Analyze the future of religion. State whether or not you agree with the author's assertion that "religion will last as long as humanity lasts," and defend your answer. (346)

📖 CHAPTER OUTLINE

EDUCATION: TRANSFERRING KNOWLEDGE AND SKILLS
I. **Today's Credential Society**
   A. A credential society is one in which employers use diplomas and degrees to determine job eligibility. The sheer size, urbanization and consequent anonymity of U.S. society is a major reason why credentials are required. Diplomas/degrees often serve as sorting devices for employers; because they don't know the individual personally, they depend on schools to weed out the capable from the incapable.
   B. Without the right credentials, a person will not get hired despite the person's ability to do the job better than someone else.
II. **Education in Global Perspective**
   A. Education in the First World: Japan
      1. Japanese education reflects a group-centered ethic. Children in grade school work as a group, mastering the same skills/materials; cooperation and respect for elders (and positions of authority) is stressed.
      2. College admission procedures are based on test scores; only the top scorers are admitted, regardless of social class.
      3. The Japanese reward schoolteaching with high pay and prestige; teachers are in the top 10 percent of the country's wage earners.

B. Education in the Second World: Post-Soviet Russia
   1. After the Revolution of 1917, the government insisted that socialist values dominate education, seeing education as a means to undergird the new political system; children were taught that capitalism was evil and communism was the salvation of the world.
   2. Education was centralized, with all schools following the same curriculum.
   3. Today, Russians are in the midst of "reinventing" education. Private, religious, and even foreign-run schools are operating, and students are encouraged to think for themselves.
   4. The primary difficulty facing the post-Soviet educational system is the rapidly changing values and world views currently underway in Russia.
C. Education in the Third World: Egypt
   1. Several centuries before the birth of Christ, Egypt was a world-renowned center of learning. Primary areas of study during this period were physics, astronomy, geometry, geography, mathematics, philosophy, and medicine. After defeat in war, education declined, never to rise to its former prominence.
   2. Today, education is free at all levels, including college; however, qualified teachers are few, classrooms are crowded, and education is highly limited. Although it is free at all levels, children of the wealthy are still several times as likely to get a college education.

III. **The Functionalist Perspective: Providing Social Benefits**
   A. A central position of functionalism is that when the parts of society are working properly, each contributes to the stability of society. For education, both manifest and latent functions can be identified.
   B. The functions of education include: (1) teaching knowledge and skills; (2) cultural transmission of values (individualism, competition, and patriotism); (3) social integration (molding students into a more or less cohesive unit); (4) gatekeeping (determining who will enter what occupations, through tracking and social placement); (5) mainstreaming (incorporating people with disabilities into regular social activities); and (6) assuming many functions previously fulfilled by the family (e.g., child care and sex education).

IV. **The Conflict Perspective: Maintaining Social Inequality**
   A. The educational system is a tool used by those in the controlling sector of society to maintain their dominance. Education reproduces the social class structure.
   B. The hidden curriculum is unwritten rules of behavior and attitude (e.g., obedience to authority, conformity to cultural norms) taught in school in addition to the formal curriculum.
   C. Conflict theorists criticize IQ (intelligence quotient) testing because they not only measure intelligence but also culturally acquired knowledge. By focusing on these factors, IQ tests reflect a cultural bias that favors the middle class and discriminates against minority and lower class students.
   D. Because public schools are largely financed by local property taxes, there are rich and poor school districts. Unequal funding stacks the deck against minorities and the poor.
   E. Regardless of ability, children of the wealthy are usually placed in college-bound tracks and children of the poor in vocational tracks. Whites are more likely to complete high school, go to college, and get a degree than African Americans and Latinos. The education system helps pass privilege (or lack thereof) across generations.

V. **The Symbolic Interaction Perspective: Teacher Expectations and the Self-Fulfilling Prophecy**
  A. Symbolic interactionists study face-to-face interaction inside the classroom. They have found that expectations of teachers are especially significant in determining what students learn.
  B. The Rist research (participant observation in an African-American grade school with an African-American faculty) found tracking begins with teachers' perceptions.
    1. After eight days--and without testing for ability--teachers divided the class into fast, average, and slow learners; social class was the basis for the assignments.
    2. Social class was the underlying basis for making assignments.
    3. Students from whom more was expected did the best; students in the slow group were ridiculed and disengaged themselves from classroom activities.
    4. The labels applied in kindergarten tended to follow the child through school.
  C. George Farkas found students scoring the same on course matter may receive different grades: females get higher grades, as do Asian Americans. Some students signal that they are interested in what the teacher is teaching; teachers pick up these signals.

VI. **Problems in U.S. Education--and Their Solutions**
  A. A variety of factors have been identified as the major problems facing the U.S. educational system today. These problems include: falling SAT scores; grade inflation, and how it relates to social promotion and functional illiteracy; and violence in schools.
  B. A number of solutions have been offered to address these problems, including creating a secure learning environment and establishing higher academic standards and expectations.

RELIGION: ESTABLISHING MEANING
VII. **What Is Religion?**
  A. According to Durkheim, religion is the beliefs/practices separating the profane from the sacred, uniting adherents into a moral community.
    1. Sacred refers to aspects of life having to do with the supernatural that inspire awe, reverence, deep respect, or deep fear.
    2. Profane refers to the ordinary aspects of everyday life.
  B. He found religion to be defined by three elements: (1) beliefs that some things are sacred (forbidden, set off from the profane); (2) practices (rituals) concerning things considered sacred; and (3) a moral community (a church) resulting from a group's beliefs and practices.

VIII. **The Functionalist Perspective**
  A. Religion performs functions such as: (1) answering questions about ultimate meaning (the purpose of life, why people suffer); (2) uniting believers into a community that shares values and perspectives; (3) providing guidelines for life; (4) controlling behavior; (5) providing support for the government; and (6) spearheading social change (on occasion, as in the case of the civil rights movement in the 1960s).
  B. War and religious persecution are dysfunctions of religion.

IX. **The Symbolic Interactionist Perspective**
  A. Religions use symbols to provide identity and social solidarity for members. For members, these are not ordinary symbols, but sacred symbols evoking awe and reverence, which become a condensed way of communicating with others.
  B. Rituals are ceremonies or repetitive practices helping unite people into a moral community. Some are designed to create a feeling of closeness with God and unity with one another.

C.   Symbols, including rituals, develop from beliefs. A belief may be vague ("God is") or specific ("God wants us to prostrate ourselves and face Mecca five times each day"). Religious beliefs include both values and a cosmology (unified picture of the world).

D.   Religious experience is a sudden awareness of the supernatural or a feeling of coming in contact with God. Some Protestants use the term "born again" to describe people who have undergone a religious experience.

X.   The Conflict Perspective

A.   Conflict theorists are highly critical of religion. Karl Marx called religion the "opium of the people" because he believed that the workers escape into religion. He argued that religion diverts the energies of the oppressed from changing their circumstances because believers focus on the happiness they will have in the coming world rather than on their suffering in this world.

B.   Religious teachings and practices reflect a society's inequalities. Religion legitimates social inequality; it reflects the interests of those in power by teaching that the existing social arrangements of a society represent what God desires.

XI.   Religion and the Spirit of Capitalism

A.   Observing that European countries industrializing under capitalism, Weber questioned why some societies embraced capitalism while others clung to traditional ways. He concluded that religion held the key to modernization (transformation of traditional societies into industrial societies).

B.   Weber concluded that:

    1.   Religion (including a Calvinistic belief in predestination and the need for reassurance as to one's fate) is the key to why the spirit of capitalism developed in Europe.

    2.   A change in religion (from Catholicism to Protestantism) led to a change in thought and behavior. The result was the Protestant Ethic, a commitment to live a moral life and to work and be frugal.

    1.   The spirit of capitalism (desire to accumulate capital as a duty, as an end in itself), which resulted from this new ethic, was a radical departure from the past.

C.   Today the spirit of capitalism and the Protestant ethic are by no means limited to Protestants; they have become cultural traits that have spread throughout the world.

XII. Types of Religious Groups

A.   A cult is a new religion with few followers, whose teachings and practices put it at odds with the dominant culture and religion.

    1.   All religions began as cults. Cults often emerge with the appearance of a charismatic leader (exerting extraordinary appeal to a group of followers).

    2.   Each cult meets with rejection from society. The message given by the cult is seen as a threat to the dominant culture.

    3.   The cult demands intense commitment, and its followers confront a hostile world.

B.   A sect is larger than a cult, but still feels substantial hostility from and toward society. If a sect grows, its members tend to become respectable in society, and the sect is changed into a church.

C.   A church is a large, highly organized religious group with formal, sedate services and less emphasis on personal conversion. The religious group is highly bureaucratized (including national and international offices that give directions to local congregations). Most new members come from within the church, from children born to existing members, rather than from outside recruitment.

D.   An ecclesia is a religious group so integrated into the dominant culture that it is difficult to tell where one begins and the other leaves off. The government and religion work together to try to shape the society. There is no recruitment of members, for citizenship makes everyone a member. The majority of the society belong to the religion in name only.

E.   Although all religions began as cults, not all varieties of a particular religion have done so. A denomination, a "brand name" within a major religion (e. g., Methodist), begins as a splinter group. On occasion a large group within a church may disagree on some aspects of the church's teachings (but not its major message) and break away to form its own organization.

XIII.   **Characteristics of Religion in the United States**

A.   Characteristics of membership in U.S. churches:

1.   Membership is highest in the South, followed by the Midwest and the East.

2.   Each religious group draws members from all social classes, although some are more likely to draw members from the top of the social class system and others from the bottom. The most top-heavy are Episcopalians and Jews, the most bottom-heavy the Baptist and Evangelicals. People who change social class are also likely to change their denomination.

3.   All major religious groups in the United States draw from various racial and ethnic groups; however, persons of Hispanic or Irish descent are likely to be Roman Catholics, those of Greek origin to belong to the Greek Orthodox church, while African Americans are likely to be Protestants.

4.   Membership rate increases steadily with age.

B.   Characteristics of U.S. Religious Groups

1.   There is a diversity of religious groups--no state church, no ecclesia, and no single denomination dominates.

2.   The many religions compete with one another for members.

3.   Today there is a fundamentalist revival because mainstream churches fail to meet basic religious needs of large numbers of people.

4.   The electronic church, in which tele-evangelists reach millions of viewers and raise millions of dollars, has grown. Some independent fundamentalist groups now subscribe to the electronic church and pay a fee in return for having "name" ministers piped "live" into their local congregation).

C.   The history of U.S. churches is marked by secularization and the splintering of religious groups.

1.   Initially, the founders of religious sects felt alienated from the general culture, their values and lower social class position setting them apart.

2.   As time passes, the members of the group become successful, acquiring more education, becoming middle class, and growing more respectable. They no longer feel alienated from the dominant culture. There is an attempt to harmonize religious beliefs with the new cultural orientation.

3.   This process is the secularization of religion, of shifting the focus from religious matters to affairs of this world.

4.   Those who have not achieved worldly success feel betrayed and break away to form a new sect.

5.   Secularization also results from modernization--industrialization, urbanization, mass education, wide adoption of technology and the transformation of

gemeinschaft to *gesellschaft* societies. Religion loses its significance as people turn to answers provided by science, technology, modern medicine, and so on.

XIV. **The Future of Religion**
   A.   Science cannot answer questions about four concerns many people have: the existence of God; the purpose of life; morality; and the existence of an afterlife.
   B.   Neither science nor political systems can replace religion, and religion will last as long as humanity lasts.

☞ GLOSSARY OF DIFFICULT-TO-UNDERSTAND WORDS

estrange: alienated; to break the bonds of loyalty (345)
freshly minted: newly issued (322)
frugal: being extremely careful with one's money (338)
interpenetrate: mutual penetration (341)
liturgy: religious rite appropriate to some event (336)
mainstream: the dominant direction of activity or influence (344)
mind-boggling: hard to understand or to comprehend (324)
papyrus: a written scroll made of the leaves of a papyrus plant (324)
permeates: spreads throughout (341)
predestined: determined beforehand; in the case of Protestantism, this term is used to signify that one's afterlife is determined even before they are born (338)
repentance: to feel sorrow or regret (346)
Resurrection: the belief in the Christian church that Church rose from death and once again lived among mortals (337)
spiraling: a spreading and accelerating increase or decrease (324)
splinter: to split into parts or factions; a group that has split off from the parent organization (345)
stampeding: rushing wildly, out of control (324)
theologians: individuals who study the works of religious bodies (333)
undergird: support (323)

☞ KEY TERMS TO DEFINE

After studying the chapter, define each of the following terms. Then check your work by referring to the answers beginning at page 221 of this Study Guide.

born again	gatekeeping	rituals
charisma	grade inflation	sacred
charismatic leader	hidden curriculum	sect
church	latent functions	secularization of religion
cosmology	mainstreaming	social integration
credential society	manifest functions	social placement
cult	modernize	social promotion
cultural transmission	profane	spirit of capitalism
ecclesia	Protestant Ethic	tracking
functional illiteracy	religious experience	

🖛 KEY PEOPLE

State the major theoretical contributions or findings of these people.

James Coleman	Thomas Hoffer	Liston Pope
Randall Collins	Benton Johnson	Ray Rist
Kingsley Davis	Karl Marx	Thomas Sowell
Emile Durkheim	Wilbert Moore	Ernst Troeltsch
George Farkas	Talcott Parsons	Max Weber

🖛 SELF-TEST

After completing this self-test, check your answers against the Answer Key beginning on page 221 of this Study Guide and against the text on page(s) indicated in parentheses.

MULTIPLE CHOICE QUESTIONS

1. Using diplomas to hire employees, even when diplomas are irrelevant to the work, is: (322)
    a. a credential society.
    b. a certification mill.
    c. employer discretion in hiring.
    d. None of the above.

2. In Japan, college admission is based on: (323)
    a. the ability of parents to pay the tuition.
    b. making a high score on a national test.
    c. being known by teachers as a "hard worker."
    d. the same procedures that prevail in the United States.

3. The function of education that funnels people into a society's various positions is: (326)
    a. functional placement.
    b. social placement.
    c. railroading.
    d. social promotion.

4. The hidden curriculum is based on: (326)
    a. functionalism.
    b. symbolic interactionism.
    c. the conflict perspective.
    d. ethnomethodology.

5. From a conflict perspective, the real purpose of education is to: (326)
    a. perpetuate existing social inequalities.
    b. provide educational opportunities for students from all types of backgrounds.
    c. teach patriotism, teamwork, and cooperation.
    d. replace family functions which most families no longer fulfill.

6. Public schools are largely supported by: (327)
    a.   state funding.
    b.   federal funding.
    c.   local property taxes.
    d.   None of the above.

7. Teacher expectations and face-to-face interactions are of interest to _____ theorists. (328)
    a.   functionalist
    b.   conflict
    c.   symbolic interaction
    d.   educational

8. Research by George Farkas focused on: (330)
    a.   education of elite children.
    b.   how teacher expectations affect a kindergarten class.
    c.   how teacher expectations are influenced by students' alleged IQ scores.
    d.   how teacher expectations affect students' grades.

9. During the past twenty to thirty years, scores on tests such as the SAT: (330)
    a.   have continued to improve.
    b.   have continued to decline.
    c.   have remained about the same.
    d.   None of the above.

10. High school graduates who have difficulty with basic reading and math are known as: (331)
    a.   "boneheads."
    b.   functional literates.
    c.   functional illiterates.
    d.   underachievers.

11. Which of the following is not a solution to the problems of the U.S. education: (331-332)
    a.   providing a safe learning environment
    b.   setting higher expectations
    c.   increasing parental involvement
    d.   eliminating the hidden curriculum

12. According to Durkheim, a church: (334)
    a.   is a large, highly organized religious group.
    b.   has little emphasis on personal conversion.
    c.   is any group of believers sharing a set of beliefs and practices regarding the sacred.
    d.   All of the above.

13. All of the following are functions of religion, except: (334-335)
    a.   encouraging wars for holy causes.
    b.   instilling the values of patriotism.
    c.   spearheading social change.
    d.   providing guidelines for daily life.

14. War and religious persecution are: (335)
    a.   manifest functions of religion.
    b.   latent functions of religion.
    c.   dysfunctions of religion.
    d.   functional equivalents of religion.

15. Religion is the opium of the people according to some: (337)
    a.   conservatives.
    b.   functionalists.
    c.   conflict theorists.
    d.   symbolic interactionists.

16. An example of the use of religion to legitimize social inequalities is: (337-338)
    a.   the divine right of kings.
    b.   a declaration that the Pharaoh or Emperor is god or divine.
    c.   the defense of slavery as being God's will.
    d.   All of the above.

17. Weber believed that religion held the key to: (338)
    a.   modernization.
    b.   bureaucratization.
    c.   institutionalization.
    d.   socialization.

18. The spirit of capitalism is: (338)
    a.   the desire to accumulate capital so one can spend it to show how one "has it made."
    b.   Marx's term for the driving force in the exploitation of workers.
    c.   the ideal of a highly moral life, hard work, industriousness, and frugality.
    d.   None of the above.

19. A cult: (340)
    a.   is a new religion with few followers.
    b.   has teachings and practices which put it at odds with the dominant culture.
    c.   often is at odds with other religions.
    d.   All of the above.

20. Although larger than a cult, a _____ may still feel substantial hostility from society. (340)
    a.   commune.
    b.   ecclesia.
    c.   sect.
    d.   church.

21. Churches: (340-341)
    a.   are highly bureaucratized.
    b.   have more sedate worship services.
    c.   gain new members from within, from children born to existing members.
    d.   All of the above.

22.　A "brand name" within a major religion is a(n): (341)
　　a.　denomination.
　　b.　faction.
　　c.　cult.
　　d.　sect.

23.　Church membership is highest in: (342)
　　a.　the South and Midwest.
　　b.　the Midwest and the West.
　　c.　the Northeast.
　　d.　the Northwest.

24.　Secularization of religion occurs as a result of: (346)
　　a.　industrialization.
　　b.　urbanization.
　　c.　mass education.
　　d.　All of the above.

25.　Questions that science cannot answer include: (346)
　　a.　is there a God?
　　b.　what is the purpose of life?
　　c.　what happens when a person dies?
　　d.　All of the above.

TRUE-FALSE QUESTIONS

T F　1.　In the United States, employers use diplomas and degrees to determine who is eligible for a job. (322)

T F　2.　Japanese schools teach the value of competition to their students. (323)

T F　3.　In Post-Soviet Russia, private, religious, and foreign-run schools are not allowed to operate. (324)

T F　4.　Because Egyptian education is free at all levels, including college, children of the wealthy are no more likely than children of the poor to get a college education. (325)

T F　5.　Education's most obvious manifest function is to teach knowledge and skills. (325)

T F　6.　American schools discourage individualism and encourage teamwork. (325)

T F　7.　Students everywhere are taught that their country is the best country in the world. (325)

T F　8.　Functional theorists believe that social placement is harmful to society. (326)

T F　9.　Functionalists emphasize the hidden curriculum in their analysis of U.S. education. (326)

T F　10.　According to conflict theorists, unequal funding for education automatically stacks the deck against children from lower income families. (327)

T F　11.　Research by Ray Rist concluded that the child's journey through school was preordained by the end of the first year of kindergarten. (329)

T F　12.　George Farkas's research demonstrated that teachers discriminate against women and some minorities because they do not fit their expectations of what a good student should be. (330)

T F　13.　Research by Coleman and Hoffer demonstrated that the superior test performance of Catholic school students was due to the higher standards that teachers maintained. (332)

T F   14.   The goal of the sociological study of religion is to determine which religions are most effective in people's' lives. (333)

T F   15.   According to Durkheim, all religions separate the sacred from the profane. (333)

T F   16.   That the U.S. flag is prominently displayed in many churches is an example of how religion instills the value of patriotism in its believers. (334-335)

T F   17.   The term "born again" is a popular term used to describe the Hindu belief in reincarnation. (337)

T F   18.   Conflict theorists believe that religion mirrors and legitimates social inequalities of the larger society. (337)

T F   19.   Emile Durkheim wrote The Protestant Ethic and the Spirit of Capitalism. (338)

T F   20.   Cults often begin with the appearance of a charismatic leader. (340)

T F   21.   The terms church and state religion mean the same thing. (340-341)

T F   22.   On any given weekend, four out of every five Americans attend a church or synagogue. (342)

T F   23.   Many religions around the world are associated with race and ethnicity. (343)

T F   24.   The racial segregation observed in church membership is based on religious teachings, not social custom. (343)

T F   25.   Fundamentalism is the belief that modernism threatens religion and that the faith as it was originally practiced should be restored. (344)

FILL-IN QUESTIONS

1.   Using diplomas and degrees to determine who is eligible for jobs, even though the diploma or degree may be irrelevant to the actual work, is a characteristic of _____. (322)

2.   _____ are the intended consequences of people's actions designed to help some part of the social system. (325)

3.   The process by which education opens and closes doors of opportunity for individuals in a society is the _____ function of education. (325)

4.   The function of _____ is intended to help people become part of the mainstream of society. (326)

5.   The unwritten goals of schools, such as teaching obedience to authority and conformity to cultural norms, is referred to as _____. (326)

6.   Many U.S. schools practice _____, the sorting of students into different educational programs based on their real or perceived abilities. (326)

7.   A high school graduate who has difficulty with basic reading and math is _____. (331)

8.   Durkheim's term for common elements of everyday life was _____. (333)

9.   Answering questions about ultimate meaning, providing emotional comfort, and social solidarity are _____ of religion. (334)

10.   For Muslims, the crescent moon and star, for Jews the Star of David, and for Christians the cross, all are examples of _____. (336)

11.   _____ is teachings or ideas that provide a unified picture of the world. (336)

12.   According to conflict theorists, religion is the _____. (337)

13.   _____ is Weber's term to describe the ideal of a highly moral life, hard work, industriousness, and frugality. (338)

14.   A(n) _____ is someone who exerts extraordinary appeal to a group of followers. (340)

15. _____ is the replacement of a religion's "otherworldly" concerns with concerns about "this world." (345)

MATCH THESE SOCIAL SCIENTISTS WITH THEIR CONTRIBUTIONS

___1. Randall Collins
___2. Ray Rist
___3. George Farkas
___4. Talcott Parsons
___5. Emile Durkheim
___6. Max Weber
___7. Karl Marx
___8. Ernst Troeltsch

a. *cult-sect-church-ecclesia typology*
b. *the gatekeeping function of education*
c. *credential society*
d. *The Elementary Forms of Religious Life*
e. *"religion is the opium of the people"*
f. *expectations of kindergarten teachers*
g. *teacher expectations in grading students*
h. *The Protestant Ethic and the Spirit of Capitalism*

"DOWN-TO-EARTH SOCIOLOGY"

1. In what ways does the educational experience of the Vietnamese immigrant (p. 329) reflect failures of the U.S. educational system to fulfill its functions? In what ways is this person's experiences different from your own? In what ways is it similar? How could education be changed to address some of her problems?

2. In his classroom Jaime Escalante has challenged many of the assumptions about educating low income students (p. 332). Is his success due to his extraordinary teaching skills or is it possible to extend his successes into classrooms across the country? If so, what changes would have to be made in education?

3. What are some of the ways in which religious beliefs permeate the culture of India (p. 341)? How have these religious beliefs proved beneficial to that society? Can you think of some examples of the secularization of religious beliefs in our own culture?

☞ ANSWERS FOR CHAPTER 13

DEFINITIONS OF KEY TERMS

born again: a term describing Christians who have undergone a life-transforming religious experience so radical that they feel they have become new persons

charisma: literally, an extraordinary gift from God; more commonly, an outstanding, "magnetic" personality

charismatic leader: literally, someone to whom God has given an extraordinary gift; more commonly, someone who exerts extraordinary appeal to a group of followers

church: According to Durkheim, one of the three essential elements of religion--a moral community of believers; used by other sociologists to refer to a highly organized religious organization

cosmology: teachings or ideas that provide a unified picture of the world

credential society: the use of diplomas and degrees to determine who is eligible for jobs, even though the diploma or degree may be irrelevant to the actual work

cult: a new religion with few followers, whose teachings and practices put it at odds with the dominant culture and religion

cultural transmission: in reference to education, the ways in which schools transmit a society's culture, especially its core values

ecclesia: a religious group so integrated into the dominant culture that it is difficult to tell where the one begins and the other leaves off; also called a state religion

functional illiteracy: a high school graduate who has difficulty with basic reading and math

gatekeeping: the process by which education opens and closes doors of opportunity; another term for the social placement function of education

grade inflation: higher grades given for some work; a general rise in student grades without a corresponding increase in learning or test scores

hidden curriculum: the unwritten goals of schools, such as teaching obedience to authority and conformity to cultural norms

latent functions: unintended consequences of people's actions that helps to keep a social system in equilibrium

mainstreaming: helping people to become part of the mainstream of society

manifest functions: intended consequences of people's actions designed to help some part of a social system

modernize: refers to a traditional society transforming into an industrial society

profane: Durkheim's term for common elements of everyday life

Protestant Ethic: Weber's term to describe the ideal of a highly moral life, accompanied by hard work, self-denial, and frugality

religious experience: a sudden awareness of the supernatural or a feeling of coming into contact with God

rituals: ceremonies or repetitive practices; in this context, religious observances or rites often intended to evoke a sense of awe of the sacred

sacred: Durkheim's term for things set apart or forbidden, which inspire fear, awe, reverence, or deep respect

sect: a group larger than a cult that still feels substantial hostility from and toward society

secularization of religion: the replacement of a religion's "otherworldly" concerns with concerns about "this world"

social integration: the degree to which people feel a part of a social group

social placement: a function of education that funnels people into a society's various positions

social promotion: passing students to the next grade even though they have not mastered basic materials

spirit of capitalism: Weber's term for the desire to accumulate capital as a duty--not to spend it, but as an end in itself--and to constantly reinvest it

tracking: the sorting of students into different educational programs on the basis of real or perceived abilities

ANSWERS FOR MULTIPLE CHOICE QUESTIONS

1. a   The use of diplomas and degrees to determine who is eligible for jobs, even though the diploma or degree may be irrelevant to the actual work is known as a credential society. (322)
2. b   In Japan, college admission is based on making a high score on a national test. (323)

3. b The function of education that funnels people into a society's various positions is social placement. (326)
4. c The hidden curriculum is based on the conflict perspective. (326)
5. a From a conflict perspective, the real purpose of education is to perpetuate existing social inequalities. (326)
6. c Public schools are largely supported by local property taxes. (327)
7. c Teacher expectations and face-to-face interactions are of interest to symbolic interaction theorists. (328)
8. d Research by George Farkas focused on how teacher expectations affect students' grades. (330)
9. b During the past twenty to thirty years, scores on tests such as the SAT have declined. (330)
10. c High school graduates who have difficulty with basic reading and math are known as functional illiterates. (331)
11. d Providing a safe learning environment, setting higher expectations, and increasing parental involvement have all been proposed as solutions to the problems of U.S. education. Eliminating the hidden curriculum has not been suggested as a solution. (331-332)
12. c Durkheim used the word church in an unusual way to refer to a group of believers organized around a set of beliefs and practices regarding the sacred. (334)
13. a The following are functions of religion: instilling the value of patriotism; spearheading social change; and providing guidelines for daily life. Encouraging wars for holy causes is a dysfunction of religion. (334-335)
14. c War and religious persecution are dysfunctions of religion. (335)
15. c Religion is the opium of the people according to some conflict theorists. (337)
16. d All of the above is correct. These are all examples of the use of religion to legitimize social inequalities: the divine right of kings; a declaration that the Pharaoh or Emperor is god or divine; and the defense of slavery as being God's will. (337-338)
17. a Weber believed that religion held the key to modernization. (338)
18. d None of the above is correct. The spirit of capitalism is the desire to accumulate capital as a duty --not to spend it, but as an end in itself. It is not the desire to accumulate capital in order to spend it and show others how one "has it made." Nor is it Marx's term for the driving force in the exploitation of workers or the ideal of a highly moral life, hard work, industriousness, and frugality (which is the Protestant ethic). (338)
19. d All of the above is correct. A cult is a new religion with few followers; has teachings and practices which put it at odds with the dominant culture; and often is at odds with other religions. (340)
20. c Although larger than a cult, a sect may still feel substantial hostility from society. (340)
21. d All of the above is correct. Churches are highly bureaucratized; have more sedate worship services; and gain new members from within, from children born to existing members. (340-341)
22. a A "brand name" within a major religion is a denomination. (341)
23. a Church membership is highest in the South and Midwest. (342)
24. d All of the above is correct. Secularization of religion occurs as a result of industrialization, urbanization, and mass education. (346)
25. d All of the above is correct. Questions that science cannot answer include: is there a God? what is the purpose of life? and what happens when a person dies? (346)

ANSWERS FOR TRUE-FALSE QUESTIONS

1. *True.* (322)

2.   *False*. In Japanese schools the value of cooperation rather than competition is stressed. (323)

3.   *False*. In Post-Soviet Russia, private, religious, and foreign-run schools are allowed to operate. (324)

4.   *False*. Despite the fact that Egyptian education is free at all levels. children of the wealthy are more likely to get an education. (325)

5.   *True*. (325)

6.   *False*. American schools encourage, rather than discourage, individualism and although teamwork is encouraged, individuals are singled out for praise when the team does well. (325)

7.   *True*. (325)

8.   *False*. Functional theorists believe that social placement is helpful, not harmful, to society because the process helps insure that the "best" people will acquire a good education and subsequently perform the most needed tasks of society. (326)

9.   *False*. Conflict theorists, not functionalists, emphasize the hidden curriculum in their analysis of American education. (326)

10.   *True*. (327)

11.   *False*. Research by Ray Rist concluded that the child's journey through school was preordained by the eighth day, not the end of the first year, of kindergarten. (329)

12.   *False*. According to Farkas's research females and Asian Americans got higher grades because they communicated to teachers through their demeanor and behavior that they were interested in what the teacher was teaching; they fit the teacher's idea of what a good student should be. (330)

13.   *True*. (332)

14.   *False*. The goal of the sociological study of religion is to analyze the relationship between society and religion and to gain insight into the role that religion plays in people's lives. It is not to determine which religions are most effective in peoples' lives. (333)

15.   *True*. (333)

16.   *True*. (334-335)

17.   *False*. The term "born again" is a term used by some Protestants to describe people who have undergone a life-transforming religious experience. (337)

18.   *True*. (337)

19.   *False*. Max Weber wrote The Protestant Ethic and the Spirit of Capitalism. (338)

20.   *True*. (340)

21.   *False*. The terms ecclesia and state religion mean the same thing, not church and state religion. (340-341)

22.   *False*. On any given weekend, **two** out of every five Americans attend a church or synagogue. (342)

23.   *True*. (343)

24.   *False*. The racial segregation observed in church membership is based on social custom. (343)

25.   *True*. (344)

ANSWERS FOR FILL-IN QUESTIONS

1.   Using diplomas and degrees to determine who is eligible for jobs, even though the diploma or degree may be irrelevant to the actual work, is characteristic of <u>CREDENTIAL SOCIETY</u>. (322)

2.   <u>MANIFEST FUNCTIONS</u> are the intended consequences of people's actions designed to help some part of the social system. (325)

3.	The process by which education opens and closes doors of opportunity for individuals in a society is the <u>GATEKEEPING</u> function of education. (325)
4.	The function of <u>MAINSTREAMING</u> is intended to help people become part of the mainstream of society. (326)
5.	The unwritten goals of schools, such as teaching obedience to authority and conformity to cultural norms, is referred to as <u>HIDDEN CURRICULUM</u>. (326)
6.	Many U.S. schools practice <u>TRACKING</u>, the sorting of students into different educational programs based on their real or perceived abilities. (326)
7.	A high school graduate who has difficulty with basic reading and math is <u>FUNCTIONALLY ILLITERATE</u>. (331)
8.	Durkheim's term for common elements of everyday life was <u>PROFANE</u>. (333)
9.	Answering questions about ultimate meaning, providing emotional comfort, and social solidarity are <u>FUNCTIONS</u> of religion. (334)
10.	For Muslims, the crescent moon and star, for Jews the Star of David, and for Christians the cross, all are examples of <u>RELIGIOUS SYMBOLS</u>. (336)
11.	<u>COSMOLOGY</u> is teachings or ideas that provide a unified picture of the world. (336)
12.	According to conflict theorists, religion is the <u>OPIUM OF THE MASSES</u>. (337)
13.	<u>THE PROTESTANT ETHIC</u> is Weber's term to describe the ideal of a highly moral life, hard work, industriousness, and frugality. (338)
14.	A(n) <u>CHARISMATIC LEADER</u> is someone who exerts extraordinary appeal to a group of followers. (340)
15.	<u>SECULARIZATION OF RELIGION</u> is the replacement of a religion's "otherworldly" concerns with concerns about "this world." (345)

<u>ANSWERS TO MATCH THESE SOCIAL SCIENTISTS WITH THEIR CONTRIBUTIONS</u>

1. c	Randall Collins: *credential society*
2. f	Ray Rist: *expectations of kindergarten teachers*
3. g	George Farkas: *teacher expectations in grading students*
4. b	Talcott Parsons: *the gatekeeping function of education*
5. d	Emile Durkheim: *The Elementary Forms of the Religious Life*
6. h	Max Weber: *The Protestant Ethic and the Spirit of Capitalism*
7. e	Karl Marx: *"religion is the opium of the people"*
8. a	Ernest Troeltsch: *cult-sect-church-ecclesia typology*

CHAPTER 14
POPULATION AND URBANIZATION

☞ CHAPTER SUMMARY

- Demography is the study of the size, composition, growth, and distribution of human populations. Almost 200 years ago Thomas Malthus observed that populations grow geometrically while food supplies increase arithmetically; he argued that the population of the world would eventually outstrip its food supply.

- Today, the basic cause of starvation is the global maldistribution of food rather than world overpopulation.

- People in the Third World have many more children than people in the First and Second Worlds because children play a very different role in Third World cultures. To project population trends, demographers use three demographic variables: fertility, mortality, and migration. The greatest challenge today is how to use the technology of the First World to help the Third World control its population and guarantee adequate food supplies to avoid malnutrition, starvation, and resource depletion.

- Urbanization, the process by which an increasing proportion of a population lives in cities, represents the greatest mass migration in human history. Cities can only develop if there is an agricultural surplus. Until the Industrial Revolution cities were small; as transportation and communication systems grew out of the Industrial Revolution, the infrastructure of modern cities developed and cities grew larger.

- Urbanization today is so extensive that some cities have become metropolises; in some cases metropolises have merged to form a megalopolis. Within the U.S., the trends are gentrification and regional migration.

- Three major models have been proposed to explain how cities expand: the concentric-zone, sector, and multiple-nuclei models. No one model is adequate in explaining completely the complexities of urban growth.

- Some people find a sense of community in cities; others find alienation. What people find depends largely on their background and urban networks. To develop community in the city, people personalize their shopping, identify with sports teams, and even become sentimental about objects in the city. Noninvolvement is generally functional for urbanites, but it impedes giving help in emergencies.

- Cities in the U.S. are subject to constant change, including disinvestment, suburbanization, and deindustrialization. Guiding principles for developing social policy are scale, livability, and social justice.

☞ LEARNING OBJECTIVES

As you read Chapter 14, use these learning objectives to organize your notes. After completing your reading, briefly state an answer to each of the objectives, and review the text pages in parentheses.

1. Discuss the Malthus theorem and identify key issues in the debate between New Malthusians and Anti-Malthusians regarding the specter of overpopulation. (352-356)
2. Explain why there is starvation. (356-357)

3. Explain why people in poor nations have so many children and note the implications of different rates of population growth. (357-359)
4. State the three demographic variables used in estimating population growth and explain why it is difficult to forecast population growth. (359-364)
5. Describe urbanization and outline the history of how cities came into existence. (365-366)
6. Identify the trends that have contributed to the growth of metropolises and megalopolises. (366-367)
7. Discuss urbanization in the U.S. (367-370).
8. Discuss the three models of urban growth and critique the models. (370-371)
9. Explain why many people feel a sense of alienation by living in large urban areas. (371-373)
10. Define the urban village and briefly describe the five different types of people who live in the city, as identified by sociologist Herbert Gans. (373-374)
11. Describe ways in which city people create a sense of intimacy for themselves in large urban areas. (374-375)
12. Explain why the norm of noninvolvement and the diffusion of responsibility, which help urban dwellers get through everyday city life may be dysfunctional in some situations. (375)
13. Outline the major changes facing U.S. cities regarding suburbanization, disinvestment, and deindustrialization. (375-378)
14. Identify the guiding principles for developing solutions to urban problems. (378-379)

☞ CHAPTER OUTLINE

POPULATION IN GLOBAL PERSPECTIVE

I. **A Plant with No Space for the Good Life?**
    A. Demography is the study of size, composition, growth, and distribution of populations.
    B. Thomas Malthus wrote *An Essay on the Principle of Population* (1798) stating the Malthus theorem--population grows geometrically while food supply increases arithmetically; thus, if births go unchecked, population will eventually outstrip food supply.
    C. New Malthusians believe Malthus was correct. The world population is following an exponential growth curve (where numbers increase in extraordinary proportions): 1800, one billion; 1930, two billion; 1960, three billion; 1975, four billion; and 1987, five billion. Right now, the world population is almost six billion.
    D. Anti-Malthusians believe that people do not blindly reproduce until there is no room left.
        1. They cite three stages of the demographic transition in Europe as an example: ;Stage 1, a fairly stable population (high birth rates offset by high death rates); Stage 2, "population explosion" (high birth rates and low death rates); and Stage 3, population stability (low birth rates and low death rates).
        2. They assert this transition will happen in the poorer countries, which currently are in the second stage.
        3. Population shrinkage (a country's population is smaller because birth rate and immigration cannot replace those who die and emigrate) has occurred in Europe.
    E. Who is correct?
        1. There is no question that the Third World is in Stage 2, but there is a question about when they will reach Stage 3. Death rates have dropped but birth rates remain high.

2.	Leaders of the industrialized world, fearing that these growing nations would upset the international balance of power, used the United Nations to spearhead global efforts to reduce world population growth.

3.	The population of the Third World is still increasing, only at a slower rater. To the New Malthusians, the catastrophe is still coming; to Anti-Malthusians, this is a sign that the Third World is approaching Stage 3.

4.	Only the future will prove the accuracy of either side's projections.

F.	Why is there starvation?

1.	Anti-Malthusians note that the amount of food produced for each person in the world has increased: famines are not the result of too little food production, but result from the global maldistribution of existing food.

2.	The New Malthusians counter that the world's population continues to grow and the earth may not be able to continue to produce sufficient food.

3.	New Malthusians promote policies that attempt to reduce the size of populations, while Anti-Malthusians concentrate on policies that focus on a more equitable distribution of food.

4.	Recently, famines have been concentrated in Africa. However, these famines are not due to too many people living on too little land. Rather, these famines are due to outmoded farming techniques and ongoing political instability.

II.	**Population Growth**

A.	Three reasons people in poor nations have so many children are: (1) the status that parenthood confers a certain status; (2) the community supports this view; and (3) children are considered to be economic assets (the parents rely on the children to take care of them in their old age). The conflict perspective stresses the domination of females by males in all spheres of life, including reproduction. This emphasis on male strength and dominance includes fathering many children as a means of achieving status in the community.

B.	Demographers use population pyramids (graphic representations of a population, divided into age and sex) to illustrate a country's population dynamics (e.g., Mexico's doubling rate is only 30 years).

1.	Different population growth rates have different implications. Countries with slow growth rates have fewer people on which to spend their resources, while countries with rapid growth rates have to cope with increased numbers of people among whom to share resources.

2.	A declining standard of living may result in political instability followed by severe repression by the government.

C.	Estimated population growth is based on three demographic variables.

1.	Fertility, measured by the fertility rate (number of children an average woman bears), is sometimes confused with fecundity (number of children a woman theoretically can bear). To compute a country's fertility rate, demographers use crude birth rate (annual number of births per 1,000 people).

2.	Mortality is measured by the crude death rate (number of deaths per 1,000 people).

3.	Migration is measured by the net migration rate (difference between the number of immigrants moving in and emigrants moving out per 1,000 population); it may be voluntary or forced. Push factors make people want to leave where they are living (e.g., poverty, persecution, lack of economic opportunity); pull factors attract people (e.g., opportunities for higher wages or better jobs in the new locale).

D. The growth rate equals births minus deaths, plus net migration.

   1. Economic changes, government policies, and behavioral changes make it difficult to forecast population growth. The primary unknown factor that influences a country's growth rate is its rate of industrialization--in every country that industrializes, the growth rate declines.

   2. Because of the difficulties in forecasting population growth, demographers formulate several predictions simultaneously, each depending on different assumptions.

URBANIZATION

III.   The Development of Cities

A. A city is a place in which a large number of people are permanently based and do not produce their own food. Small cities with massive defensive walls existed as far back as 10,000 years ago; cities on a larger scale originated about 3500 B. C. as a result of the development of more efficient agriculture and of a surplus.

B. The Industrial Revolution drew people to cities to work. Today urbanization not only means that more people live in cities, but also that today's cities are larger; about 300 of the world's cities contain at least one million people.

C. Urbanization is the process by which an increasing proportion of a population lives in cities. There are specific characteristics of cities, such as size and anonymity, that give them their unique urban flavor.

   1. Metropolis refers to cities that grow so large that they exert influence over a region; the central city and surrounding smaller cities and suburbs are connected economically, politically, and socially.

   2. Megalopolis refer to an overlapping area consisting of at least two metropolises and their suburbs, connected economically, socially, and sometimes politically.

IV.   Urbanization in the United States

A. In 1790, only about 5 percent of Americans lived in cities; by 1920, 50 percent of the U.S. population lived in urban areas; today, 80 percent of Americans live in urban areas, and about 200 U.S. cities have more than 100,000 inhabitants.

   1. The U.S. Census Bureau divided the country into 283 metropolitan statistical areas (MSAs)--which consist of a central city and the urbanized counties that are linked to it.

   2. Over half of the entire U.S. population lives in just 44 MSAs.

B. As Americans migrate in search of work and better life styles, distinct patterns appear. The general movement is from the North and East to the West and the South--from the "snow belt" to the "sun belt."

C. As Americans migrate and businesses move to serve them, edge cities have developed (a clustering of service facilities and residential areas near highway intersections).

D. Gentrification, the movement of middle-class people into rundown areas of a city, is another major U.S. urban pattern.

V.   Models of Urban Growth

A. Robert Park coined the term human ecology to describe how people adapt to their environment (known as "urban ecology"); human ecologists have constructed three models which attempt to explain urban growth patterns.

B. Ernest W. Burgess proposed the concentric-zone model, which views the city as a series of zones emanating from its center, with each characterized by a different group of people and activity: Zone 1, central business district; Zone 2, in transition with deteriorating housing and rooming houses; Zone 3, area to which thrifty workers have moved to escape the zone in transition, yet maintain access to work; Zone 4, more expensive apartments, single-family dwellings, and exclusive areas where the wealthy live; and Zone 5, commuter zone consisting of suburban areas or satellite cities that have developed around rapid transit routes.

C. The sector model sees urban zones as wedge-shaped sectors radiating out from the center. A zone might contain a sector of working-class housing, another sector of expensive housing, a third of businesses, and so on, all competing with one another for the same land. In an invasion-succession cycle, when poor immigrants move into a city, they settle in the lowest-rent area available and, as their numbers grow, begin to encroach on adjacent areas. As the poor move closer to the middle class, the middle class leave, expanding the sector of lower-cost housing.

D. The multiple-nuclei model views the city as comprised of multiple centers or nuclei, each of which focuses on a specialized activity (e.g., retail districts, automobile dealers, etc.).

E. Cities are complex, and no single model yet developed does justice to this complexity; the models do not make allowances for the extent to which elites influence the development of cities.

VI. **Experiencing the City**

A. For some, cities provide a sense of community--a feeling that others care about what happens to others, and they depend upon one another. For others, the city is alienating.

B. Louis Wirth argued that the city undermines kinship and neighborhood, which are the traditional bases of social control and social solidarity.

    1. Urban dwellers live in anonymity, their lives marked by segmented and superficial encounters which make them grow aloof from one another and indifferent to other people's problems.

    2. This is similar to the idea that *gemeinschaft* (a sense of community that comes from everyone knowing everyone else) is ripped apart as a country industrializes, and *gesellschaft* (a society characterized by secondary, impersonal relationships which result in alienation) replaces it.

C. Some sociologists use the term urban village to refer to an area of the city that people know well and in which they live, work, shop, and play.

D. Herbert Gans identified five types of people who live in the city.

    1. Cosmopolites--intellectuals and professionals, students, writers, and artists who live in the inner city to be near its conveniences and cultural benefits.

    2. Singles--young, unmarried people who come seeking jobs and entertainment.

    3. Ethnic villagers--live in tightly knit neighborhoods that resemble villages and small towns, united by race and social class.

    4. The deprived--the very poor, the emotionally disturbed, and the handicapped who live in neighborhoods more like urban jungles than urban villages.

    5. The trapped--who consist of four subtypes: those who can not afford to move when their neighborhood is invaded by another ethnic group; downwardly mobile persons who have fallen from a higher social class; elderly people who have drifted into the slums because they are not wanted elsewhere and are powerless to prevent their downward slide; and alcoholics and drug addicts.

E.   Sociologists have analyzed how urban dwellers build community in the city.
1.   City people create a sense of intimacy for themselves by personalizing their shopping (by frequenting the same stores and restaurants, people become recognized as "regulars").
2.   Spectator sports also engender community identification.
3.   City dwellers develop strong feelings for particular objects and locations in the city such as trees, buildings, rivers, lakes, parks, and even street corners.
F.   Urban dwellers are careful to protect themselves from the unwanted intrusions of strangers.
1.   They follow a norm of noninvolvement--such as using of a newspaper or a Walkman to indicate inaccessibility for interaction--to avoid encounters with people they do not know.
2.   They use a variety of filters to prevent unwanted stimuli from reaching them, including unlisted telephone numbers, telephone answering machines, and post office boxes instead of revealing home addresses.
G.   The more bystanders there are to an incident, the less likely people are to help because people's sense of responsibility becomes diffused. The norm of noninvolvement and the diffusion of responsibility may help urban dwellers get through everyday city life, but they are dysfunctional because people do not provide assistance to others.

VII.   **The Decline of the City**
A.   Suburbanization--the movement from the city to the suburbs--has had a profound effect on U.S. cities.
1.   People have moved for over 100 years to towns next to the cities in which they worked; today the speed and extent to which people have left the city is new.
2.   Central cities have lost residents, businesses, and jobs, causing the cities' tax base (which supports essential city services and schools) to shrink; people left behind are those with limited financial means.
3.   According to William Wilson, the term ghetto reflects a social transformation; groups represented in these areas today are more socially isolated than those who lived in these communities in the past.
4.   Suburbanites prefer the city to keep its problems to itself and fight movements to share suburbia's revenues with the city. However, the time may come when suburbanites may have to pay for their attitudes toward the city.
B.   By the 1940's, the movement to suburbs began to undermine the cities' tax base, a problem accelerated as huge numbers of poor rural migrants moved into northern cities. As the tax base eroded, services declined, buildings deteriorated, and banks began red lining (drawing a line on a map around problem areas and refusing to make loans to living and working in these areas). This pushed these areas into further decline.
C.   The development of a global market has led to deindustrialization. Manufacturing firms have relocated from the inner city to areas where production costs are lower. The inner-city economies have not been able to provide alternative employment for poor residents, thereby locking them out of the economy.

VIII.   **Social Policy: Failure and Potential**
A.   Social policy usually takes one of two forms.
1.   Urban renewal involves tearing down and rebuilding the buildings in an area. As a result of urban renewal, the areas residents can no longer afford to live in the area and are displaced to adjacent areas.

2.   Enterprise zones are economic incentives to encourage businesses to move into the area. Most business, however, refuse to move into high- crime areas.

B.   If U.S. cities are to change, they must become top agenda items of the U.S. government, with adequate resources in terms of money and human talents focused on overcoming urban woes.

C.   Flanagan suggests three guiding principles for working out specific solutions to urban problems: (1) regional and national planning is necessary; (2) growth needs to be channeled in such a way that makes city living attractive; and (3) social policy must be evaluated by its effects on people. Finally, unless the root causes of urban problems-- housing, education, and jobs--are addressed, solutions will only serve as band-aids that cover the real problems.

☞ GLOSSARY OF DIFFICULT-TO-UNDERSTAND WORDS

amniocentesis: a surgical procedure in which a needle in inserted into the uterus of a pregnant woman and a small amount of amniotic fluid is extracted and analyzed in order to detect birth defects as well as the sex of the fetus (363)

barren: unable to conceive a child (358)

beamed: smiled with joy (352)

catcalls: whistles and comments, generally directed at a woman by men (377)

crucible: a container capable of withstanding high temperatures, used for melting a substance (377)

deplorable: bad or wretched (378)

deteriorating: run down; in poor condition (370)

distended: inflated (352)

docksiders: a type of shoe worn by sailors (377)

ecstatic: very happy (355)

gangsters: members of a gang of criminals; racketeers (370)

haphazard: not kept in a meaningful manner (360)

hybrid: the offspring of two plants of different varieties (355)

infrastructure: the underlying foundation or basic structure (366)

irrefutable: unable to be disputed (356)

mind-boggling: an idea or thought that overwhelming your thinking (354)

mushroomed: having increased very rapidly (355)

pastoral: relating to the countryside (372)

precariously: depending upon known circumstances (354)

quintuple: reach four times its present size (361)

ravishing: exceptionally attractive (357)

spigot: water faucet or valve (372)

squatter settlements: places where people live without paying any rent or other fees, having claimed a right to the space (372)

volatile: unstable, and likely to explode (355)

☞ KEY TERMS TO DEFINE

After studying the chapter, define each of the following terms. Then check your work by referring to the answers beginning at page 239 of this Study Guide.

alienation	enterprise zone	metropolis
basic demographic equation	exponential growth curve	net migration rate
city	fecundity	population pyramid
community	fertility rate	population shrinkage
crude birth rate	gentrification	redlining
crude death rate	growth rate	suburb
demographic transition	human ecology	suburbanization
demography	invasion-succession cycle	sun belt
disinvestment	Malthus theorem	urban renewal
edge city	megalopolis	urbanization

☞ KEY PEOPLE

State the major theoretical contributions or findings of these people.

Ernest Burgess	Chauncey Harris	Edward Ullman
Paul and Ann Ehrlich	Homer Hoyt	Louis Wirth
William Flanagan	Thomas Malthus	
Herbert Gans	Robert Park	

☞ SELF-TEST

After completing this self-test, check your answers against the Answer Key beginning on page 239 of this Study Guide and against the text on page(s) indicated in parentheses.

MULTIPLE CHOICE QUESTIONS

1.   The proposition that the population grows geometrically while food supply increases arithmetically is known as the: (352)
   a.   food surplus equation.
   b.   Malthus theorem.
   c.   exponential growth curve.
   d.   demographic transition.

2.   The New Malthusians point out that the world's population is: (353)
   a.   in the midst of the demographic transition.
   b.   becoming increasingly more urban.
   c.   experiencing zero population growth.
   d.   following an exponential growth curve.

3. Anti-Malthusians believe that: (354-355)
   a. people will blindly reproduce until there is no room left on earth.
   b. it is possible to project the world's current population growth into the indefinite future.
   c. most people do not use intelligence and rational planning when it comes to having children.
   d. None of the above.

4. The three-stage historical process of population growth is known as the: (355)
   a. demographic equation.
   b. demographic transition.
   c. exponential growth curve.
   d. implosion growth curve.

5. The process by which a country's population becomes smaller because its birth rate and immigration are too low to replace those who die and emigrate is: (355)
   a. population transfer.
   b. population annihilation.
   c. population shrinkage.
   d. population depletion.

6. According to Anti-Malthusians, people are starving because: (356)
   a. there are too many people.
   b. there is too little food.
   c. there is a mismatch between where the greatest supply of food is and where the greatest demand for it is.
   d. people are greedy.

7. Poor nations have so many children because: (358)
   a. parenthood provides status.
   b. children are considered to be an economic asset.
   c. the community encourages people to have children.
   d. All of the above.

8. Factors that influence population growth: fertility, mortality, and net migration are: (359-360)
   a. demographic variables.
   b. demographic transitions.
   c. demographic equations.
   d. demographic constants.

9. The annual number of deaths per 1,000 population is the: (360)
   a. crude death rate.
   b. crude mortality rate.
   c. crude life expectancy rate.
   d. net death rate.

10.   Factors pushing someone to migrate include: (361)
        a.   poverty.
        b.   lack of religious and political freedom.
        c.   political persecution.
        d.   All of the above.

11.   According to your text, it is difficult to forecast population growth because of: (363-364)
        a.   government programs.
        b.   dishonesty in reporting data.
        c.   lack of computer programs to deal with data adequately.
        d.   All of the above.

12.   Today's rapid urbanization means that: (366)
        a.   more people live in cities.
        b.   today's cities are larger.
        c.   about 300 of the world's cities contain at least one million people.
        d.   All of the above.

13.   The process by which an increasing proportion of a population lives in cities is: (366)
        a.   suburbanization.
        b.   gentrification.
        c.   megalopolitanism.
        d.   urbanization.

14.   Edge cities: (369)
        a.   consist of malls, office parks, and residential areas near major highway intersections.
        b.   overlap political boundaries and include parts of several cities or towns.
        c.   provide a sense of place to whose who live there.
        d.   All of the above.

15.   The movement of middle-class people into rundown areas of a city is called: (369)
        a.   urban renewal.
        b.   urban homesteading.
        c.   gentrification.
        d.   reverse migration.

16.   The _____ model suggests that land use in cities is based on several centers. (371)
        a.   sector model.
        b.   concentric-zone model.
        c.   multiple-nuclei model.
        d.   commerce model.

17.   According to Gans's typology, the trapped includes: (374)
        a.   downwardly mobile persons.
        b.   elderly persons.
        c.   alcoholics and drug addicts.
        d.   All of the above.

18. The Kitty Genovese case in an example of: (373)
    a. ethnic villagers.
    b. cosmopolites.
    c. alienation.
    d. community.

19. Alienation can result in societies characterized by: (373)
    a. *gemeinschaft.*
    b. *gesellschaft.*
    c. norms of non-involvement.
    d. diffusion of responsibility.

20. Suburbanization is the: (375)
    a. movement from the suburbs to edge cities.
    b. movement from the city to the suburbs.
    c. movement from rural areas to suburbs.
    d. displacement of the poor by the relatively affluent, who renovate the former's homes.

TRUE-FALSE QUESTIONS

T F 1. Thomas Malthus was a sociologist at the University of Chicago in the 1920s. (352)
T F 2. The exponential growth curve is based on the idea that if growth doubles during approximately equal intervals of time, it accelerates in the latter stages. (353)
T F 3. There are four stages in the process of demographic transition. (355)
T F 4. The major reason why people in poor countries have so many children is because they do not know how to prevent conception. (358)
T F 5. Population pyramids represent a population, divided into race, age, and sex. (358)
T F 6. Demographers analyze fertility, mortality, and migration to project a country's population trends. (359-360)
T F 7. Migration rates do not affect the global population. (360)
T F 8. It is difficult for demographers to forecast population growth. (364)
T F 9. The rapidity and extent of urbanization which has occurred in recent years is new to the world scene. (366)
T F 10. In the United States today, the fastest growing cities are in the South and West. (368)
T F 11. The concentric-zone model is based on the idea that cities expand radially from their central business district. (371)
T F 12. The multiple-nuclei model is the most accurate model of urban growth. (371)
T F 13. According to Herbert Gans, the author of *The Urban Villagers*, people in cities are always alienated because they lack a sense of community. (373-374)
T F 14. Sports teams often engender community identification in urban areas. (374)
T F 15. When banks engage in the practice of redlining the quality of life in neighborhoods generally improves. (376)

FILL-IN QUESTIONS

1. _____ is the study of the size, composition, growth, and distribution of human populations. (352)

2.	A pattern of growth in which numbers double during approximately equal intervals, thus accelerating in the latter stages is the _____. (353)

3.	A(n) _____ is a graphic representation of a population, divided into age and sex. (358)

4.	The _____ refers to the number of children that the average woman bears. (359)

5.	The basic demographic equation is *growth* = _____ - _____ + _____. (363)

6.	_____ is a place in which a large number of people are permanently based and do not produce their own food. (365)

7.	An overlapping area consisting of at least two metropolises and their many suburbs is a _____. (367)

8.	The displacement of the poor by the relatively affluent, who renovate the former's homes is _____. (369)

9.	_____ is the relationship between people and their environment. (370)

10.	_____ is a place people identify with, where they feel a sense of belonging. (371)

MATCHING

___1. Thomas Malthus	a. *theorem on population growth*
___2. Ernest Burgess	b. *human ecology*
___3. Herbert Gans	c. *concentric-zone model*
___4. Homer Hoyt	d. *urban villagers*
___5. Robert Park	e. *sector model*

"DOWN-TO-EARTH SOCIOLOGY"

1.	After reading "Where the United States Population is Headed" on page 361, how will institutions like schools, government, hospitals and churches have to change as our population becomes more diverse? Should the U.S. government cut off immigration?

2.	Why is the practice described in "Killing Little Girls: An Ancient and Thriving Practice" (p. 363) common in certain cultures and not others? How does it reflect deep-rooted sexism? What social, economic or political changes would help to eliminate this practice?

3.	How do the images painted in "Urbanization in the Third World," on page 372, compare with your own "picture" of the Third World? Why are so many people moving into cities? Do the lives of people in the Third World have any bearing on your life?

4.	After reading "You Can Work for Us, But Don't Live Near Us" on page 377, do you agree with the strategies of exclusion being adopted by native-born residents? Has your own community become more racially and ethnically diverse in recent years? If it has, what has been the reaction of long-term residents? What can we do to resolve some of the tensions that can potentially develop when different cultural groups live together?

☞ ANSWERS FOR CHAPTER 14

DEFINITIONS OF KEY TERMS

alienation: a sense of not belonging, and a feeling that no one cares what happens to you

basic demographic equation: growth rate = births - deaths + net migration

city: a place in which a large number of people are permanently based and do not produce their own food

community: a place people identify with, where they sense that they belong and that others care what happens to them

crude birth rate: the annual number of births per 1,000 population

crude death rate: the annual number of deaths per 1,000 population

demographic transition: a three-stage historical process of population growth; first, high birthrates and high death rates; second, high birthrates and low death rates; and third, low birthrates and low death rates

demography: the study of the size, composition, growth, and distribution of human populations

disinvestment: the withdrawal of investments by financial institutions, which seals the fate of an urban area

edge city: a large clustering of service facilities and residences near a highway intersection that provides a sense of place to people who live and shop there

enterprise zone: the use of economic incentives in a designated area with the intention of encouraging investment there

exponential growth curve: a pattern of growth in which numbers double during approximately equal intervals, accelerating in the latter stages

fecundity: the number of children that women are theoretically capable of bearing

fertility rate: the number of children that the average woman bears

gentrification: the displacement of the poor in a section of a city by the relatively affluent, who renovate the former's homes

growth rate: the net change in a population after adding births, subtracting deaths, and either adding or subtracting net migration

human ecology: Robert Park's term for the relationship between people and their environment (natural resources such as land)

invasion-succession cycle: the process of one group of people displacing a group whose racial-ethnic or social class characteristics differ from their own

Malthus theorem: an observation by Thomas Malthus that although the food supply increases only arithmetically (from 1 to 2 to 3 to 4 and so on), population grows geometrically (from 2 to 4 to 8 to 16 and so forth)

megalopolis: an urban area consisting of at least two metropolises and their many suburbs

metropolis: a central city surrounded by smaller cities and their suburbs

net migration rate: the difference between the number of immigrants and emigrants per 1,000 population

population pyramid: a graphic representation of a population, divided into age and sex

population shrinkage: the process by which a country's population becomes smaller because its birthrate and immigration are too low to replace those who die and emigrate

redlining: the officers of a financial institution deciding not to make loans in a particular area

suburb: the communities adjacent to the political boundaries of a city

suburbanization: the movement from the city to the suburbs

sun belt: the southern and western states to which most U.S. migrants move

urban renewal: the rehabilitation of a rundown area, which usually results in the displacement of the poor who are living in that area

urbanization: the process by which an increasing proportion of a population live in cities

ANSWERS FOR MULTIPLE CHOICE QUESTIONS

1. b The proposition that the population grows geometrically while food supply increases arithmetically is known as the Malthus theorem. (352)
2. d According to the New Malthusians, the world's population is following an exponential growth curve, which means that after doubling during approximately equal intervals of time, the world's population growth suddenly accelerates. (353)
3. d None of the above is correct. Anti-Malthusians do not believe that people will blindly reproduce until there is no room left on earth, or that it is possible to project the world's current population growth into the indefinite future. They believe that most people do use intelligence and rational planning when it comes to having children. (354-355)
4. b The three-stage historical process of population growth is the demographic transition. (355)
5. c The process by which a country's population becomes smaller because its birth rate and immigration are too low to replace those who die and emigrate is population shrinkage. (355)
6. c According to the Anti-Malthusians, starvation is due to a mismatch between where the greatest supply of food is and where the greatest demand for it is. Those areas of the world where populations are growing at a slow rate also produce an oversupply of food, while those areas of the world that are growing at a fast rate are not able to produce enough food. (356)
7. d All of the above is correct. Poor nations have so many children because parenthood provides status, children are considered to be an economic asset, and the community encourages people to have children. (358)
8. a Factors that influence population growth (fertility, mortality, and net migration) are demographic variables. (359-360)
9. a The annual number of deaths per 1,000 population is the crude death rate. (360)
10. d All of the above is correct. The factors pushing someone to emigrate include poverty, lack of religious and political freedoms, and political persecution. (361)
11. a According to your text, it is difficult to forecast population growth because of government programs that impact on fertility. (363-364)
12. d All of the above is correct. Today's urbanization means that more people live in cities, today's cities are larger, and about 300 of the world's cities contain at least one million people. (366)
13. d Urbanization is when an increasing proportion of a population lives in cities. (366)
14. d All of the above is correct. Edge cities consist of a cluster of shopping malls, hotels, office parks, and residential areas near the intersection of major highways; they overlap political boundaries and include parts of several cities or towns; and they provide a sense of place to whose living there. (369)
15. c Gentrification is the movement of middle-class people into rundown areas of a city. (369)
16. c The model which is based on the idea that land use in cities is based on several centers, such as a clustering of restaurants or automobile dealerships is the multiple-nuclei model. (371)
17. d All of the above is correct. According to Gans's typology, the trapped includes downwardly mobile persons, elderly persons, and alcoholics and drug addicts. (374)
18. c The Kitty Genovese case in an example of alienation. (373)
19. b *Gesellschaft* societies are characterized by secondary, impersonal relationships; the end result of this can be alienation. (373)

20. b   Suburbanization is the movement from the city to the suburbs. (375)

ANSWERS FOR TRUE-FALSE QUESTIONS

1.   *False.* Thomas Malthus not a sociologist at the University of Chicago in the 1920s. He was an English economist who lived from 1766 to 1834. (352)
2.   *True.* (353)
3.   *False.* There are three stages, not four, in the process of demographic transition. (355)
4.   *False.* The major reason why people in poor countries have so many children is not necessarily because they do not know how to prevent conception. The reason is more sociological in nature, including the status which is conferred on parents for producing children, as well as the need for children to take care of a person when she or he is old. (358)
5.   *False.* Population pyramids represent a population, divided into age and sex--but not race. (358)
6.   *True.* (359-360)
7.   *True.* (360)
8.   *True.* (364)
9.   *True.* (366)
10.   *True.* (368)
11.   *True.* (371)
12.   *False.* No one model is considered to be the most accurate because different cities develop and grow in different ways, especially if there are certain kinds of natural barriers such as rivers or mountains. (371)
13.   *False.* Herbert Gans, the author of *The Urban Villagers*, found that people living in large cities created a sense of community through their involvement in extensive social networks, thereby avoiding feelings of alienation. (373-374)
14.   *True.* (374)
15.   *False.* When banks engage in the practice of redlining the quality of life in neighborhoods generally deteriorated. (376)

ANSWERS FOR FILL-IN QUESTIONS

1.   DEMOGRAPHY is the study of the size, composition, growth, and distribution of human populations. (352)
2.   A pattern of growth in which numbers double during approximately equal intervals, thus accelerating in the latter stages is the EXPONENTIAL GROWTH CURVE. (353)
3.   A(n) POPULATION PYRAMID is a graphic representation of a population, divided into age and sex. (358)
4.   The FERTILITY RATE refers to the number of children that the average woman bears. (359)
5.   The basic demographic equation is *growth = BIRTHS - DEATHS + MIGRATION*. (363)
6.   CITY is a place in which a large number of people are permanently based and do not produce their own food. (365)
7.   An overlapping area consisting of at least two metropolises and their many suburbs is a MEGALOPOLIS. (367)
8.   The displacement of the poor by the relatively affluent, who renovate the former's homes is GENTRIFICATION. (369)
9.   HUMAN ECOLOGY is the relationship between people and their environment. (370)
10.   COMMUNITY is a place people identify with, where they feel a sense of belonging. (371)

ANSWERS TO MATCHING

1. a   Thomas Malthus: *theorem on population growth*
2. c   Ernest Burgess: *concentric-zone model*
3. d   Herbert Gans: *urban villagers*
4. e   Homer Hoyt: *sector model*
5. b   Robert Park: *human ecology*

CHAPTER 15
SOCIAL CHANGE: TECHNOLOGY, SOCIAL MOVEMENTS AND THE ENVIRONMENT

☞ CHAPTER SUMMARY

- Social change, the alteration of culture and society over time, is a vital part of social life. Social change has included four social revolutions, as well as a change from *gemeinschaft* to *gesellschaft* societies, capitalism and industrialization, modernization, and global stratification.

- William Ogburn identified technology as the basis cause of social change. The processes of social change are innovation, discovery, and diffusion.

- The types of technology are primitive, industrial, and postindustrial. Technology is a driving force in social change, and it can shape an entire society. This is evident when the impact that the computer have had on American society is analyzed. Major concerns about the computer focus on the potential for its abuse, the invasion of privacy, the integration of misinformation into computerized records, and use as an instrument for social control.

- Other theories of social change include: evolutionary theories, cyclical theories, and conflict theories.

- Social movements usually involve more people, are more prolonged, are more organized, and focus on social change. Depending on whether their target is individuals or society and whether the amount of change desired is partial or complete, social movements can be classified as alterative, redemptive, reformative, or transformative.

- Because the mass media are the gatekeepers for social movements, their favorable or unfavorable coverage greatly affects a social movement and tactics are chosen with the media in mind.

- Social movements go through distinct stages. Resource mobilization theory accounts for why some social movements never get off the ground while others enjoy great success. Social movements seldom solve social problems because they focus on problems deeply embedded in society which do not lend themselves to easy solutions.

- Social change has often had a negative impact on the natural environment. As a result of industrialization, today we face such problems as acid rain, global warming, and the greenhouse effect.

- Environmental problems are worldwide, brought about by industrial production and urbanization, the pressures of population growth, and inadequate environmental regulation. In response a worldwide environmental movement has emerged, which seeks solutions in education, legislation, and political activism. If we are to survive, we must seek harmony between technology and the environment.

- Environmental sociology is an attempt to study the relationship between humans and the environment.

☞ LEARNING OBJECTIVES

As you read Chapter 15, use these learning objectives to organize your notes. After completing your reading, briefly state an answer to each of the objectives, and review the text pages in parentheses.

1.   Describe the four major social revolutions which have occurred. (384)

2. Describe *gemeinschaft* and *gesellschaft* societies, explain the relationship between capitalism and Protestantism and social change, and explain the relationship between these forces and modernization. (384-386)
3. Identify the shifts in the global map and discuss the threats to the global map. (386-387)
4. Discuss how the different types of technology have produced social change. (387-388)
5. Identify and define Ogburn's three processes of social change, and explain what is meant by "cultural lag." (388-389)
6. Discuss the impact of computers on our society, including both the advances that computers have made and the concerns that we have about them. (389-393)
7. Explain how computers have contributed to cultural leveling. (393)
8. Explain evolutionary, cyclical, and conflict theories of social change, and note the advantages and disadvantages of each. (393-394)
9. State the major reasons why social movements exist. (394)
10. Compare and contrast proactive and reactive social movements. (394-395)
11. List the four types of social movements. (395)
12. Define propaganda and discuss the role of the mass media in social movements. (395-396)
13. Identify the five stages that social movements go through as they grow and mature. (396-397)
14. Describe the environmental problems facing the world today, noting differences between the First, Second, and Third Worlds. State ways in which First World countries may have contributed to these problems. (399-401)
15. Discuss the goals and activities of the environmental movement. (401-403)
16. List the assumptions of environmental sociology. (403-404)
17. Describe some of the actions which would be necessary to reach the goal of harmony between technology and the environment. (404)

☞ CHAPTER OUTLINE

I. **Social Change: An Overview**
    A. Social change is a shift in the characteristics of culture and societies over time.
    B. There have been four social revolutions: the domestication of plants and animals, from which pastoral and horticultural societies arose; the invention of the plow, leading to agricultural societies; the industrial revolution; and now the information revolution, resulting in postindustrial societies.
    C. The shift from agricultural to industrial economic activity was accompanied by a change from *gemeinschaft* (daily life centers on intimate and personal relationships) to *gesellschaft* (people have fleeting, impersonal relationships) societies.
    D. Karl Marx identified capitalism as the basic reason behind the breakup of feudal (agricultural) societies. Max Weber saw religion as the core reason for the development of capitalism: as a result of the Reformation, Protestants no longer felt assured that they were saved by virtue of church membership and concluded that God would show visible favor to the elect.
    E. Modernization (the change from agricultural to industrial societies) produces sweeping changes in societies. Modern societies are larger, more urbanized, and subject to faster change. They stress formal education and the future and are less religiously oriented. They have smaller families, lower rates of infant mortality, and higher life expectancy; they have higher incomes and more material possessions.

1.   When technology from the industrialized world is brought into the Third World, the impact on society is evident, as demonstrated by introduction of medicine.
2.   The export of Western medicine to Third World nations reduced death rates but did not affect high birth rates. Rapidly increasing populations strain Third World resources, leading to widespread hunger and starvation, and the mass migration to cities and to First World countries.

F.   Already in the 16th century today's First and Third Worlds had begun to emerge. As capitalism developed, the industrialized nations exploited the resources of those nations that did not industrialize.
1.   Dependency theory asserts that because the Third World countries have become dependent on the First World, they are unable to develop their own resources.
2.   The world's industrial giants (the United States, Canada, Great Britain, France, Germany, Italy, and Japan--the G7) have decided how they will share the world's markets; by regulating global economic and industrial policy they guarantee their own dominance, including continued access to cheap raw materials from the Second and Third Worlds.

G.   The resurgence of ethnic conflicts, for example the conflict in Bosnia, threatens the global map as conceived by the G7.

II. **How Technology Changes Society**

A.   There are three types of technology: primitive (adaptation of natural items for human use); industrial (uses machines powered by fuels); and postindustrial (centers on information, transportation, and communication).

B.   William Ogburn identified three processes of social change: (1) inventions, which can be either material (computers) or social (capitalism); (2) discovery, which is a new way of seeing things; and (3) diffusion, which is the spread of an invention, discovery, or idea from one area to another. Ogburn coined the term cultural lag to describe the situation in which some elements of a culture adapt to an invention or discovery more rapidly than others.

C.   The computer is an example, changing medicine, the military and war, education, the workplace, and interpersonal relationships.
1.   Computers have produced multiskilling, the addition of skills over and above those already possessed by the worker.
2.   Computers also have resulted in "deskilling," reducing the skills necessary to do a job (e.g., a master baker who is replaced by an unskilled employee who needs only to press a button to start the mixing process).

D.   With computers the world is linked by almost instantaneous communication, national boundaries now mean nothing, and information is not contained.
1.   The term information superhighway carries the idea of information traveling at a high rate of speed around the world.
2.   The implications of the information superhighway are enormous; on a national level, a new dimension of inequality could emerge--the information "have-nots," while on an international level the question is "who will control the information superhighway?"
3.   During the Tiananmen Square massacre in Beijing, Chinese students faxed reports to Americans, and tele-communications was one of the many factors that contributed to the collapse of the Soviet empire.

4.   Computer programs now make it more difficult for people in power to snoop and pry into the private affairs of others, whether those others are private citizens or foreign governments.

E.   Computers shrink the world in terms of both time and space. With the information superhighway homes and businesses are connected by a rapid flow of information. The implications of this superhighway for national and global stratification are severe.

      1.   On a national level, we may end up with information have-nots among inner-city and rural residents, thus perpetuating existing inequalities.

      2.   On a global level, the First World will control the information superhighway thereby destining the Third World to a perpetual pauper status.

III.   **Other Theories of Social Change**

A.   Evolutionary theories are unilinear or multilinear.

      1.   Unilinear theories assume that all societies follow the same path, evolving from simple to complex through uniform sequences.

      2.   Multilinear theories assume that different routes can lead to a similar stage of development, thus, societies need not pass through the same sequence of stages to become industrialized.

      3.   Both unilinear and multilinear theories assume the idea that societies progress toward a higher state. These theories are now being discredited, and seeing one's own society as the top of the evolutionary ladder is now considered unacceptably ethnocentric. Furthermore, because of the crises in Western culture today, these assumptions have been cast aside and evolutionary theories have been rejected.

B.   Cyclical theories examine great civilizations, not a particular society; they presume that societies are like organisms, they are born, reach adolescence, grow old, and die.

      1.   Arnold Toynbee proposed that at first a civilization is able to meet challenges, yet when it has become an empire, the ruling elite loses its capacity to keep the masses in line "by charm rather than by force," and the fabric of society is then ripped apart.

      2.   Oswald Spengler proposed that Western civilization was on the wane; some analysts think the crisis in Western civilization may indicate he was right.

C.   Marx's conflict theory viewed social change as a dialectical precess, in which a thesis (the status quo) contains its own antithesis (opposition), and the resulting struggle between the thesis and its antithesis leads to a new state or synthesis. Thus, the history of a society is a series of confrontations in which each ruling group creates the seeds of its own destruction (e.g., capitalism sets workers and capitalists on a collision course).

IV.   **Social Movements as a Source of Social Change**

A.   Social movements consist of large numbers of people, who, through deliberate and sustained efforts, organize to promote or resist social change. At the heart of social movements lie grievances and dissatisfactions.

      1.   Proactive social movements promote social change because a current condition of society is intolerable. In contrast, reactive social movements resist changing conditions in society which they perceive as threatening.

      2.   To further their goals, people often develop social movement organizations. Examples of proactive social movements are National Organization of Women (NOW) and the National Association for the Advancement of Colored People (NAACP); an example of reactive social movements is the Klu Klux Klan (KKK).

3.   Mayer Zald suggests that a cultural crisis can give birth to a wave of social movements. According to Zald, when a society's institutions fail to keep up with social changes, many people's needs go unfulfilled, massive unrest follows, and social movements come into being to bridge the gap.

B.   David Aberle classified social movements into four broad categories according to the type and amount of social change they seek.

1.   Two types seek to change people but differ in terms of the amount of change desired: alterative social movements seek to alter only particular aspects of people (e.g., the Women's Christian Temperance Union); while redemptive social movements seek to change people totally (e.g., a religious social movement such as fundamental Christianity that stresses conversion).

2.   Two types seek to change society but also differ in terms of the amount of change desired: reformative social movements seek to reform only one part of society (e.g., animal rights or the environment); transformative social movements seek to change the social order itself and to replace it with their own version of the ideal society (e.g., revolutions in the American colonies, France, Russia, and Cuba).

C.   Leaders of social movements try to manipulate the media in order to influence public opinion about some issue.

1.   Propaganda is a key to understanding social movements. Propaganda simply means the presentation of information in an attempt to influence people.

2.   The mass media play a critical role in social movements. They have become, in effect, the gatekeepers to social movements. If those who control and work in the mass media are sympathetic to a "cause," it will receive sympathetic treatment. If the social movement goes against their own biases, it will either be ignored or receive unfavorable treatment.

D.   Social movements have a life course, that is, they go through five stages as they grow and mature.

1.   Unrest and agitation grow because people are upset about some social condition; at this stage leaders emerge who verbalize people's feelings

2.   Leaders mobilize a relatively large number of people who demand that something be done about the problem; charismatic leaders emerge during this stage.

3.   An organization emerges with a division of labor with leadership that makes policy decisions and a rank and file that actively supports the movement.

4.   Institutionalization occurs as the movement becomes bureaucratized and leadership passes to career officials who may care more about their position in the organization than about the movement itself.

5.   The organization declines, but there may be a possibility of resurgence. Some movements cease to exist; others become reinvigorated with new leadership from within or from coming into conflict with other social movements fighting for the opposite side of the issue, (e. g., social movements relating to abortion).

V.   Social Change and the Natural Environment

A.   Industrialization, while viewed as good for the nation's welfare, has led to a major assault on the environment.

1.   Industrial growth came at a high cost to the natural environment.

2.   Many of today's problems--ozone layer depletion, acid rain, the greenhouse effect, and global warming--are linked to our dependence on fossil fuels.

3.   There is an abundant source of natural energy that would provide low-cost power and therefore help to raise the living standards of human across the globe. Better technology is needed to harness this energy supply. From a conflict perspective, such abundant sources of energy present a threat to the energy monopoly ruled by multinationals. We cannot expect the practical development and widespread use of alternative sources of power until the multinationals have cornered the market on the technology that will harness them.

3.   Racial minorities and the poor are disproportionately exposed to air pollution, hazardous waste, pesticides and the like. To deal with this issue a new specialty known as environmental poverty law is developing.

B.   Environmental degradation is also a problem in the Second World.

1.   Pollution was treated as a state secret in the former Soviet Union. With protest stifled, no environmental protection laws to inhibit pollution, and production quotas to be met, environmental pollution was rampant.

2.   For the most part, the protests which occurred after dissolution of the Soviet Union fell on deaf ears, and pollution continues because of the Second World's rush to compete industrially with the West, the desire to improve its standard of living, and the lack of funds to purchase expensive pollution controls.

C.   The combined pressures of population growth and almost nonexistent environmental regulations destine the Third World to become the earth's major source of pollution.

1.   Some First World companies use Third World countries to dump hazardous wastes and to produce chemicals no longer tolerated in their own countries.

2.   The consequences for humanity of the destruction of the tropical rain forests are unknown. With rain forests disappearing at a rate of 2500 acres every hour, it is estimated that 10,000 species are becoming extinct every year.

D.   Concern about the world's environmental problems has produced a worldwide social movement.

1.   In some countries, the environment has become a major issue in local and national elections (e.g., Germany, Great Britain, and Switzerland).

2.   This movement often transcends social class, gender, and race, and generally seeks solutions in education, legislation, and political activism.

E.   Environmental sociology examines the relationship between human societies and the environment. Its basic assumptions include: (1) the physical environment is a significant variable in sociological investigation; (2) humans are but one species among many that are dependent on the environment; (3) because of intricate feedbacks to nature, human actions have many unintended consequences; (4) the world is finite, so there are potential physical limits to economic growth; (5) economic expansion requires increased extraction of resources from the environment; (6) increased extraction of resources leads to ecological problems; (7) these ecological problems place restrictions on economic expansion; and (8) the state creates environmental problems by trying to create conditions for the profitable accumulation of capital.

F.   If we are to have a world that is worth passing on to the coming generations, we must seek harmony between technology and the natural environment. As a parallel to development of technologies, we must develop a greater awareness of their harmful effects on the planet, systems of control giving more weight to reducing technologies' harm to the environment than to lowering costs, and mechanisms to enforce rules for the production, use, and disposal of technology.

☞ GLOSSARY OF DIFFICULT-TO-UNDERSTAND WORDS

apparatus: equipment (388)
arable: suitable for cultivation (400)
drudgery: work, viewed as a chore or grind (390)
espouse: to take up and support a cause (403)
exuberant: joyful (394)
grievances: complaints (394)
harnessing: to make use of something (388)
hawk: to sell something by calling out in the street (397)
hogtied: to be made helpless (403)
honing: making something more effective (390)
indigenous: coming from a particular region (398)
microchip: the electronic device on which information and directions are stored in a computer (384)
on-line: being connected to a mainframe computer from a remote terminal by means of a modem (391)
polarizing: reaching opposite extremes (398)
pristine: being free and clean, untouched (399)
recurring: taking place again and again(394)
saloons: establishments in which alcoholic beverages are sold and consumed (395)
subtle: difficult to distinguish; elusive (397)
surveillance: watching specific people or places, as by the police, without being seen (391)
zap: to use speed or force to impart something (391)

☞ KEY TERMS TO DEFINE

After studying the chapter, define each of the following terms. Then check your work by referring to the answers beginning at page 254 of this Study Guide.

acid rain
alterative social movement
cultural lag
cultural leveling
dialectical process
diffusion
discovery
environmental sociology
global warming
greenhouse effect
ideal type

industrial technology
information superhighway
invention
job deskilling
job multiskilling
modernization
postindustrial technology
primitive technology
proactive social movement
propaganda
public opinion

reactive social movement
redemptive social movement
reformative social movement
resource mobilization
social change
social movement
social movement organization
technology
transformative social movement

☞ KEY PEOPLE

State the major theoretical contributions or findings of these people.

David Aberle
William Ogburn
Karl Marx

Oswald Spengler
Arnold Toynbee
Max Weber

Mayer Zald
Shoshana Zuboff

☞ SELF-TEST

After completing this self-test, check your answers against the Answer Key beginning on page 254 of this Study Guide and against the text on page(s) indicated in parentheses.

MULTIPLE CHOICE QUESTIONS

1.   A shift in the characteristics of culture and society over time is: (384)
     a.   social transformation.
     b.   social metamorphose.
     c.   social alternation.
     d.   social change.

2.   Max Weber identified _____ as the core reason for the development of capitalism. (385)
     a.   religion
     b.   industrialization
     c.   politics
     d.   None of the above.

3.   Third World countries have become reliant on the First World and they are unable to develop their own resources according to: (386)
     a.   dependency theory.
     b.   capitalist exploitation theory.
     c.   evolutionary theory.
     d.   multilinear evolution theory.

4.   Which of the following does the author of the text identify as a threat to the global map that was drawn up by the G7? (387)
     a.   stricter environmental controls in the Third World.
     b.   stiffer tariff regulation world-wide.
     c.   resurgence of ethnic conflicts.
     d.   ecosabotage.

5.   The adaptation of natural items for human use is: (388)
     a.   primitive technology.
     b.   industrial technology.
     c.   postindustrial technology.
     d.   new technology.

6.   The idea of citizenship is an example of: (388)
     a.   invention.
     b.   discovery.
     c.   diffusion.
     d.   innovation.

7.   The situation in which some elements of a culture adapt to an invention or discovery more rapidly than others is: (389)
    a.   cultural downtime.
    b.   cultural lag.
    c.   cultural delay.
    d.   cultural drag.

8.   Changes were brought about by the computer in: (389-392)
    a.   education and medicine.
    b.   the military and war.
    c.   the workplace.
    d.   All of the above.

9.   A surprising consequence of telecommunications is: (392)
    a.   an increase in academic achievement scores.
    b.   an increase in ethnic hostilities.
    c.   weakening of national boundaries.
    d.   a strengthening of powerful leaders to maintain secrecy.

10.   _____ theories assume that all societies follow the same path, evolving from simple to complex through uniform sequences. (393)
    a.   Cyclical
    b.   Uniformity
    c.   Unilinear evolution
    d.   Multilinear evolution

11.   The history of a society is a series of confrontations in which each ruling group creates the seeds of its own destruction, according to: (394)
    a.   Karl Marx.
    b.   William Ogburn.
    c.   Pitirim Sorokin.
    d.   Max Weber.

12.   The National Organization of Women is an example of a _____ while the Klu Klux Klan is an example of _____. (394)
    a.   reactive social movement/proactive social movement
    b.   redemptive social movement/reactive social movement
    c.   proactive social movement/reactive social movement
    d.   proactive social movement/alternative social movement

13.   Social movements that seek to change people totally are: (395)
    a.   alterative social movements.
    b.   redemptive social movements.
    c.   reformative social movements.
    d.   transformative social movements.

14. A social movement that seeks to change society totally is a(n): (395)
    a.   alternative social movement.
    b.   redemptive social movement.
    c.   reformative social movement.
    d.   transformative social movement.

15. How people think about some issue is: (395)
    a.   irrelevant to most social scientists.
    b.   public opinion.
    c.   propaganda.
    d.   mass-society theory.

16. Advertising is: (396)
    a.   a type of propaganda.
    b.   an organized attempt to manipulate public opinion.
    c.   a one-sided presentation of information that distorts reality.
    d.   All of the above.

17. Raising money, recruiting people with needed skills, acquiring equipment, and gaining the attention of the media are all part of the process of: (398)
    a.   organization building.
    b.   bureaucratization.
    c.   resource mobilization.
    d.   organizational decline.

18. Which groups in U.S. society are disproportionately exposed to environmental hazards? (400)
    a.   office workers and factory workers
    b.   racial minorities and the poor
    c.   farm workers and lumberjacks
    d.   racial and ethnic groups

19. The major source of pollution in the future is likely to be: (401)
    a.   the Third World.
    b.   the Second World.
    c.   the Third World.
    d.   another planet.

20. Environmental sociology examines: (403)
    a.   how the physical environment affects human activities.
    b.   how human activities affect the physical environment.
    c.   the unintended consequences of human actions.
    d.   All of the above.

TRUE-FALSE QUESTIONS

T F   1.   The rapid social change that the world is currently experiencing is a random event. (384)
T F   2.   Modernization is the change from agricultural to industrial societies. (385)

T F 3. The resurgence of ethnic conflicts in Europe, North and South America, Africa, and Asia do not really threaten the global map that has been carefully partitioned by the world's industrial giants. (387)

T F 4. Technology is not a very powerful force for social change. (388)

T F 5. Industrial technology centers on information, transportation, and communication. (388)

T F 6. Invention, discovery, and diffusion are Ogburn's three processes of social change. (388)

T F 7. Technology usually changes first, followed by culture. (389)

T F 8. The use of computers in education will significantly reduce existing social inequalities between school districts. (391)

T F 9. Job multiskilling and deskilling are the result of advances in computer technology. (392)

T F 10. Unilinear evolutionary theories assume that all societies follow the same path. (393)

T F 11. Cyclical theories assume that civilizations are like organisms. (394)

T F 12. According to Max Weber, the history of a society is a series of confrontations in which each ruling group sows the seeds of its own destruction. (394)

T F 13. All social movements seek to change society. (394)

T F 14. The environmental movement is an example of a transformative social movement. (395)

T F 15. Propaganda and advertising are defined quite differently from one another. (395-396)

T F 16. In the final stage of a social movement, decline is certain. (398)

T F 17. The lack of environmental protection laws in Third World countries has contributed to their becoming dumping grounds for hazardous wastes. (401)

T F 18. The worldwide environmental movement often transcends social class, gender, and race. (402)

T F 19. Environmental sociology examines the relationship between human societies and the environment. (403)

T F 20. According to environmental sociologists, governments are not to blame for environmental problems because they actively set limits on the conditions for the profitable accumulation of capital. (404)

FILL-IN QUESTIONS

1. An _____ is a composite of characteristics based on many specific examples. (385)

2. The combination of existing elements and materials to form new ones results in _____. (388)

3. William Ogburn used the term _____ to describe human behavior that lags behind technological innovations. (389)

4. Reducing the amount of skills that a job requires is referred to as _____. (392)

5. _____, which occurs when Western industrial culture is imported and diffused into developing nations, is a threat to traditional ways of life. (393)

6. Broadly speaking, a _____ consists of large numbers of people who organize to promote or resist social change. (394)

7. The Women's Christian Temperance Union is an example of a _____ social movement. (395)

8. The presentation of information in an attempt to influence people is _____. (396)

9. The _____, the buildup of carbon dioxide in the earth's atmosphere that allows light to enter but inhibits the release of heat, is believed to cause _____. (400)

10. _____ examines how human activities affect the physical environment and how the physical environment affects human activities. (403)

MATCHING

___1. Karl Marx a. *religion led to the development of capitalism*
___2. David Aberle b. *capitalism produces alienation of workers*
___3. William Ogburn c. *cyclical theory predicting the decline of Western civilization*
___4. Max Weber d. *three processes of cultural innovation*
___5. Oswald Spengler e. *classified social movements by type and amount of social change*

"DOWN-TO-EARTH SOCIOLOGY"

1. After reading "Tricks of the Trade: The Fine Art of Propaganda" on page 397, listen carefully to politicians and leaders of social movements who advocate a particular idea. Are they using some of the techniques described? If yes, which ones?

2. Read "Which Side of the Barricades? Prochoice and Prolife as a Social Movement" on page 398. Do you agree with the author that no issue divides Americans as abortion does? How does each side see this issue? Why does the author say that there is no way to reconcile the opposing views? In what ways are these social movements different from others? How do you feel about this issue?

3. After reading "Lost Tribes, Lost Knowledge" on page 402, why do you think the West is becoming more concerned about the loss of tribal knowledge? Do you think "cultural ignorance" is a valid defense for crimes committed against groups with diverse cultural backgrounds? Why or why not?

4. Do you think "Ecosabotage," as described on pages 403, is ever justified? Why or why not? Do you think radical acts can do more harm than good? Do they alienate people who support the movement, rather than unite them?

☞ ANSWERS FOR CHAPTER 15

DEFINITIONS OF KEY TERMS

acid rain: rain containing sulfuric and nitric acid
alterative social movement: a social movement that seeks to alter only particular aspects of people
cultural lag: William Ogburn's term for human behavior lagging behind technological innovation
cultural leveling: the author's term for the process by which cultures become similar to one another, and especially by which Western industrial culture is imported and diffused into developing nations
dialectical process: each arrangement, or thesis, contains contradictions, or antitheses, which must be resolved; the new arrangement, or synthesis, contains its own contradictions, and so on
diffusion: the spread of invention or discovery from one area to another; identified by William Ogburn as a major process of social change
discovery: a new way of seeing reality; identified by William Ogburn as a major process of social change

environmental sociology: a subdiscipline of sociology that examines how human activities affect the physical environment and how the physical environment affects human activities

global warming: an increase in the earth's temperature due to the greenhouse effect

greenhouse effect: the buildup of carbon dioxide in the earth's atmosphere that allows light to enter but inhibits the release of heat; believed to cause global warming

ideal type: a composite of characteristics based on many specific examples; "ideal" in this case means a description of abstracted characteristics, not what one desires to exist

industrial technology: technology centered on machines powered by fuels instead of natural forces such as wind and rivers

information superhighway: carries the idea of information traveling at a high rate of speed among homes and businesses

invention: the combination of existing elements and materials to form new ones; identified by William Ogburn as a major process of social change

job deskilling: reducing the amount of skills that a job requires

job multiskilling: adding skills to those a worker already possesses

modernization: the transformation of traditional societies into industrial societies

postindustrial technology: a society based on information, services, and high technology, rather than on raw materials and manufacturing

primitive technology: the adaptation of natural items for human use

proactive social movement: a social movement that promotes social change

propaganda: in its broad sense, the presentation of information in the attempt to influence people; in its narrow sense, one-sided information used to try to influence people

public opinion: how people think about some issue

reactive social movement: a social movement that resists social change

redemptive social movement: a social movement that seeks to change people totally

reformative social movement: a social movement that seeks to reform some specific aspect of society

resource mobilization: a theory that social movements succeed or fail based on their ability to mobilize resources such as time, money, and people's skills

social change: the alteration of culture and societies over time

social movement: consists of large numbers of people who organize to promote or resist social change

social movement organization: the organization developed to further the goals of a social movement

technology: often defined as the applications of science, but can be conceptualized as tools, items used to accomplish tasks

transformative social movement: a social movement that seeks to change society totally

ANSWERS FOR MULTIPLE CHOICE QUESTIONS

1. d   The shift in the characteristics of culture and society over time is social change. (384)
2. a   Max Weber identified religion as the core reason for the development of capitalism. (385)
3. a   Third World countries have become dependent on the First World and they are unable to develop their own resources according to dependency theory. (386)
4. c   The current resurgence of ethnic conflicts, particularly in Bosnia, threatens the global map drawn up by the G7. (387)
5. a   The adaptation of natural items for human use is primitive technology. (388)
6. c   According to William Ogburn, the idea of citizenship is an example of diffusion. (388)
7. b   The situation in which some elements of a culture adapt to an invention or discovery more rapidly than others is cultural lag. (389)

8. d   All of the above is correct. Changes were brought about by the computer in education and medicine, the military and war, and the workplace. (389-392)
9. c   A surprising consequence of telecommunications is the weakening of national boundaries. (392)
10. c   Unilinear evolution theories assume that all societies follow the same path, evolving from simple to complex through uniform sequences. (393)
11. a   The history of a society is a series of confrontations in which each ruling group creates the seeds of its own destruction, according to Karl Marx. (394)
12. c   The National Organization of Women is an example of a **proactive social movement** while the Klu Klux Klan is an example of **reactive social movement**. (394)
13. b   Social movements that seek to change people totally are redemptive social movements. (395)
14. d   A social movement that seeks to change society totally is a transformative social movement. (395)
15. b   How people think about some issue is public opinion. (395)
16. d   All of the above is correct. Advertising is a type of propaganda, an organized attempt to manipulate public opinion, and a one-sided presentation of information that distorts reality. (396)
17. c   Raising money, recruiting people with needed skills, acquiring equipment, and gaining the attention of the media are all part of the process of resource mobilization. (398)
18. b   Racial minorities and the poor are disproportionately exposed to environmental hazards. (400)
19. c   The major source of pollution is likely to become the Third World. (401)
20. d   All of the above is correct. Environmental sociology examines how the physical environment affects human activities; how human activities affect the physical environment; and the unintended consequences of human actions. (403)

ANSWERS FOR TRUE-FALSE QUESTIONS

1.   *False.* The rapid social change that the world is currently experiencing is not a random event. It is the result or fundamental forces unleashed many years ago. (384)
2.   *True.* (385)
3.   *False.* The resurgence of ethnic conflicts in Europe, North and South America, Africa, and Asia does threaten the global map that has been carefully partitioned by the world's industrial giants; of special concern is the continued economic and political stability in countries that provide the essential raw materials for the G7's industrial machine. (387)
4.   *False.* Technology is a very powerful force for social change because it highlights problem areas within a society. (388)
5.   *False.* Industrial technology centers on machines powered by fuels; postindustrial technology information, transportation, and communication. (388)
6.   *True.* (388)
7.   *True.* (389)
8.   *False.* The use of computers in education is likely to increase, rather than decrease, the social inequality between school districts, because poor districts will not be able to afford the hardware. (391)
9.   *True.* (392)
10. *True.* (393)
11. *True.* (394)
12. *False.* It was not Max Weber but rather Karl Marx who believed that the history of a society is a series of confrontations in which each ruling group sows the seeds of its own destruction. (394)
13. *False.* Not all social movements seek to change society; some seek to change people. (394)

14.   *False.* The environmental movement is an example of a reformative, not a transformative, social movement. (395)

15.   *False.* Propaganda and advertising are not quite different from one another. In essence, advertising is a type of propaganda because it fits both the broad and the narrow definition of propaganda perfectly. (395-396)

16.   *False.* In the final stage of a social movement, decline is not always certain. Sometimes an emerging group with the same goals and new leadership will take over the "cause." (398)

17.   *True.* (401)

18.   *True.* (402)

19.   *True.* (403)

20.   *False.* According to environmental sociologists, governments are often to blame for environmental problems because they try to create conditions for the profitable accumulation of capital. (404)

ANSWERS FOR FILL-IN QUESTIONS

1.   An <u>IDEAL TYPE</u> is a composite of characteristics based on many specific examples. (385)

2.   The combination of existing elements and materials to form new ones results in <u>INVENTION</u>. (388)

3.   William Ogburn used the term <u>CULTURAL LAG</u> to describe human behavior that lags behind technological innovations. (389)

4.   Reducing the amount of skills that a job requires is referred to as <u>JOB DESKILLING</u>. (392)

5.   <u>CULTURAL LEVELING</u>, which occurs when Western industrial culture is imported and diffused into developing nations, is a threat to traditional ways of life. (393)

6.   Broadly speaking, a <u>SOCIAL MOVEMENT</u> consists of large numbers of people who organize to promote or resist social change. (394)

7.   The Women's Christian Temperance Union is an example of a <u>ALTERATIVE</u> social movement. (395)

8.   The presentation of information in an attempt to influence people is <u>PROPAGANDA</u>. (396)

9.   The <u>GREENHOUSE EFFECT</u>, the buildup of carbon dioxide in the earth's atmosphere that allows light to enter but inhibits the release of heat, is believed to cause <u>GLOBAL WARMING</u>. (400)

10.   <u>ENVIRONMENTAL SOCIOLOGY</u> examines how human activities affect the physical environment and how the physical environment affects human activities. (403)

ANSWERS TO MATCHING

1. b   Karl Marx: *capitalism produces alienation of workers*

2. e   David Aberle: *classified social movements by type and amount of social change*

3. d   William Ogburn: *three processes of cultural innovation*

4. a   Max Weber: *religion led to the development of capitalism*

5. c   Oswald Spengler: *cyclical theory predicting the decline of Western civilization*